In the Name of Allah,
Most Gracious, Most Merciful

JOURNEY TO MY SOUL

EYE
OF THE
HEART

Niyah Press
Detroit, MI

EYE OF THE HEART: JOURNEY TO MY SOUL
Copyright © 2017 by Sommieh Stephanie Flower.

Published in the United States by Niyah Press,
www.niyahpress.com

www.sommiehflower.com
www.sitara-institute.org

Cover by Lisa Amowitz

FIRST EDITION

ISBN: 978-1-945873-05-8

Praise for Eye of the Heart

"Reading *Eye of the Heart* is like experiencing a wonderful, deep dream; the further you go the longer you want to stay. A paradoxical journey from elite Manhattan life to teaching slum children in Pakistan, Stephanie Flower invites her reader along for an intimate ride that will open your own heart's eye."
—*Chris Abdul Rahman Blauvelt, Founder and CEO of Launchgood.com*

"There are many ways to read Sommieh Flower's memoir, but the most important one is not her conversion story, nor the contrast between the family and society into which she was born, and the societies in which she has lived during her adult life. For me as an educator, the most enduring contribution of the author is the vision of education--how to engage the young in an altruistic and uplifting kind of schooling. She has long been a person of vision with the even rarer ability to implement that vision with teachers and students, and to communicate it to others in a way that lets it live and spread. The story of her well-rounded humanities education and her embrace of Islam that led her into this vision of participatory, child-centered, empathetic and outward-looking education is one that the Muslim community should take to heart and embrace. Like the wider American community, the Muslim community abroad and in the US has mistakenly erred on the side of regimented education with an overemphasis on the STEM fields. Her example, pursued with dogged persistence, lights the way to a different possibility."
—*Susan Douglass, curriculum developer, education outreach provider at Georgetown University, and fellow-traveler in the same vision.*

"This expansive baring of the soul is likened to a roller coaster ride. It begins smooth, sometimes folds back on itself, at times it turns upside down but finds its footing just before the next loop. There is a hesitation at the crest and a hair-raising ride down, only to be taken back up again to new heights. *Eye of the Heart* will let you know who the author is, as very little is held back. May Allah bless Sommieh in her endeavor."
—*Loretta J. Poisson, author (Between a Pyramid and a Hard Place, Interview with Death, and Unearthing Hidden Jewels.)*

"The Eye of the Heart: Journey to My Soul" is indeed a journey which author Flower invites us to join; it's the voyage of an American youth, wife and mother, educator and a believer in Allah's universality through Islamic teachings.

This is a memoir of simplicity, intimacy and compassion easy to share, even though the life that unfolds, page by page, is in many ways unique. Stephanie Flower takes us from her early years as a typical American child, through her sometimes aimless, but mostly determined path towards the divine and her own personal maturity. That path involved conversion into a new faith, Islam, marriage and motherhood, becoming a successful educator, remarriage and a new career along with a new way of being Muslim.

Sister Flower's sometimes understated social and spiritual encounters make her life less exotic and more normal than one might expect—so that becoming Muslim and living Islam are entirely natural and reveal Flower's forever evolving heart and spirit. Engaging in this journey with her is an endearing experience."
—*Barbara Nimri Aziz, anthropologist, journalist and former producer at Pacifica-WBAI Radio, NY*

Contents

Prologue

Me, age three

My earliest stories are apocrypha from family retellings, like the time I slept over my Grandma and Grandpa's house when my brother was born. Grandma and Grandpa lived on Ocean Parkway in Brooklyn close to a Carvel Ice Cream store. The store had a twirling silver cone on its roof. I loved seeing it from Grandma's living room window. It made me think of ice cream. Yum! On the day my parents came to take me home, Grandma dressed me in a pretty white party dress. My parents were taking too long, and soon I was whining for chocolate ice cream. Not being ones to tell me *no*, Grandma and Grandpa dutifully took me to Carvel. The inevitable result was chocolate ice cream on a white party dress, sticky chocolate fingers, and no time to change before Mommy and Daddy arrived with the shriveled, red, and wrinkled creature that was my new baby brother, Andrew Michael Flower.

Fast forward fifty years, and I'm in the park with my children and grandchildren at a summer festival. It's a hot day, and there's ice cream for sale. I get Bilal and Bayan one cone each, chocolate and vanilla twists. I come to realize these are my grandchildren's first cones ever. What fun! Out comes the camera to capture the moment of ice cream is smeared everywhere in all its glorious stickiness. We try to wash up before heading home to their mama. If she scolds them, I have pictures to prove that she made the same mess at their age, just as I had once done. The first ice cream cone is a rite of passage, is it not?

Reaching forward and reaching back is what life and memories are all about. How did Stephanie Ann Flower, a/k/a Stephy, Steffi, and Steph become Sommieh Uddin, Sommieh Stephanie Flower, and Stef? What parts of myself did I lose and gain along the way? Or, more accurately, what kind of evolution/revolution took place so that I became Sommieh?

There is a hadith, or quotation of Prophet Muhammad 🕮, which says, "If Allah (God) loves a person, He calls the angel Gabriel, saying, 'Allah loves so and so, O Gabriel, love him.' So Gabriel would love him and then would make an announcement in the Heavens: 'Allah has loved so and so therefore you should love him also.' So all the dwellers of the Heavens would love him, and then he is granted the pleasure of the people on the earth."

All my life, I've been loved and supported by those around me. From my small, tight-knit family to the people in the schools and communities where I've lived and worked, I've encountered respect, fellowship, and love. All those blessings come from Allah. It's to Him that I dedicate this book. Besides Him, there are many to thank, but none more so than my parents who first taught me to recognize beauty in all its forms.

For those who will read to find themselves among these pages, I hope you'll not be disappointed by my inadequacies as a first-time author or by what I might or might not say. As for my family and friends, I love you all.

Writing a memoir is a challenge of sustaining effort over a relatively long period of time. There is also the dilemma of whether or not it's worth the risk of putting myself on the line in the first person. Why not change everyone's names, including my own, to protect the innocent? (Is anyone truly innocent?) A good answer to these questions pertains to voice. Who is the one *really* speaking through these pages? Read on, and find out.

*A note on the quotes: each chapter begins or ends with one or two. They are a mixture of verses from the Holy Quran, sayings of the Prophet Muhammad 🌿, and poetry that has influenced my life at various stages. When quoting the Quran, I will cite the Arabic name of the chapter, or *sura* (S.), and the specific verse quoted.

*🌿 This notation is used to honor the name of the prophet Muhammad 🌿. It means "May Allah's peace and blessings be upon him."

*(SWT) is used after the word Allah, which is the Arabic name for the one true God. It is the abbreviation of *Subhanahu wa Ta'ala*, which means Glory to the Most High.

I pray in the words of Moses (on him be peace) when he was told by God to confront Pharaoh: *"Oh Allah, expand me my chest and loosen a knot from my tongue, that they may understand me."* (S. Taha, v. 25-28)

If my words and my story can help someone else find the eye of *their* heart, then this little effort will have been worthwhile.

JOURNEY TO MY SOUL

EYE

OF THE

HEART

SOMMIEH STEPHANIE FLOWER

Part I.

Seeking

Our birth is but a sleep and a forgetting:
The Soul that rises with us, our life's Star,
Hath had elsewhere its setting,
And cometh from afar:
Not in entire forgetfulness,
And not in utter nakedness,
But trailing clouds of glory do we come
From God, who is our home:
Heaven lies about us in our infancy!
Shades of the prison-house begin to close
Upon the growing Boy,
But he beholds the light, and whence it flows,
He sees it in his joy;
The Youth, who daily farther from the east
Must travel, still is Nature's priest,
And by the vision splendid
Is on his way attended;
At length the Man perceives it die away,
And fade into the light of common day.

—William Wordsworth,
excerpt from Ode: Intimations of Immortality, 1804

CHAPTER 1

Seeking the Spheres

Me, three-months-old

*My soul is from elsewhere, I'm sure of that, and I intend to end up
there.*
—*Jalaluddin Rumi (translated by Coleman Barks)*

If this is life, I want to go back!

My newborn eyes squeeze tightly shut to block out the glaring light.
Cold air and the grasp of chilly hands shock and stiffen my body. My face
contorts as my first anguished cry ironically brings joyful relief to the de-
livery room, but not to me. *I want to go back!* I'm passed to a second set of

rubbery hands and plunged into a steely basin of water. I'm poked and prodded—all these sudden invasions.

Where is my warm, peaceful abode? I struggled mightily to leave it, pushing, pushing head first for an eternity of time, only to be released into this? Where am I and who are these alien beings? Only one seems vaguely familiar as but a voice whose rhythms I've heard before; though now I hear it from a distance, not inside my being.

Methodical, efficient hands cleanse me in the basin and lift me back into the coldness. They wrap me in something soft and warm, restoring a small measure of comfort. I'm placed in the arms of the person speaking with the familiar voice. My pitiful cries of loss gradually weaken. Mother's arms hold me close. I settle down to the warmth of her body. The pounding panic in my chest subsides as my heartbeat synchs with hers.

My infant brain tries to grasp some shreds of memory. In some time past, my essence had been placed in a vessel that had grown inside my mother's womb. It had been a warm, familiar, happy home. But now both vessel and spirit together have been dislodged from that home into a cold and terrifying place. *God, are you here? How will I survive?* I cry out wordlessly. From the place of peaceful stillness comes the answer. *You will be safe here. I am always near, and your angels will not leave you. Your parents will love you and cherish you, fulfilling their trust as it has been written. Allahu Akbar, Allahu Akbar, La illaha il Allah. (God is great, God is great. There is no God but Allah.)* Since nobody calls these words from the outside, reassurance echoes strongly from within.

I don't remember my baby days. Photos and family recollections tell me enough to piece together a narrative: I was a chubby, happy baby who grew into a mischievous and energetic toddler. I had curly hair, dimples, and a shy but willing smile for the camera. I was curious about everything and asked many questions. My parents showered me with loving care and concern for my happiness and development. I'd had a mobile for my crib, a playpen, bedtime stories, and plenty of toys. I lacked nothing that my parents could provide. I was safe, happy, warm, well-fed, and loved. These blessings set the foundation for a good life.

My spiritual life also thrived because of my family's love and attention, but it also developed from hidden, unseen places. The *fitrah,* my human nature and my birth right, lived within.

> *Every child is born on the fitrah. It is his parents that make him a Christian, a Jew, or a Magian.*
> —Hadith of Prophet Muhammad ﷺ

CHAPTER 2

A Sense of the World

Age five

I have been birthed into this world called Earth where life is lived through the senses. Meanings and memories build from my eyes, my ears, my nose, my tongue, and my fingertips.

In my earliest memory, I'm lying on my stomach, knees bent, with my feet waving in the air above me, as only a small child can do. I lie midway between the speakers that pour out the music. My hands pat the carpet and roll fluffy gray balls from its fibers. I gaze up at a canvas of pastel-painted trees floating in a misty landscape. I hear the music and ponder the tall trees. Together they form the backdrop to my imagination as my mind paints a landscape of its own.

Mommy changes the records on the turntable in the hall. I know I'm not supposed to touch the record player. "The needle goes around these grooves on the record and makes a sound," she tells me. "You have to be careful not to scratch it or you'll ruin the record." The little needle traces the record as it rotates—slower and faster—teasing me, tempting my hands to touch it just once. Can I change the speed of the turntable or disrupt the progress of the needle? When Mommy goes upstairs I reach out my fingers. *Scrratchhhhhhhh.* The sound it makes is not musical. What if Mommy hears it too?

Many things my nose detects and fingers have to try. The brown powder in the red jar on the kitchen counter smells so delicious; it must be chocolate! Furtively, I swipe some with a spoon and thrust it in my eager mouth. Uggh, so bitter! Not chocolate after all. I rinse my mouth out many times to get rid of the bitter taste. Funny about smells: coffee smells rich and deep like chocolate, but it doesn't taste that way at all when eaten from a spoon!

Daddy's pipe rack sits front and center on his desk. My brother Andrew and I know not to touch the papers or disturb their order... but the pipes! We can't resist their sweet and pungent scent, like musty apples. We put the pipe stems to our lips as if to smoke like daddy, then giggle at the acrid aftertaste that doesn't match their delicious smell.

There's also a big, old trunk in Daddy's study closet filled with photos of people we don't know. We drag Daddy by the hand to his study and ask him who the people in the pictures are. He tells us their stories. "This one is my father, who was in the Russian army and escaped on a boat to America." We stare at the picture of a grandpa we have never known. He wears an army uniform, a tall, furry hat, and boots. His bushy eyebrows arch over almond-shaped eyes, his expression fierce and confident.

We squeal when we discover a naked baby boy lying prone on a divan. His hair is beautifully combed, and he smiles with pleasure. "It's Daddy! What a silly baby!" we exclaim. In Mommy's baby picture, she is fully dressed—a chubby little girl transfixed in time. She's gazing intently at a toy ball, looking like a genius in disguise.

When we reach the limits of Daddy's closet, Andrew wanders off to watch television. I head for the shelves and pull out picture books to wonder over. My favorite is *The Family of Man,* an oversized book of photos. I gaze into the lives of families from around the world: mothers and children, fathers and children, brothers and sisters, and children alone. I imagine myself in these pictures. Reading is another way to discover secrets.

As I grow older, I start to read, first tracing the titles on the books' bindings and sounding out the letters. *T ro pic of C an cer.* I know that cancer is some kind of sickness people only mention in whispers, like the word *divorce.* The thought that someone would write a book about cancer gives me a little thrill of fear. But in my Daddy's study nothing bad will come to me. My world is protected by the sturdy red leather of his easy chair, the soft green grass in our yard, and the gentle voice of my mother's bedtime stories. With a sigh of contentment, I curl up in the big cozy chair and slip into the world between the book covers.

I was born on the *fitrah* and this knowledge stays within me to this day, lodged like a seed in my psyche and my soul. During my childhood, it's not mentioned by my parents. God isn't a part of their picture. But then, as now, I have eyes and ears to see and hear the beauty of the world.

As a young child I roam my backyard, a former forest of stately old trees, flowering lilacs, forsythia, and rhododendrons that bloom in the spring. The bright green grass is my carpet. I wander from tree to bush to flower, enjoying the scents of evergreen and the taste of honeysuckle and grass. I'm a child nurtured by nature. As I wander, I sing little songs to myself and know I am part of this beauty: a part of all that is.

One day after it rains and the air is fresh, I play with friends on my neighbor's driveway. The rain has made small, oily puddles that glisten with tiny colorful rainbows—purple, green, and blue. I squat down for a closer look and become absorbed into the colors; I'm in them and they're in me. A moment of transcendence in a private separate world... Then, just as suddenly, I'm back playing. *You're a part of it all. You're a part.*

Our home is on Secatogue Lane, one long block leading down to the bay. Large, leafy trees line each side of our lane. Their supple branches arch toward each other, their tips like delicate wrists cuffed in leaves. The leaves make a canopy of sunlight and shade. I shut my eyes and bask in the greenness as my parents drive my brother and me to and fro on countless errands and outings. Going out, the trees usher us off to diversions. Coming home, they gather us in under night skies. Their rustling branches whisper the comfort of cozy beds... Just a few moments more to reach up and murmur, "Daddy, can you carry me?"

At age five, Daddy is my hero. But I don't want to share him, especially not with my little brother Andrew. When Daddy comes to say good night, he spends a few minutes at each of our bedsides. He goes to Andrew's room first. I wait impatiently in my room, trying to eavesdrop on their conversation. *Why is Andrew hogging all of Daddy's time?* I wonder jealously. I am sometimes hurt when Daddy doesn't take as much time to talk with me. Sometimes I'm even jealous of my mom. I have the usual girlhood fantasies where both mom and Andrew conveniently disappear, and I get Daddy all to myself. It's the female version of the Oedipus complex.

One day, I notice Davey Cross, a neighbor boy, up in a tree adjacent to our property. He is hammering into the tree and building something. Davey Cross fascinates me. He's rough and tough, older, and wiser. A big boy compared to little five-year-old me. I want to know everything about him. I tip my head back to look up at him, way up in the tree, and call out, "Davey, what are you doing?"

"Building a treehouse," he calls down.

"What's a treehouse?"

No answer, so I stand there with my neck craned, watching. After a few moments, something makes a *pinging* sound as it bounces off the top of my head. It doesn't hurt, exactly, it's just unusual, so I reach up and touch my crown to investigate. When I draw back my hand, it's covered with blood! Soon, bright red blood is trickling down the sides of my face. The crown of my head begins to throb, dully at first, as I run screaming toward the house.

Both of my parents are at work. Only our Costa Rican housekeeper, Matilda, is home looking after my brother and doing the laundry. She takes one look at me and her skin blanches white. "*Ay Dios!*" she cries out, then begins muttering to herself in Spanish. In trying to decide what to do, she grabs a comb, loosens my waist length pigtails, and combs through my hair to identify the source of the blood. That makes it flow more, so I scream even louder. I'm frightened by the sight of my blood. Matilda calls Daddy's office. Between his rudimentary Spanish and her broken English, an emergency is declared, and he comes rushing home. Upon arriving, he scoops me up, bloody shirt and all, and throws me into the car. We are in Good Samaritan's emergency room in five minutes flat. The doctor explains to Daddy that heads bleed a lot, so the superficial wound might seem worse than it really is. "It's just a scratch," Daddy says to comfort me. I receive a few stitches on the top of my head and a lollipop before we go home. Once again, Daddy saved the day. I was happy to have his undivided attention, even if it meant losing blood and shedding tears.

> *To see the world in a grain of sand*
> *And heaven in a wildflower*
> *To hold infinity in the palm of your hand*
> *And eternity in an hour*
> *—William Blake, excerpt from Auguries of Innocence and Experience,*
> *1794*

> *To children, things are never as they seem, but as they imagine them*
> *in their dreams...*
> *—S. Flower, 1975*

Me, age six

CHAPTER 3

Family Ties

My parents, Edward and Marilyn Flower, 1955

My parents are Jews without God. For them, being Jewish is an ethnic distinction. God is either optional or irrelevant to the discussion; He was mostly left back in the old country before World War II and the Holocaust. My maternal and paternal grandparents were already safely ensconced on the Lower East Side of New York in the early twentieth century, so the horror they felt for the Jewish Holocaust in Europe was tinged with guilt over being powerless to stop it. And of course they would have questioned, "Why did God let the Holocaust happen?" Lack of a good answer, compounded by a public-school education that encouraged "scientific thinking," lead my father to become first an agnostic, then an atheist.

I never got to know my paternal grandparents because they died in my infancy. I inherited my almond-shaped eyes with their tendency to crinkle into slits when I smile from my grandpa. That, and my love of horseback riding. My dad even saw his father ride bareback once, in the tradition of our distant Mongolian ancestors. We are descendants of the Khazhar tribes who came from what is now Kazakhstan. Grandpa Isidore came to Ellis Island by boat, escaping from the Russian army, fleeing centuries of Jewish persecution in Eastern Europe. In Russia, we were the family *Tchatchka*, a small knickknack meant for display. I'm glad for the mistranslation. "Flower Power" was a groovy nickname in the sixties, and I was a bud with lots of potential. Also, Flower is much easier to spell and much more American sounding than *Tchatchka!*

My parents, Edward and Marilyn, grew up during the Great Depression and World War II. People were so poor back then that cigarettes were often sold singly instead of in packs. A nickel could get you a ride on the subway and two factory workers would share one lunch. My dad still has among his mementos ration cards issued during the war for items like shoes, stockings, and meat.

Isidore, my paternal grandfather, owned a grocery store and delicatessen called The Epicure. Dad's mother, Rose, married Isidore and became Rose Flower—a happy coincidence. She was a housewife and a loving mother. My dad's earliest memory is of rolling a ball back and forth across the floor with her. According to my Aunt Dotty, Rose treated my father like a prince. He was her oldest child and the only son. The Flower family lived in a series of modest apartments in Long Island City, a part of Queens, New York.

During the Depression, the Flowers took in a boarder and shared a hallway bathroom with another family. Dad shared a room with his younger sister Dotty until his adolescence, when he moved to the living room couch. His youngest sister Annette wasn't born until dad was fifteen, although they share the same birthday. The Flowers were poor by today's standards, yet better off than most people because they owned a store. More importantly, their household was a happy one.

As a boy, my dad was called Eddie and later Ed for short. In his early adolescence, he worked with his father and his uncle Murray at The Epicure, getting items for customers, slicing cold cuts for sandwiches, and making lunch-time deliveries to the factories. Uncle Murray was Rose's much younger half-brother from another mother. Only seven years older than Dad, he was like a brother to him, taking him to ball games and double feature movies, and just looking out for him in general.

Dad was independent from a young age, riding the subway all over the Tri-borough area and Manhattan, and holding a variety of jobs while attending high school and college. He was a very bright student in all subjects, except handwriting. "My teachers knew I was brilliant," he once told me. "So even if they couldn't read my compositions, they still gave me A's." He went on to Stuyvesant High School, a public school in New York City for gifted and talented students, and eventually started his adult career as a teacher. When he realized a teacher's salary would not support the lifestyle he aspired to, he began attending law school at night.

My mother Marilyn's family was smaller and more insular than Dad's and not as happy. Her maternal grandparents, Lina and Gershon, immigrated to the United States from Russia around 1910 with their two-year-old daughter Sarah. Lina had married Gershon, a house painter, when she was just fifteen years old. They came to America, as everyone did, with big dreams of a better life. Sarah was their only child, and she and her young mother grew very close.

My paternal and maternal grandfathers were both named Isidore. Grandpa Izzy, on my mom's side, came to America as a young man. He finished high school and went on to become a pharmacist with his own drug store and soda fountain. He married Sarah and they raised two daughters, my mother Marilyn, born in 1930, and her sister Gail, who is nine years her junior. Their age difference meant they would not grow to be close childhood friends. When my eighty-six-year-old mom talks in her sleep, taking care of her sister is a recurring topic in her monologues.

At some point, and for reasons unknown to me, Izzy gave up the drug store. During the war years, he became a fabric cutter in a coat factory run by his mother-in-law's brother. He was a sensitive, gentle man easily overpowered by his wife and in-laws. They all lived in the same house on Ocean Parkway in Brooklyn, a fairly nice address for the time. Mom and Gail grew up there. But it was not a happy home. There was fighting and constant stress in the household. They had enough to live on, but the anxiety of "not enough" was ever present. Lina was jealous of her only child's close marital relationship. She and Gershon fought bitterly and were never close companions the way Sarah and Isidore were. In his later years, when I was an infant, Gershon broke his leg and could no longer work as a house painter. He grew so despondent about his life that he hung himself in the family basement.

When he was forty-seven, my grandpa Izzy had a stroke. Now there was the worry of his illness on top of the other domestic problems. My Aunt Gail recalls that the household was never happy or joyful, but always somber and quiet. "Your mother had it hard," she commented. "So did I, but I didn't come till nine years later, and I was tougher than she was." Sarah and Lina were the dominant figures in the household, and they also fought with each other. Mom was sometimes caught in the middle as she tried to please them both, losing her own budding identity in the process. She became what they wanted her to be and did as she was told. Music, luckily, was a positive influence in her life. She learned to play the piano and played it beautifully. She loved classical music and wanted to be a concert pianist. She later made sure my brother and I learned to play the piano and always took care to surround us with beautiful music.

My mother was a very intelligent woman, but she lacked confidence. Her high school guidance counselor told her she "wasn't college material," but she proved him wrong and got her bachelor's degree in education and later two masters' degrees. She went into teaching because her mother and grandmother insisted that it was a good career for a woman to fall back on if her husband fell ill or lost his job. That had been Sarah's own experience and that was also the thinking of the times.

My parents met at Green Mansions, an upstate New York resort. My mother saw my dad sitting by the side of the lake. He was drying himself with a towel when she asked, "Have you been in the water?"

"Yes," he replied. "Why don't you sit down?"

So she did, and a conversation that would continue for decades to come began. He was smiling and handsome; his wet shoulders and hair glistened in the sun. My mother didn't swim but was stylish in a pair of shorts that showed off her great legs and nice curves. They began a courtship that continued once they returned to the city. Both families gave the couple their blessing and life plans were made. My dad was in law school, and my mom was soon to graduate and begin teaching. Each of them had been engaged before and knew the ups and downs of love; they knew what they were getting themselves into.

Marilyn and Ed married and moved to West Islip on Long Island on November 24, 1955. He started practicing law, first in the garage of their modest house on Pine Avenue, then later taking on partners and opening an office. He was hard-working, energetic, and optimistic about the future. She taught at a local elementary school, devoting her time to her students with compassion and concern. They met other young couples, played bridge and Monopoly, and enjoyed short vacations.

I enter the picture three years later. I'm born on January 19, 1958, the first child and grandchild in the family. I'm given all the love and attention in the world. Great grandma Lina comes to stay with us to help my mother. Both sets of grandparents, Uncle Murray and his new wife, Pixie, and various other family members visit our little house on Pine Avenue. Grandpa Izzy, his bad leg dragging behind him, never refuses me a horsey ride on his knee, and Aunt Gail's new husband, Uncle Vic, seems like the tallest man in the world whenever he lifts me up to touch the ceiling.

Dad gets briefly involved in local politics, running for Islip town supervisor. One night he gets an angry phone call from his Republican rival. It seems that Mom and her best friend Simone have been spotted around town climbing telephone poles and removing the Republican party campaign posters. As they say, "You can take the girl out of Brooklyn but you can't take Brooklyn out of the girl." Mom's actually pregnant with my brother Andrew at the time this escapade occurs. He's born on October 31, 1959. Dad loses the election.

Dad, though, does well enough in his law practice to buy a new house for our young family. He invests in the stock market, but daily checking the ups and downs of the market adds stress without pleasure to his life and aggravates his ulcer. After he settles his first large case in 1966, he makes the momentous decision to switch from investing in stocks to investing in art instead. Collecting becomes a passion he and Mom will share together. They begin by acquiring paintings and prints by American and European artists of the nineteenth and twentieth centuries, and soon broaden their acquisitions to include small sculptures and ceramics. As soon as we are old enough to behave, Andrew and I begin accompanying our parents to art galleries, museums, auction houses and flea markets. Visual art, drama, and music become our family's preferred forms of entertainment. New York City is our playground.

It is also during this time that Murray and Pixie often round out our Saturdays. Though he was actually my great uncle, Murray was *everyone's* uncle in our family. He and Pixie, formally known as Rita, married relatively late in life. They choose to be childless yet lavish love on all their nieces, nephews, and friends' kids instead. They travel the world, delighting my cousins and I with wonderful anecdotes and unique gifts. Their cozy Manhattan apartment is open to family and friends alike for joyful holiday gatherings. I love to exit the elevator on their building's fifth floor and smell the delicious aromas wafting down the hallway from their tiny New York kitchen. Their home is a paradise of memorabilia from their travels, exotic green plants, and books, books, books tumbling from the shelves and stacked and piled everywhere. Murray is an English teacher par excellence, adored by all his students at the High School of Performing Arts. Pixie is an executive secretary at a prominent New York law firm with celebrity clientele. It is Pixie who takes me by the hand on Saturdays and leads me on adventures to the American Museum of Natural History. In her musical voice she tells me all about the Native Americans who lived on the island of Manhattan, right where we now stand.

Saturdays are for the city and Sundays are for family visits. The front lawn is where Andrew and I wait for the visitors we most want to see: the ones who will bring us presents! Andrew and I wait on the lawn chanting a little song as we watch each passing car: "Grandma, Grandpa, Grandma, Grandpa." We repeat this mantra again and again until they arrive. What have they brought me this time? Is it a doll, a book, a necklace, or a stuffed animal? I go through phases of desire, and Grandma never disappoints. I learn to say "thank you" before running off to my room to start reading the latest Nancy Drew or to nestle the new doll into my burgeoning collection.

If we visit Grandma and Grandpa, we often go to their dress shop, Rozelle Fashions. Behind the shop is a large work room where three seamstresses make customized alterations on fancy dresses. That back room is a gold mine to Andrew and me. We fight for command of the magnetized "magic" wand that picks up the pins from the floor. We love taking home fabric scraps, sequins, and buttons, and we jealously guard our personal collections from one another.

My father does exceptionally well in his law practice. Long Island is booming with real estate development and road construction—he is in the right place at the right time and is making good money. He likes to drive and favors big, comfortable cars that we take on road trips around the country, stopping at historic restorations and recreational sites. I see most of the fifty states during my childhood. The summer when I'm five, we travel cross country to California in a big Cadillac with fins, but no air conditioning. We go to Yellowstone National Park in Wyoming and see real live bears and geysers gushing from the ground. We visit the Grand Canyon, and Native American reservations in the Southwest. In national parks with scenic views, I marvel at the grand scale of nature.

Between outings and travels, my mother trains my ears through music, and my father trains my eyes to see the beauty of the world. "Look at the sunlight on the water!" he exclaims as we cross the Brooklyn Bridge. The dappled sunlight on the water sparkles just like diamonds and the cables of the bridge itself are glinting in the sun. There is beauty in unexpected places too, like the urban factories with their smokestacks set against the blue background of the sky. I learn that beauty is in the eye of the behold-er, though, thanks to a print hanging in our front hallway called *Businessman's Bath*. I am embarrassed by the sight of naked old men chomping on cigars in a public bathhouse in turn of the century New York. But to my father, it's a piece of artful history. He laughs when I ask him to at least remove it from our front hall!

I'm finishing this chapter in my parents' Long Island home. It's not the one I grew up in, though it is only five minutes from Southside Hospital where I was born. I watch my eighty-six-year-old father as he leans over my frail mother, seated in a wheelchair. He strokes her beautiful silvery hair and gives her a kiss. Nowadays, she accepts his affections and gazes after him as he leaves the room. When I was a child, her common retort to him was, "Get your greasy hands off me!" as she stood at the kitchen sink, and he came up behind her with an after-dinner hug. In their sixty-year-old marriage, I see patterns of argumentative, yet loyal and loving behavior. My mother suffers from dementia, but let Dad tell any of his many stories, and she's right there, listening. When he finishes, she'll come out with a one liner like, "Are you happy now?" or "Are you crazy?" Sometimes it's just one word, like "Really?" but it's dripping with sarcasm. We all prefer her sardonic comments at the dinner table to the days when she's eating with her eyes closed. Dementia has made her a shadow of her former self. It's scary and depressing to go through the progression of this illness with her, especially for my dad. He keeps his sanity by going to his law firm, working out with his personal trainer at the YMCA, and continuing to add works of art to his substantial collection. He's become an expert at "cook-ing with a credit card," as he says. He plans and prepares catered meals for my mom, himself, and the aides who attend to her twenty-four hours a day, doing everything from bathing to changing to feeding her.

Mom's been suffering from non-Alzheimer's dementia for the past five years. Unlike Alzheimer's, dementia is not fatal, but it is progressive. At this point in time, she recognizes me, my father, and the people who see her on a daily basis, but there may come a time when she will no longer know who we are. She stands up and walks only with the assistance of her physical therapist. She still enjoys an occasional wheelchair ride around the neighborhood for fresh air and listening to music or looking at pictures of her grandchildren and great grandchildren, though she doesn't always know who they are. She enjoys her meals, as long as someone feeds her. At least she doesn't worry about calories anymore! She hates being changed or washed, and the worst thing is having to brush her teeth. My dad is very fortunate to be able to afford homecare for my mom. He's done his utmost to provide the best of everything for her, just the way he's done their entire married life.

Mom lived as many women of her generation, as a helpmate to her husband, revolving her life around his schedule and the needs of her family. When she worked on her master's degree in library science, I was in high school. I sense that she was trying to come into her own at that time, to build her own identity and career, but maybe she lacked the confidence or the financial need to carry it through. She worked mainly as a volunteer in the local library because her life with my father was too full of vacations and trips to Manhattan to hold down a regular job. In her fifties, she suffered some anxiety problems that gradually caused her to stop driving. She never learned to use a computer. Perhaps the lack of motivation or confidence to try new things even contributed to the development of her dementia.

I cherish the pictures I have of my mother. There's the intense little baby staring at her ball, the mischievous kindergartner in her overalls, the demure high school graduate, the classically beautiful bride, and the giggling newlywed on her honeymoon. I miss her smile!

My eighty-seven-year-old father is still the family patriarch, taking care of all our needs as much as he can. Is this sense of responsibility what has kept him looking so young? We all depend on this man who has worked hard all his life and is still working for all of us. He overflows with generosity and love. Our family couldn't be more blessed than to have him. He is the patriarch but he doesn't expect rigid obedience in return for his patronage and never attaches strings to his gifts. He's let us each grow in our own way, but helps us financially whenever he can. In 2010, I announced to my family that I was traveling to Pakistan to be with my new husband. In such times of political turmoil, social injustice, and violence, it's natural that they'd worry. I called my uncle Murray. By now, he and Pixie were both in their nineties. He used the occasion to tell me about the circle of concern that exists in a family—among one of many ties that bind a family together. He spoke about how everyone shares joys, sorrows, and worries. That's what family is all about. I thank God for my family because without their care, I would not be who I am today.

Thy Lord hath decreed that ye worship none but Him, and that ye be kind to parents. Whether one or both of them attain old age in thy life, say not to them a word of contempt, nor repel them, but address them in terms of honor. And out of kindness, lower to them the wing of humility, and say: "My Lord! bestow on them Thy Mercy even as they cherished me in childhood." (S. Bani Israel, v. 23–24)

CHAPTER 4

Raising a Reader

Age five

"*The Little White House* is too easy for her. She read it at home last year. She needs to be reading *On Cherry Street*. I want her reading group changed." Mom was talking on the phone to my first-grade teacher, while I eavesdropped. Then she turned to me and said, "Make sure you read loudly and clearly when the teacher calls on you. There's nothing to be afraid of."

After that conversation, I try my best and do get placed in the more advanced reading group. I am shy and quiet, but smart. Between bedtime stories and bookshelf browsing, I've learned to read.

In the pale pink bedroom of my childhood, books are piled everywhere, library books as well as my own. I spend countless hours happily reading, completely immersed in the world of *The Five Little Peppers and How They Grew*, as well as *The Uptown Family*, and when I get older, *Little Women*, and *Little House on the Prairie.* The books I read over and over are fantasies and fairytales, such as *Charlie and the Chocolate Factory, A Little Princess,* and *Hans Christian Andersen's Fairytales.* I love the details of each character's life: what they ate and wore, and who they shared their bed and their secrets with. Andrew and I share our secrets at night until one or the other falls asleep. We whisper loudly across the landing—me in my pink room and him in his blue one—until Mom or Dad comes down the hall or calls from their bedroom, "Be quiet and go to sleep."

Andrew's room, having first been our father's study, has wall-to-wall built in shelving and a treasure trove: three kinds of encyclopedias. There is dad's old red *Encyclopedia Britannica,* bought with his own money when he was still in high school. Then there are *World Book* and *Childcraft.* A salesman had shown us those books in our own living room, pointing out the glossy pages with their color illustrations and transparencies that overlap to show the different systems of the human body or the structure of an atom. *Childcraft* is perfection. It has fifteen wonderful volumes. I love them all but my favorites are *Stories and Fables, Holidays and Customs, Make and Do,* and *How Things Change.* I devour them on rainy or wintry days, going back to read my favorite entries over and over.

My room is on the north side of the house. It has a large picture window, and it's usually cold. We use a space heater during the winter months to keep it cozy. I sit on the floor with my back on the warm baseboard and an apple in hand, reading for hours. Andrew is elsewhere, maybe watching TV. Mom and Dad are somewhere in the kitchen or the study. I am in my own little orbit, reading. Whenever Mom calls upstairs for me to set the table, take the laundry up, or put away the groceries, I hear her but pretend not to, or I call down, "Just a minute," then read on to finish another chapter or two.

Having a mother who works as a teacher in the school district has both advantages and disadvantages. I'm a January baby, born in the new year of 1958. But the school year begins in September and the public school has age requirements. A child has to be five years old by November in order to start kindergarten in September, and I am only four and a half.

My parents don't want to wait the extra year, so they find a private school that waives the age requirement and send me there for kindergarten. The school is not in our town, but it does provide bus service. After spending my first day in the old, Tudor-style school building, which I find a bit scary, I board the bus to go home. It's a big bus, but it's not full. After a long while, I am the last one on the bus, a four-year-old girl with pigtails whose little legs don't even hang over the edge of the seat. I'm in the back, a long way from the driver. Does he even know I'm back here? I wonder. Suddenly, he turns around and asks, "Little girl, where do you live?" I'm silent. *Where do I live? I don't know.* "What's your address?" he asks. Again, I say nothing, because I don't even know what an address is.

For some reason, I'm not afraid. I'm just wondering when and how I'm going to get home. Finally, the driver stops to use a pay phone to call someone who can tell him where I live. Of course, Mommy's upset with me when I walk in the door. "Why didn't you tell him your address?"

"Because I don't know it," I reply calmly. "What's an address?"

The next day, there's no school for me, but I still need to learn two things. "My address is 211 Secatogue Lane, West Islip, NY," I keep repeating after Mommy until I can say it on my own. "211 Secatogue Lane, 211 Secatogue Lane." At the same time, I'm learning how to go up and down the stairs without stopping on each step, like babies do. Mommy wants me to know these two things before returning to school, so I keep marching up and down the stairs, saying "211 Secatogue Lane, 211 Secatogue Lane," in a sing-song voice in time with my footsteps.

Near the end of kindergarten, the school gives me a strange kind of test. I have to circle boxes, make Xs, and draw things. Mom and dad use this test to convince the public school that I am ready for first grade even though I won't be six until January. My parents get what they want, and I begin first grade at age five.

In second grade, I have Mrs. Anderson, who is young and inexperienced. She doesn't know how to handle the many social situations second graders need help navigating. I'm only six while most of my peers are seven. I'm introverted and quiet, as likely to play alone with my dolls as I am my classmates. One day, I bring my new Thumbelina baby doll to school.

A bully of a girl named Tracy grabs the doll away from me and won't give it back. I start crying and Mrs. Anderson finally takes notice. She approaches the scene and says, "Only babies bring dolls to school and then cry about them. You're not a baby, are you?" Tracy is delighted to have escaped notice for her behavior and begins calling me a baby on a regular basis. She makes the rest of that year miserable for me. I withdraw further into myself to avoid conflict with some of the bigger, tougher kids like Tracy.

I do not tell my parents about the doll incident; instead, I pretend not to care if other kids bother me. After all, I am better than them. My father is richer than theirs, I have better toys and clothes than they do, and I'm smarter. Our family eats out every weekend and goes to the city in a Cadillac, not on the train. An attitude of superiority begins to cloak my shyness and reserve at school. I am a princess like the ones in the books I read—a secret princess—and those kids that bother me are nobodies.

Third grade brings a different set of problems. My teacher is also my mom's close friend and that means my daily behavior and struggles are under closer scrutiny than ever before. I am certainly struggling with math. Multiplication tables have to be memorized and this proves very hard for me because I don't really understand what multiplication is all about: I don't get the concept. My teacher Mrs. Maurer wants us to rattle off the tables in front of the class while she times us to see who can recite them the fastest and most accurately. I can do neither, and I'm nervous about it. Mom and her friend agree a tutor is necessary. So off I go to a well-intentioned tutor a few days a week after school. I try to improve, but my eyes just glaze over, and I feel sleepy whenever she starts to explain anything to me.

Unlike math, reading is my favorite pastime; wherever I am, I devour books. I am especially interested in fantasies and stories of children from other times and places. When I'm eight years old, my family and I take a scenic trip to Vermont to see the changing of the autumn leaves. As we drive, Mom keeps calling back to me, "Stephy, look out the window," but I'm too engrossed in the fat new book Grandma has given me to bother glancing up. The book is two stories in one, and Heidi's mountain adventures and Hans Brinker's skates prove more compelling than real life!

There is no Frigate like a Book
To take us Lands away
Nor any Coursers like a Page
Of prancing Poetry —
This Traverse may the poorest take
Without oppress of Toll —
How frugal is the Chariot
That bears the Human Soul —
—Emily Dickinson, 1873

CHAPTER 5

Lenore-Owaissa Bluebird

At camp in 1968

In the summer of 1967, my parents send me to sleep-away camp. Lenore-Owaissa is nestled in the Berkshire Hills of Massachusetts. A beautiful, peaceful green pervades the atmosphere here, from the rolling hills to the wide campus lawns. Our uniforms are green with a white bluebird logo. Even the blanket on my camp bed is a bright, kelly green. I love lying on it on warm summer afternoons, writing long, descriptive letters home.

Steffi comes alive at camp; two Fs instead of a ph make all the difference. Steffi is a bolder, more fearless, more active, and more mature version of Stephy. She's more confident and more popular—more of everything that counts in my little world.

I spend eight summers at Lenore-Owaissa and love every moment there, from the chilly morning walks to the blazing evening campfires. I belong at camp in a way I've never belonged anywhere before. Ninety-eight percent of the girls there are Jewish—not religious, but ethnically Jewish, like my family. We share a common culture. The camp directors, Dotty Langer and Joe, have skillfully designed an environment that has just the right mix of everything a young girl might need, including spirituality. Friday nights mean white dress uniforms with Sabbath candle lighting, and Bible story reenactments performed by young girls in rusty old costumes.

Big and Little Sisters is one of the most significant activities at camp. We girls spend the first few weeks of the summer in anticipation of the important night when our big or little sister gets assigned. Each young camper is assigned a big sister, an older girl she can go to for sisterly love and advice. We little sisters are treated almost like cute and amusing pets. In exchange for our cuteness, we're allowed to perch on our big sisters' beds and learn as much as we can about being a teenager. I have no sisters at home, so this is very important to me. I want to know how to apply lipstick and what kind of music is cool.

My first big sister is a glamorous girl named Joanie. She is absolutely beautiful, and I want to be just like her. Sandy is my big sister for several years after Joanie. Sandy's a jock, not a glamour girl. She plays tennis well and becomes my role model for women and sports. I become a fair tennis player myself over the next few years, and Sandy helps me with my strokes. Though Sandy is not the beauty Joanie is, I find her heart is very warm and beautiful.

Dotty Langer makes each camper feel special, and I blossom at camp. I discover a passion for horseback riding and swimming, enjoy arts and crafts, and discover that I'm a fairly good artist when I give myself half a chance.

Honor Camper awards are issued weekly to the girls who behave best and are the most cooperative and helpful to others. One year I am particularly determined to win such an award and focus especially hard on being good and helping my counselor. I do get an award; however, the following week I go down to the lake without permission—a serious offence—which gets me thrown off the honor roll. From that experience, I learn that doing good just for the sake of a reward is insincere—it's not a good reason to behave well. I now recognize that intrinsic motivation holds more value than extrinsic motivation for me.

At camp, I am not the smallest, the quietest, or the weakest. I am well-liked and popular. But there's an insecurity in that status. It can easily change if you don't read all the right magazines and comics, like *MAD* and *Archie*, listen to the most popular songs, or generally know when to say the right thing at the right moment. Every year, there is someone in our bunk who is weaker than the rest of us, and though I know from my experiences at school what it's like to be bullied, I still do my fair share of harassing whichever girl we choose as our scapegoat. I am not moral or noble in this regard. One of the people I hurt most is my own cousin, Patty. Although I am nice to her at home, I want nothing to do with her at camp and tease her along my other bunkmates. Sad to say, I chose popularity over loyalty.

The campers at Lenore-Owaissa are ninety-eight percent Jewish, but our counselors are from all backgrounds and all regions of the United States. We even have tennis and riding instructors from Ireland and England. The year I'm nine, my counselor is from Missouri. Her accent is very different from the East Coast English I'm familiar with. One day it starts to rain and Pat instructs us to "Get our *tayls* in." I think she's telling us to come in out of the rain, so I do. But she keeps saying, "Steffi, get your *tayl* in," while gesturing outside at the rain. Get your *tayl*, your *tayl!*" I am confused and really don't know what she means. So finally I say in all seriousness, "But I don't have a tail!" So she marches me outside to the clothesline so I can retrieve my *towel* before it gets soaking wet.

Many camps have color wars, but Lenore-Owaissa has a special activity called SING. It is a performance-based activity that is eagerly anticipated and takes weeks of planning. The part I like best about SING is writing the songs' lyrics. We choose popular tunes and write our own words for them based on themes. I discover a talent for this and begin writing songs that set my own poetry to music. When I am SING co-captain during my senior year at camp, I write:

"Back through the hour glass the sands will flow,
Touching on memories from long ago.
The spirit of Lenore Owaissa will live on
Within our hearts though signs of youth are gone"

My favorite activity at camp is horseback riding. The horses are magnificent beings of substance, power, and beauty in glossy browns, blacks, beiges, and whites. I especially enjoy stroking their muzzles; they're so velvety soft. Atop our mounts, we amble over winding trails, through dense green woods on paths worn smooth by horses' hooves. It is there that I experience another "green" moment, when the entire world dissolves into splendor, enveloping my senses and the very sense of who I am. The trees are draped with hanging vines. Dappled sunlight dances on the leaves. Everything in that moment is part of one Unity. All is perfect, peaceful, and serene. These moments keep my face turned toward the light and keep my feet walking toward God, though my innocent mind and heart seem unaware of the destination that awaits me.

And the earth, We spread it out and cast therein firmly set mountains
and made grow therein something of every beautiful kind
(S. Qaf, v. 7)

At camp with my mother and grandparents, Visiting Day, 1968

CHAPTER 6

School Days

Williamsburg, VA. 1966

After my summers at camp, I return to school each fall full of confidence. For the next eight years, my dad willingly drives me all over Long Island and even to New Jersey for sleepovers and parties with my camp friends. My social world and my school world have become two separate entities.

Fifth grade is the year of Mr. Gaggin, my first male teacher (male elementary school teachers being quite a rarity circa 1968). We students really don't know what to make of him initially, but it's Mr. Gaggin who pushes me to write my first book. I had just read *Follow My Leader*, the story of a boy who was blinded in an accident and gets a guide dog. The book makes a big impression on me, so I decide to write my own story based on the same theme. Mr. Gaggin encourages me, and the secretary in Dad's office even types up my manuscript. It's more than ten pages! I'm very proud but wonder why nobody realizes that I've copied the idea from someone else's book? Or, if they have realized, why doesn't anyone say anything? Perhaps they don't want to crush my dream of being a future, famous author!

Whatever their reasons, they worked. Writing becomes a lifelong activity of mine—both writing for pleasure and to gain insight into myself and others. Travelogues, diaries, and more than thirty journals written during my adulthood attest to this fact, though I admit much of the evidence has been destroyed to protect the innocent!

In addition to writing, singing is also something I learn to love in school. The best part about elementary school music class with Mrs. Cunningham is getting ready for our school holiday concerts around Easter and Christmas. There is usually one Hanukkah selection thrown in, but it's vastly overshadowed by the beautiful Christmas carols we learn to sing. I secretly love Christmas, even though it's not my holiday. A feeling of peace seems to come over everyone at that time of year, and it's so beautiful, especially if it snows. Hanukkah pales by comparison.

Mrs. Pescuma is the queen of teachers, the one all the professional parents want their child to have. As a school district insider, my mother makes sure I'm in Mrs. Pescuma's sixth-grade class. In a suburban Long Island school system, she's at the vanguard of teaching. All learning in her classroom is based on projects designed by the students. She makes sure our classroom is filled with music, art, and light. When it's time to practice our cursive writing, she puts multicultural songs from the countries we're studying on the record player, and we write the lyrics in our best handwriting, singing to ourselves as we go.

Best of all, Mrs. Pescuma accepts each student as he or she is, working with their strengths to bolster their weaknesses. Whenever I freeze at the blackboard, trying to remember how to do long division, Mrs. Pescuma is right beside me, shielding my mistakes from the view of my classmates and walking me calmly through the math problems, step by step. She has thick, dark hair, and olive skin. She talks with her hands and is energetic, animated, and creative. All of us love her. She makes it a joy to come to school. She even talks to us girls on the playground about such womanly subjects as the pros and cons of shaving our legs! (She's against shaving at a young age, as is my mother.)

Our class writes two original plays featuring the Peanuts gang. One play is about pollution, and the other is called *The Peanuts Gang Goes to Australia.* I land one of the main parts as Charlie Brown's little sister, Sally. Linus is played by the most hyper boy in the class. Snoopy is played by the boy who stopped talking when his mother died suddenly in the middle of the school year. Mrs. Pescuma knows all sorts of secrets to bring children out of their shells, help them cope with their lives, and let them glimpse their future potential.

When I eventually study education, I realize just how far ahead of her time Mrs. Pescuma was. I try to model my own teaching practices on her example and have her ever in mind when I design professional development courses and workshops for teachers.

> *Do not debilitate your hearts. Seek for them creative and fun ways to teach wisdom, for they tire like your bodies do.*
> — *Hazrat Ali ibn Abu Talib (r.a.)* *

*Abbreviation for Radthi Allahu Anhu - may Allah be pleased with him. This is as a term of respect for companions of the Prophet ﷺ.

CHAPTER 7

Neighbors

Melissa Cheply in my bedroom, 1968

When I was nine years old, bulldozers cleared away the last remaining bit of woods next to our house. From the time we could first play alone in the yard, we children had been warned away from those woods by our parents and neighbors. "If you go in there, the winos will get you!" Or, "The boogeyman lives in there. If he catches you, you'll never see your parents again." With the woods gone, we could see some broken glass bottles and the remains of a few campfires, so maybe those stories were true.

The men work for many days, clearing the land, cutting down trees, and pulling out stumps. Like our own backyard, many large, mature trees are left standing in the dirt, the basis of another beautiful yard to be. Andrew and I watch the whole process. Many days find us glued to our front lawn, watching cement mixers and men working in a huge rectangular hole in the ground. "They're pouring the foundation for a new house," Daddy explains. "Soon a house will be there, and then we'll have next door neighbors." *Neighbors! Where before only trees stood, now there will be a house and people. I'm sure they'll have children, a dog, and a girl my age. We'll be best friends for life and... and... and...* My imagination spins out a whole best-friend scenario, and Andrew's does the same, as we wait every day for builders to arrive with their hammers, nails, and sheetrock. But they never come.

Disappointed, we give up watching for a house to be built over the rectangular hole in the ground. But just as soon as we give up waiting, one day, all of a sudden, a house arrives—an entire house pulled by a trailer! Somehow it's secured to the foundation. We're amazed to come home from school and find a house already standing where there had been just a hole in the ground that very morning.

The house is followed by a family. They are the Cheplys: Bob and Geri, and their children, Keith, Craig, and Missy. They soon adopt a white German shepherd puppy called Holly. She and Tiny, our St. Bernard puppy, devise their own racetrack running parallel to either side of the fence separating our yards. Up and down they run, incessantly, snarling and barking like sworn enemies in a never-ending, do-or-die race to the finish that wears dirt paths on both sides of the fence—paths that are still visible forty years later.

The boys are much older than Andrew and I, especially Keith, but Missy is only one grade ahead of me in school, and we become best friends up until high school, where we drift apart. Our afternoons are filled with games in our two big backyards: hide and seek, SPUD, and our very own Olympic games complete with gold, silver, and bronze medals of distinction. One of the events is walking on a barrel until you fall off, while someone carefully keeps time. Then we issue medals according to who balanced the longest. Missy usually gets the gold, me silver, and Andrew bronze.

We enjoy lazy afternoons swinging in the Cheply's hammock, slung between two shady old trees to catch some coolness on a summer day. The hammock can fit two if necessary, but nobody wants to share, so we take turns and time each other. If someone gets too greedy, we swing the hammock back and forth violently until the occupant is inevitably dumped to the ground.

The Cheplys spend much more time at home than our family does. They also live more simply. They drive Volkswagens with stick shift transmissions, the economy cars of the times. The Cheplys have both a Beetle and a van. They also do their own landscaping and cultivate a beautiful flower garden in their front yard. Andrew and I often help them plant the seeds and seedlings.

Mrs. Cheply becomes our second mother. Andrew and I regularly run into her warm, motherly arms so she can tend to our little cuts and bruised egos. We can always count on her sympathy, often followed by a bowl of vanilla ice cream with honey. I relish that delicious, sweet confection sliding down my throat.

Mrs. Cheply is a master at making ends meet. She sews clothes for her family, and makes curtains and slipcovers. She's creative and artistic, decorating for each holiday with ceramic Christmas trees and gaily painted ceramic bunnies and eggs. The Cheply's house is warm and festive, whereas ours is stylish and elegant. Andrew and I are frequent guests at their dinner table, where summer salad, bread, and beans are served after saying grace. One of Mrs. Cheply's favorite expressions is "You have to eat a peck of dirt before you die." She would use this expression to address some of our childish complaints and problems.

The Cheplys are Baptists and try their best to put religion into practice. The summer I'm eleven, Missy sets out to save my soul and get me baptized. Through her own religious training, she's convinced that if I don't get baptized, I will go to Hell. I'm her best friend, and she loves me sincerely and wants me to be in Heaven with her and all the good people. That summer, while I'm away at camp, she encourages me to write her Sunday school teacher with all of my questions. This I do, sending letters full of questions: "How do you know there is a God? Why was Jesus his son and not the other prophets? What happens to us when we die?" Missy's teacher writes back and a dialogue begins. But the idea of Jesus as the son of God is too foreign and strange for me to believe. I am, after all, Jewish. When I ask Dad about Jesus, he tells me, "If he really existed, he was just a man who believed in doing good. A religion, Christianity, was started by those who followed his teachings. If God exists, He has no son because He wasn't a human being. Each person is responsible for his own behavior, which should be based on morals and ethics, not religious doctrine."

Missy's continues her mission of trying to get me to accept Jesus Christ as my personal savior and to have me baptized. I wonder if her parents had known what she was up to! A few years later, when I'm in junior high, the record *Jesus Christ Superstar, a Rock Opera,* is released. I am fascinated by its lyrics—which I memorize—and its storyline. The rabbi at Sinai Reform Temple does his best to speak out against the record, saying it rehashes the myth of the Jews as the killers of Jesus. We kids just think it's cool music.

In 1981, when my first child is born, Missy Cheply and I are both home visiting our parents. She comes to see the baby and the new, Muslim me. I thank her for her child-like optimism in loving me enough to want me baptized and to save me from Hell. Neither of us knew it at the time, but her Christian love kept my footsteps moving on the path toward recognizing God's role in my life. The Cheply family had nurtured more than plants in their garden. They'd nurtured this "Flower" girl as well.

And there are certainly,
Among the People of the Book,
Those who believe in God,
In the revelation to you
And in the revelation to them,
Bowing in humility to God;
They will not sell
The Signs of God
For a miserable gain!
For them is a reward with their Lord,
And God is swift in account.
(S. Al Imran, v.199)

CHAPTER 8

Looking for God

My Bat Mitzvah, 1971

Who was God and what did He have to do with me? Not much, according to Daddy. "If there was a God, He created the universe and then disappeared."

"If there is a God, why are there so many problems in the world?" my mom would add.

"If he does exist, then how can you explain the Holocaust?" asked my dad. That question usually ended the discussion.

Only Grandma had told me, with some measure of certainty, "Yes, Stephy, there is a God and he lives in Heaven." The Cheplys believed that too. But their God was Jesus and he wasn't a Jew. Or was he? I was confused and wanted answers, not questions!

None of my close relatives were religious in the sense of actually practicing the faith. We did have one branch of my mother's family in California that had converted to Hebrew Christianity back in the 1940s. My grandma's Cousin Annie was a staunch follower. They considered themselves Jews who had accepted Jesus as their savior. Annie promoted the faith with her own radio show. She had tried to convert my mother when my mother was a young woman, but Mom's father had forbidden such a heretical act. Annie came to New York in 1981 when my grandmother was dying and read the New Testament at her bedside. When I showed up there with a Quran she told my grandma that I was worshipping a false God! Both Grandma and her Cousin Annie have since passed away. I wish them God's mercy in their afterlife.

The rest of my paternal and maternal relatives identified being Jewish as a socio-cultural distinction more than a religious one. The previous generation had left much of their Jewishness in the "old country" of Eastern Europe. My dad, his uncle, and his sister Dotty all went to Hebrew school and the boys had their bar mitzvahs because that coming of age ceremony was an important part of Jewish cultural tradition. My mom studied Hebrew as an elective at Brooklyn College. They both fulfilled their families' expectations by marrying Jewish spouses and trying to raise children who knew the most significant features of their heritage.

My parents join Sinai Reform Temple in Bayshore when I'm about ten years old. They do so to keep Andrew and me in touch with our roots and perhaps so we will socialize more with Jewish friends. After all, Jews are in the minority in the West Islip school system—most of our classmates are of Irish and Italian, Protestant, and Catholic descents. The weekly and holiday services at Sinai are mostly in English with a few Hebrew prayers left in for tradition's sake. Andrew and I go to Sunday School and take Hebrew classes on Tuesday evenings. In Sunday school, we learn the history of the Jewish people, chosen by God around the time of Abraham because they recognized that there was only one God. A very significant prayer in Judaism is the *Shema*. It's first line translates as: "Hear O Israel, The Lord Your God, The Lord is One." It is very similar to the 111th chapter in the Quran—which begins, "Say He is Allah, He is One"—especially when you look at the Arabic and Hebrew texts side by side.

In Sunday school, I learn that the Jewish people believe in one God. But I get a different message at home, where belief is optional. I am learning about the Jewish holidays in Hebrew school and want to celebrate them with full observance at home. Consequently, I am disappointed when my family attaches almost no religious significance to these days. They are just a time to get together with our relatives. Family is important, but ritual practices are not. My Jewish home life never matches up with what I am learning in Hebrew School. This dichotomy frustrates me.

Our family attends religious services on the High Holy Days of Rosh Hashanah, Yom Kippur, and Passover, the three major holidays of the Jewish calendar. I love Rosh Hashanah, the Jewish New Year, which comes in the fall, along with a new year of school. Rosh Hashanah means new fall clothes and beautiful autumn colors. It also means apples dipped in honey and honey cake to herald a sweet new year. Perhaps my lifelong love of honey stems from that single tradition. Coming home from school I'd drink a very large mug of tea with lots of honey in it. To this day, I've always preferred honey over sugar, even in coffee.

I like the songs and the ritual prayers in temple, the call and response between rabbi and congregation. The cantor has a voice that turns the Hebrew verses into a song so beautiful that it doesn't matter if I can't understand the meaning. There's the mournful *kaddish*, the prayer to remember the dead, one of the few that my father recites because it commemorates his parents and relatives who've passed away. The best part of the service is the blessing at the end. With the fingers of both hands spread in what the kids called the *Star Trek* blessing, Rabbi Dobin asks God to bless us, and make us like Jacob, Ruth, and Esther.

Going to temple gives me the sensation of being cleansed. Whatever worries and problems I carry in are somehow washed away while I'm there.

More so than the chanting of ritual prayers, it is this feeling of being uplifted and released from mundane concerns that stays with me. I go through my adolescence searching for, but rarely finding, that sensation of transcendence and relief anywhere else.

For a few years we attend Friday night services. Attendance at some services is required of all prospective bar and bat mitzvah children and their families. I am determined to have a bat mitzvah, even though traditionally this coming-of-age ceremony is only for boys. The Jewish religion is as sexist and patriarchal as any other traditional faith in that regard. However, due to the feminist movement in the latter half of the twentieth century, bat mitzvahs for girls have gained acceptance, and I want mine, though mainly for the presents and the party! I want to wear the cut velvet, salmon pink midi dress my grandma has made for me, with shoes dyed to match. Looking back at my bat mitzvah photos, I see a thin girl with long hair and braces smiling awkwardly, standing next to proud parents, a grimacing brother, and a grandmother who was in mourning because her husband had died a few months earlier.

Grandpa's death is the first death I've experienced. Andrew and I don't attend the funeral because the grownups think we're too young for such a solemn occasion. I cannot sleep well after his death. I keep thinking, *What will happen when I die?* Mom and Dad have no answers to quell my fears. When I go to their room, scared and crying with exhaustion, they ask if I am worried about *them* dying and I say, "No, I am worried about myself." Mom tells me I am selfish and that they will probably die long before I will. It isn't a comforting thought! After many days of insomnia, mom finally gives me half a sleeping pill. It knocks me out for quite a long time, and I wake up, feeling groggy and sick.

To say, "We don't really know, but the body goes into the ground and eventually disintegrates. The person doesn't exist anymore!" is of little comfort to a child who wants to know where her soul will go after she dies. I don't understand how I'd been wondering about my soul back then, because the word *soul* didn't exist as part of my daily vernacular. What I did seem to know during those early adolescent years is that life felt empty. It wasn't just my grandpa's death that led me to that conclusion, it was everything.

In the weeks and months following my grandpa's death and my bat mitzvah, I begin to understand that new clothes, jewelry, and other material goods bring only momentary satisfaction at best. The same is true of entertainment: movies and plays end once you leave the theater. And what about all the expectations we have for our futures? *There has to be more to life than this. Being a good student, getting into a good college, getting married, and raising a family...Is life really just this meaningless process we go through only to die at the end? If so, it is not enough.*

These feelings of emptiness, lack of satisfaction and fear of death becomes a recurring train of thought that leaves me apprehensive and afraid. I start experiencing breathlessness. My stomach aches after eating anything, I can't sleep and I'm full of anxiety. Mom takes me to our family doctor, Dr. Frankel, the same man who delivered both Andrew and I. After examining me, he finds nothing wrong and implies that the cause may be psychological.

In the car on the way home, I sit in the backseat and broach the subject of my feelings with mom.

"Ma, is this all there is to life?"

"I don't know Steph. What do you mean?"

"I mean, trying to be a good girl, do well in school, get As, go to college and get a job..."

"Those are all very important things," she interrupts, surprised by the turn of this conversation.

"I know they're important, Ma. But if this is all there is to life..." I take a deep breath, then blurt it out: "If this is really all there is to life, then I don't want to live."

I know I've gone too far. My own words reverberate in the sudden silence.

Mom looks at me sharply in the rearview mirror, her eyebrows arched behind her glasses, her lips pressed together in a pained expression. Her hands grip the steering wheel tightly as she measures her words: "Stephanie, are you saying this because you mean it or just for effect?" She thinks this is some kind of drama I've planned to upset her.

More silence. How should I answer? I don't know why I feel this way, but it's real, isn't it? We are both on tiptoes now, both trying to back away from the abyss I've uncovered. How can I explain what I can't put into words? What can I say that won't upset her even more?

I stay very still in the back seat as I struggle for the safe response that will put everything back where it was before our trip to Dr. Frankel's office.

I affect a tone of reassurance that masks my resignation.

"No, ma. I don't mean it."

And nothing is the life of this world but a play and a passing delight;
and the life in the hereafter is far better for all who are conscious of
God. Will you not then, use your reason? (S. Al-An'am, v. 32)

CHAPTER 9

Learning to Breathe

1973

It's the early seventies. Students at the high school have staged a sit-in to earn the right for girls to wear pants to school. They win, but many of our teachers don't support this change in the dress code. We junior high students start to wear jeans to school, like the guys. Always first in style, thanks to my mom, I proudly wear my tie-dyed bell bottom blue jeans to school. My social studies teacher, an otherwise cool guy, decides to embarrass me in front of the class. He actually has me stand up while he cracks a joke at my expense.

"Miss Flower, I think your mother put too much bleach in the wash and ruined your jeans."

I turn red with embarrassment at being singled out but I say nothing. At least none of the other kids tease me over this incident. Rather, they're on my side. Within a week, almost all the girls in our class are wearing tie-dyed jeans to school.

In junior high, I'm still hanging out with my neighbor, Missy. We walk to school together, once I get her up in the morning. Missy just does not like to wake up. So when I arrive at her house about half an hour before we have to leave, I help her mother get Missy moving. She especially does not want to dress in the clothes she has, many of which have been designed and sewn by her mother.

Alicia, another friend of mine in junior high, lives down the block from me in Willets Point. I attend her communion; it's the first time I ever step foot in a church. I'm impressed by the hushed sanctity of the place, very similar to our temple, and realize that a church is also a place of God. I visit my friend's home just a few times. She has two older sisters and a father. I learn that her mother has a problem with alcohol and observe firsthand how that affects Alicia and her family. After seeing her mother yell and scream and curse, I'm afraid to visit her at home again.

In junior high, I take up the French horn. I want to play the flute but can't do so with braces on my teeth. The clarinet looks too hard, and the trumpets are all taken. I like the shape of the French horn and the sound it makes, so that is that. Band practice begins. Our music teacher works hard to whip us into shape for school concerts. My mother is very happy I'm playing music. It has always been a love in her life. I start private lessons with a local teacher and later have lessons with a musician who plays in Broadway musicals. He lives a bit far from our home and my lessons are early in the morning on Saturdays. My mother is very devoted to my music and practice, more so than I am. I enjoy playing in the school marching band and most of all in a high school performance of *South Pacific*. The overture at the beginning of the play starts with a very small French horn solo, and I am chosen to play it. But I drop the French horn when I get to university and never play again. In one of her prophetic dreams, my moth-

44

er sees my French horn abandoned in a tree, and that's how she knows I'm no longer playing!

By the time I'm in high school, my parents have already seen most of Europe on trips they've taken while Andrew and I are at summer camp or home with a babysitter. They decide, finally, that we are mature enough to join them when I'm in tenth grade. On my first trip to Europe, we go to London, Copenhagen, Moscow, and Leningrad. To travel in the Soviet Union, we need visas, and we also must stick to a strictly guided tour. Americans are not free to wander there in 1974. We attend a ballet and marvel at the St. Petersburg cathedral and the artwork in the museums and the subway. The food is terrible and my mother ends up with a parasitic infection that takes months, perhaps even years, to cure. Copenhagen, the capital of Denmark, has beautiful tulip gardens and a statue of *The Little Mermaid* on the bay in honor of their native son, Hans Christian Andersen. London, meanwhile, is full of history but it is a rainy Easter weekend when we get there, and most places are closed! We do, however, tour the city on a double-decker bus.

The best trip we take is when I'm fifteen years old, and we travel to the French Riviera. Andrew and I sit on the balcony of our room at the Hotel Negresco eating flaky croissants with jam and honey every morning. The view overlooks the Mediterranean Sea, whose water is turquoise in comparison to the wilder, gray-blue Atlantic of our Long Island home. I eat rabbit, bouillabaisse, and blood oranges that flow with a red, sweet juice. We rent a car and tour all the sites associated with the famous artists Monet, Picasso, Cocteau, and Matisse. I fall in love with those artists and their spaces, especially a little fisherman's chapel with stained glass windows designed by Jean Cocteau. I think, *My father always travels in style*, and I can't help feeling very princess-like and privileged in his care.

But despite the luxuries of world travel, access to culture and basically anything money can buy, the thought *is this all there is to life?* stays with me all through my adolescence and into early adulthood. I continue to search for whatever might give more meaning to my life. Most of the time, I look in the wrong places. When you miss your connection to God, there's a void in your life that can only be filled by Him. Try as you might to fill it with material possessions, intellectual pursuits, or hedonistic pleasure, you will not succeed. Those things are all temporary. They do not satisfy the eternal soul.

Some bright flashing glimmer in the darkness of the void. In high school, my friend Lisa and I decide to try TM, transcendental meditation. Meditation is something different and cool. Indian gurus abound on Long Island, trying to raise the consciousness of little white boys and girls one mantra at a time. The two of us save our allowance for the introductory session and go to the Indian temple, which is really just a small office complex with lots of incense burning in corners of rooms, and smiling men and women ready to be of service.

We attend an introductory session about the benefits of meditation. Each initiate is given a secret mantra, supposedly theirs alone, never to be revealed to anyone. The practice is to sit comfortably for twenty minutes and try to reach beyond the day-to-day world into another plane of reality. I attempt this while relaxing in the easy chair in my father's study, the darkest, most peaceful room in the house, the one that has always been a haven for me.

Breathe in, breathe out. I sit in the leather recliner, deepen my breathing, close my eyes and begin to chant my mantra. Twenty minutes is a long time, but eventually I succeed in stilling the chatter of my mind and feel at peace—in another zone, so to speak. It's a new and beneficial experience for me. My body is still in the chair, but there's another part of me that's going somewhere else. *Is that my soul?* I wonder.

"Stephanie! Come and set the table!"

Ma is yelling from the kitchen, jolting me back to reality. She doesn't like this new activity I've found. She doesn't say so, but she finds a way to interrupt me every time.

High school is a time to figure out who I am, though my self-definitions change daily. I want to fit in somewhere, with some group. But that sense of belonging always eludes me. I admire the cool kids, but I'm not one of them. I'm certainly not a jock, though I do play JV tennis, enjoy gymnastics, and square dancing in gym class. I can't be a nerdy kid because I'm not good at math. So, I end up having friends and acquaintances from most of these groups, but no one I can call a "best friend" in school. Missy and I have grown apart by the time we hit high school. It's sometimes lonely riding my bike to and from school by myself, but at least I have other social outlets, like camp and youth group, where the kids are Jewish and more like me.

I continue to excel in English and social studies, taking honors and AP-level courses in those subjects, but regular classes in science and math. We read *The Bell Jar* in ninth grade—way too depressing and suicidal a book for impressionable adolescents—but my teacher has some kind of fixation on Sylvia Path. Tenth grade is American literature, eleventh is British, taught by another wonderful teacher who is an Anglophile. Along with our Shakespeare lessons, I learn much British royal history that year. In an effort to have afterschool activities on my college applications, I join the school literary magazine, which prints several of my poems and a short story.

In the spring of junior year, the honors class is assigned a major independent research project. I choose to do mine on William Blake, the mystic British poet. His life and work fascinate me for many months. My mother encourages my interest by taking me to the New York Public Library to do some serious research and look at Blake's illuminated manuscripts. I am writing about symbolism, allegory, and Blake's unique imagery, very little of which I really understand. But this study whets my appetite for mystics and mysticism. I like writers who look deep below the surface and into the hearts of people to get a glimpse of hidden truths. As Jalaluddin Rumi says, *Enjoy being washed with this knowing and not knowing.*

Twelfth grade brings another wonderful teacher into my life for AP English, Mr. Plummer. He introduces the Bible as literature, which intrigues me. I've never read the Bible before. I also choose Emily Dickinson as my research topic for AP English, and I become overwhelmed by Emily's writings as I try to balance my school work with my social life and two serious boyfriend relationships. Guess which wins out? When I go to him crying, but without my completed paper, Mr. Plummer gives in to my tears and grants me an extension. That kind old man even gives me his handkerchief to blow my nose. There is a lesson in this, but not the one he'd wanted to impart: Tears really do garner sympathy and help you get what you want! Of course, I already knew this by senior year. It's just that now I use this women's weapon to my advantage. I sometimes think if Mr. Plummer had been more hardnosed with me, it would have served me better in future situations.

It isn't until high school that I get a good math tutor. He's Mr. Sweezey, my trigonometry teacher. Mr. Sweezey is the stuff of high school girls' fantasies. He has curly, dirty-blond hair and glasses that make him look like a professor. But he's also ultra-cool, riding his Honda motorcycle to school and to my house for tutoring sessions. He has a great smile and is full of praise when I answer correctly. If you can't learn your math from him you're really were dumb, no two ways about it. In eleventh grade he's my classroom teacher as well as my tutor, so at least I pass my math Regents Exam. However, I never really get over my math anxiety. I only get a C in a basic math class in college, and that's with a tutor as well. For years afterward, I have that recurring dream of cutting my math course and being totally unprepared for a major exam.

One thing I cannot credit the West Islip High School with is an unbiased political education. In high school, I have two male teachers for modern history and international relations. They both believe the Arabs are the bad guys and that Israel is a hero on the world stage. Mr. Zuckerman teaches us the maps of the Middle East and Africa by making up puns about the country names, and Dr. Carroll blasts the African and Arab rulers every chance he gets, calling them "Idiot Amin" and "Muammar Gadfly." Both these teachers reinforce common stereotypes about Arabs in my mind and make me see Islam as a foreign religion and Allah (SWT) as a different God than the one Jews and Christians worship. As I will later realize, nothing could be further from the truth.

Know then Oh man, that there is no deity except God. (S. Muhammad, v. 19)

CHAPTER 10

Into the Void

High School Yearbook, 1975

In the seventies, suburban Long Island was a hotbed of sex, drugs, and rock and roll. I was an adolescent in those years. My parents were liberal Jewish thinkers, although more conservative than my younger aunts and uncles were. They were not the kind of parents who laid down the law regarding social activities and relationships. In most cases, my friends and I took our cues from older kids. When the high school girls staged a sit-in for the right to wear pants, we junior high girls followed suit. When the college-aged chaperones at our youth group events didn't stop us, we got high and made out with our boyfriends right under their noses. It wasn't a problem.

My junior high held a special mother-daughter tea sponsored by the Modess Company. A Modess representative ushered us into the school cafeteria with our moms to show us a film about how our bodies were changing. We were transforming from little girls into beautiful young women and needed to prepare for our future roles as wives and mothers. Essentially, the film was about menstruation and the convenience of using Modess sanitary napkins to stay clean during "that time of the month."

I'm sure that movie made it much easier for most mothers to discuss the topic of where babies come from with their daughters. I know I had a lot of questions for my mom, though I don't remember ever asking them. As for sex, all I had to do was go to the bookshelf in my parents' bedroom and read. Of course, their books, such as the *Joy of Sex*, *Sexual Politics*, and *Portnoy's Complaint*, were written for adult audiences. But that didn't stop my curious adolescent mind from becoming fascinated with those books. I borrowed them from my parents' bookshelf one by one and hid them in my bedroom closet.

I start dating around age twelve. "Dating" meant going to boy-girl parties in friends' basements or going to the movies, bowling, or skating with someone special. I was intrigued and excited by my early dating experiences, but also a little bit shy and afraid. *What if a boy wants to do more than kiss?* I often wondered.

When I'm 15, I go out with a boy who is two years older than me. He is acting in a local play, and I go to see it. There is a party after the play where we both drink a bit. Then he takes me back to his house. His parents aren't home. He wants to have sex with me but I feel threatened and scared. As he is trying his best to persuade me, my mom calls on his home phone. "Stephanie, where are you?" Talk about saved by the bell! I don't hear from him again. I want him to call, though, because he's an older guy and that excites me. I am afraid to have sex, but it doesn't mean I'm not interested in further contact. My hormones are just getting started.

In high school, I join U.S.Y. (United Synagogue Youth), a youth group sponsored by the Jewish community. There I meet Lisa, who becomes my best friend. Lisa is an only child. Her home is always open to me, and her mom is always friendly and cheerful. We spend hours in her bedroom, listening to Elton John, Jethro Tull, And *Tommy* by The Who, and we attend thrilling live concerts together. Lisa is always working on some art project or other. She has boundless creative energy. She enjoys spending time in my house discussing great art with my father, who really influences her views and tastes. I admire her talent, but become annoyed when we go to museums together and she says, "Oh, I could do that," about almost any work of art. The thing is, she *can* do it. After high school she gets a scholarship to Carnegie Mellon in Pittsburgh, Pennsylvania and goes on to become a graphic arts instructor, young-adult fiction author, and book cover illustrator. (The cover of this book was designed by Lisa.)

U.S.Y. is purely a social organization. The adults in charge say its purpose is for Jewish youth to form lasting friendships with other Jewish youth. But if you ask us, it's a place to hook up with guys and hang out. Basketball games, road trips, amusement parks, skating, bowling, and hanging out with friends are my preferred activities on weekends. It's like a sleepaway camp. I've found a place where I belong.

U.S.Y. becomes the center of my social life and dating activities. Most, but not all, the boys I date are Jewish. I date or have crushes on a few guys from my high school, but those are not long-term relationships. By long-term, I mean a few months of being exclusive with one guy or "going steady." It is normal for us to meet guys and girls in a group at various social events that are arranged for us and then get together privately with a boy who interests us.

Most of our parents are very accommodating. The psychobabble of the time tells them to let us "do our own thing" and respect our privacy. Maybe they prefer not to know what we're doing, or maybe they just don't understand. As kids, we still think we're the center of our parents' world so we sneak around when we think we're doing something wrong. But in reality, they sometimes don't have a clue what we're up to until something major occurs, like a teenage pregnancy or a call from the police station.

Once we can drive and have cars and vans of our own, there are plenty of opportunities for fun. I enjoy my teenage life of partying, concerts, and movies. Sex is reserved for very serious relationships. It has always been up to the girl to say *no* in these situations. Thank God, I am never with a guy who tries to force me beyond where I want to go.

As young women in the age of women's liberation, we absorb the message that we should be just as free as the guys to do what we want with our lives, our careers, and our bodies. Our role models, including Simone de Beauvoir, Gloria Steinem, Susan Brownmiller, and Helen Gurley Brown, are fighting to do away with the double standard. Empowered by what of their message trickles down to us, we feel freer than previous generations to engage in sex without guilt and without the consequences of being considered a "bad girl." Also, birth control has become widely available, and all the guys we date carry condoms, just in case they get lucky.

On the surface, we embrace the message of sexual freedom. We feel we *should* be liberated enough to do as our hormones please. But in hindsight, I know there were age-old patterns at work that told us otherwise. Most women want the security of having one special man who will marry them and raise a family. Even as a young, "liberated" woman in high school, the fantasy of a knight in shining armor was lodged in my psyche.

By contrast, most young men are encouraged to leave their family home, see some of the world and get some experience before they settle down to one woman and the responsibilities of family life. This idea is embedded in the male psyche. Therefore, any serious premarital relationship carries this conflict of interest, albeit on a subconscious level.

I begin dating Gary in my senior year of high school. He is cute, curious, passionate and intelligent. He wants to be a lawyer like my father. He has his own car, and we go everywhere together from Central Park for concerts to the tip of the Long Island for daytime camping trips. We talk deep into the night and share many common interests. We write poetry for each other. What could be more romantic?

My parents don't like the seriousness of our relationship and they are not particularly friendly to Gary. He is hurt that they don't take more of an interest in him. My father thinks I could do better, though I never care to ask him what he means. It's Gary and I against the world, if need be. I am in love.

Although he loves me, Gary is also a product of the times. The Allman Brothers are singing "Lord, I was born a rambling man," and Jack Kerouac has gone *On the Road*. Gary is determined to do the same. At the end of senior year, instead of going to the prom and attending my senior graduation party, he leaves for an extended road trip with friends. It's his last breath of freedom before the grind of university life sets in, but to me, it's the end of the world. I'm miserable and heartbroken.

Before he leaves on his road trip, Gary and I have a conversation that makes me change direction in my life. He says he wants to take a year off before college and go to Israel but doesn't have the money. His father owns a hardware store and is not particularly well off, so he'll be attending a New York state university in the fall. I think, *If he can travel, so can I!* Senior year has been rough for me, both emotionally and academically, with the pressures of AP courses, Regents Exams, and having to get into a good college. I've been accepted at several schools I've applied to and have chosen Hamilton-Kirkland, a small and prestigious private liberal arts college in upstate New York.

I'm feeling burned out on school and not ready to jump into college, so I ask my father's permission to go to Israel. After some consideration, he agrees. He himself had traveled to the new state of Israel in 1952 to meet some relatives he'd never seen before. In the early 1900s, his father and his uncle left Russia and went in separate directions. My grandfather came to America, and his brother immigrated to Palestine and raised a whole family there.

My mother is relieved that I'm going. She and I had been fighting a lot during my last two years of high school; our screaming matches were many. I'm ashamed to admit that she slapped me across the face, and I slapped her back! It will do us both some good to be apart for a while.

When I remember the disrespect I showed my mother in our arguments during my teenage years, I wish I could somehow revoke my angry words. When I say she was generally unhappy and displeased, I mean this is what came across in her daily demeanor. She was a nervous, high-strung, and pessimistic person. But she was also loving, compassionate, and generous. She could be funny in a sarcastic way. She was most likely frightened for the safety of the rebellious, independent daughter she was raising. She also worried about my reputation. My genereation and I were so different than hers, at least on the surface. Years later, she would confide in me about the mistakes she had made as a young woman, and I would realize we were not so completely different after all.

Before I leave for Israel, my father offers me some advice: "You are not part of their country just because you are a Jew. Don't let anyone pressure you into wanting to stay there. You need to come home and get your degree." He speaks from his own experience. In 1952, he traveled to the newly formed State of Israel to visit his father's brother. His uncle urged him to think about staying to help build the country. He's afraid I might give in to a similar kind of pressure. And yet he respects my independence enough to let me go and even funds the entire experience! My father is a rare breed among men.

I solemnly agree with what he says. I'm impatient to be traveling on my own and want to leave as soon as possible. My college admission is deferred for one year, and I select a group to travel with. Youth trips are very popular among Jewish kids in the United States. Israel welcomes worldwide Jewish youth, viewing them as potential Israeli citizens.

I'm very excited. This will be my first trip overseas without my parents. I will be joining a group of fifteen to twenty American kids in their late teens and early twenties. We'll be placed on a *kibbutz* to learn Hebrew and Israeli culture. We'll take frequent trips to historic sites, spend time in Jerusalem, and also study for four weeks at Haifa University. Everything is well organized and supervised. I can't wait to leave.

The eye of the heart, though closed in fallen man, is able to take in a glimmering of light, and this is faith. But any way of living causes a covering like rust to accumulate over the heart so it cannot sense the Divine origin of Allah's message.
—Abu Bakr Siraj-ud-Din a/k/a Martin Lings, Sufi writer, and scholar

Part II.

Finding

A Noiseless Patient Spider

A noiseless patient spider,
I mark'd where on a little promontory it stood isolated,
Mark'd how to explore the vacant vast surrounding,
It launch'd forth filament, filament, filament, out of itself,
Ever unreeling them, ever tirelessly speeding them.

And you O my soul where you stand,
Surrounded, detached, in measureless oceans of space,
Ceaselessly musing, venturing, throwing,
seeking the spheres to connect them,
Till the bridge you will need be form'd, till the ductile anchor hold,
Till the gossamer thread you fling catch somewhere, O my soul.

—Walt Whitman, published in Leaves of Grass, 1891

CHAPTER 11

The Holy Land

In the Upper Galilee, 1976

The land of Palestine is ancient and holy. One can feel it in the air, in the way the sky hugs the ground and the hills rise up. For nine months, I lived in the valley below the hills of Galilee, the same hills walked by the Prophet Jesus (upon him be peace). As I went about my daily life, I trod on sacred ground, heedless and unaware.

A *kibbutz* is a collective farm. It's the Israeli version of a socialist commune. On the *kibbutz*, children are raised both in nurseries and at home. Parents have the option of having their children sleep at home, especially when they are babies, but the nursery is there to take care of all the babies while the parents work. Older children may sleep at home or in children's houses, where all boys and girls of the same age group live together. They visit with their parents daily but live with their peers and the adult caretakers who supervise and teach them. They're schooled on the *kibbutz* all the way up to high school. As young adults, they retain very close bonds with those they were raised with as brothers and sisters. However, there is a high degree of sexual experimentation among the youth, and marital infidelity is common and widely accepted.

There are religious *kibbutzim* (pl.) in Israel, but Garin Yarden, where I am placed, is not one of them. There are no religious services or daily prayers. Holiday celebrations are more secular than spiritual in tone. Traditional foods still are served during Hanukkah and at Passover in the spring. There is a contemporary aspect to the ancient Passover story of Moses leading his people out of Egypt. That ancient event has become connected to the Jewish exodus from Europe when Israel became a state in 1948.

The Israelis have written a history for themselves that marginalizes the Palestinians, making them basically just tenant farmers on lands owned by the Ottoman Turks prior to World War I. They use the persecution of the Jews in Europe and Hitler's Holocaust as justification for statehood. Israel's statehood in 1948 was the Nakba for the Palestinians, the time when thousands of them were forced to flee their ancient homeland. In 1976, none of this means much to me, an ethnically Jewish girl from Long Island. My consciousness would only be raised little by little over the years that follow.

I enjoy living on the *kibbutz* in some regards and dislike it in others. The volunteer community is quite international. I meet Maurice and Francois from Paris; Valerie, Suzanne, and Richard from the United States; and Gary from Canada. Short-term volunteers also join us from New Zealand, Australia, Denmark, England, and France. Since we are near the Lebanese border, there are also Israeli soldiers stationed here. The soldiers are very interested in American girls, believing we are very liberal in our morals.

There is strong communal life and the warmth of people living, working, and enjoying their lives together on the *kibbutz*. Nobody worries about money or salaries because everyone gets the same pay and has their needs for food, clothing, and shelter met by the collective. This is true for the residents, not the volunteers. For the *kibbutzniks*, collective farming is a permanent and viable way of life. For us, it is a working vacation, a temporary respite from our "real" lives back home, an inexpensive way to travel, and a lifeline to our ancient ethnic roots. Volunteers come from all over the world, for different reasons. Some of them end up staying and making the *kibbutz* their home. I actually consider that possibility during my nine-month stay, but remember my father's talk when he'd emphasized that Israel wasn't my country and that I should feel no obligation to make it my home simply because I was a Jew.

Regardless, while living on the *kibbutz*, I enjoy the communal living and the manual labor; it's a refreshing change from years of schooling. I like the freedom to travel on my own or with small groups of friends. Making my own decisions is exhilarating, although depending only on myself for answers is sometimes frightening. I do not like the loneliness that results from being so far away from home and family. The *kibbutzniks*, especially those my age, can be very cliquish and volunteers come and go, so it's hard to form significant, lasting relationships with either group.

All volunteers are expected to learn Hebrew, the national language of Israel. When we first arrive on the *kibbutz*, we are given a six-week crash course in modern standard Hebrew. This is a very intensive course of study called an *ulpan*. Its main purpose is to get us to speak the language as soon as possible, using what we learn in our daily life and work activities. In spite of high school language studies, I've never been much good at picking up languages, but the *ulpan* course is so good, one can't help but learn. The teachers are excellent and demanding. There's plenty of homework. And then, most of the *kibbutzniks* don't speak English, so if I don't learn, I risk sounding like a fool when I want to communicate.

One day I make a major language error. I find my job assignment on the job board—I'm scheduled to serve meals in the cafeteria that day. I wheel a cart around, tell people the different choices, and serve them what they request. One of the choices at lunch is sweetbreads, called *qalb* in Hebrew. The *qaf* and the *kaf* sounds in Hebrew and Arabic are hard for a westerner to differentiate. *Kalb* means dog, which is what I told everyone we were serving for lunch! After more than a few diners start laughing or refusing to eat, somebody lets me in on the joke. My face turns red, of course, but at least I never make that mistake again!

Every adult works on the kibbutz. Jobs are assigned and rotated as necessary. Long-term residents eventually specialize in the work that best suits them. Volunteers experience a variety of jobs as we're rotated through the job roster. During my time at Garin Yarden, I work in the apple orchards, the dairy, the canning factory, the kitchen, the dining room, and the nursery.

I particularly love working in the apple orchards because the work is outside and the fresh air is exhilarating. We rise early in the morning and have Turkish coffee, known as "mud coffee" because of the thick sediment that settles at the bottom of the cup. We drive by Jeep to the fields where we tie the branches of young saplings to wires that will train the direction of their growth. From the apple orchards, we can see the actual border with its rolls of barbed wire. In between the Israeli and Lebanese borders is a kind of no man's land, a white road that is patrolled by U.N. forces. During my nine-month stay, there are no skirmishes, explosions, or shootings across the border, although we can see occasional gunfire in the distance. The *kibbutzniks* work with guns beside them, just in case.

Toward the end of my stay on the *kibbutz*, a position opens up for a cook to work in the field kitchen of the orange and grapefruit groves. The men who work there mostly handle machinery and supervise the Palestinian women who come to pick the fruit every day. I wonder how those women feel, harvesting fruit for settlers on land that might have belonged to their own families in the past. However, I have no opportunity to interact with them. There's an unspoken barrier between us that has nothing to do with language. It's almost as if we exist in separate spheres.

The men start their workday at about 4:00 am and finish at 2:00 pm. By 8:00 in the morning, they need a hearty breakfast. I cook omelets and make toast, and after a while, I get to know how each of the twenty men like their eggs and can cook them accordingly, with two or three frying pans going at once on the stove. It's challenging and fun. In the long run, it makes me more competent in the kitchen, at least at cooking breakfast!

It's also a boost to my confidence at a time when I have much self-doubt about the next stage of my life in college. My work takes only a few hours and then I'm free for the rest of the day to wander around the kibbutz, visit people, nap, or read. There are also excursions to local sites of interest for the volunteers.

In Israel in 1975, all male and female citizens have to serve in the army, air force, or navy. They also have the right to carry arms. It is a very strange sight for me to see men and women storing their guns on the luggage racks of buses and picking them up as they depart. The *kibbutz* has a well-stocked bomb shelter. There's a beautiful mural painted on its exterior wall. I'm given a tour of the shelter, but it is never used under threat of attack during the time that I'm there. Even though the country is surrounded by enemies, I feel safe. This is often the case in countries where the threat of war or attack is imminent. Life just proceeds normally because what other choice do people have? I write to my parents and unwisely describe the barbed wire and guard towers surrounding the *kibbutz*, but personally, I'm having too many new and fascinating experiences to worry about warfare. I reflect on my experiences in my journal. In October of 1975, I write the following:

> *It's a problem to be a girl volunteer on the kibbutz. Men are so much more important to them: manpower! I don't like it, but I think once the kibbutzniks get to know me better and maybe if I work a little bit harder, I'll become more important to them. Guys have an automatic, natural advantage. It's a macho attitude accentuated by Middle Eastern culture. Israel is a Western state with an Eastern background and the culture is really a mixture of the two. The equality situation is horrible in the Middle East and the East. It's really only in the West that the question of equality has even come up!*

I first encounter Arabs and Muslims in Israel. 1975–76 is a fairly peaceful time, at least in the Upper Galilee. Palestinian men and women are hired as day laborers in the fields and on the *kibbutz*. The Arab men usually work on construction projects. They are often joined by poor Yemeni laborers. The Yemenis are Jews from the east called *Sephardim*. Jewish immigrants of European and western origin are called *Ashkenazim*. A vast class difference exists between the two groups, with the poorer Sephardim working lower paying jobs like construction alongside the Muslim and Christian Arabs.

It's in the cities where I glimpse what it means to be Palestinian in the state of Israel. We spend six weeks at Haifa University studying the history and culture of the country. At Haifa, I have my first encounter with Palestinian students, a group of boys who study and dorm at the university. They're very curious about me as an American woman and invite me for tea in their dorm. But their anger at the occupation and their insistence that I, as an American, can do something about it, feels threatening, as does their obvious interest in me as an "easy" American woman. I quickly size up the situation and leave. I have one other experience with Palestinians in Israel when I go with my friends to Nabawiya, in the south, near Mount Sinai. The area is famous for its nude beach. As we sunbathe there, a gang of boys come running through the sand, gesturing toward our naked bodies and telling us, "*Haram, haram*! Cover yourselves and be decent!"

I visit Jerusalem twice, including once with my family, who come for a three-week visit in the winter of 1975. I love to wander in the old *suq*, or bazaar, and discover the site's ancient history. In Jerusalem there is tension. The city is divided into sectors: the old city, or East Jerusalem, is mainly for the Palestinians and the more modern West Jerusalem is for the Israelis. I visit some distant relatives and an old friend while I'm there. Both parties feel the need to justify the importance of the state for the survival of the Jewish people. They seem willing to defend it, right or wrong, against the Palestinians. It's a very complicated issue, one that has certainly worsened over time.

The Dome of the Rock and the Wailing Wall are always fully manned with soldiers. I am very fortunate to be able to visit both. I visit the Wailing Wall and push a piece of paper with a prayer into a crack in the wall, as is customary, though doing this does not make me feel any more Jewish than before.

I wish I had known more about The Dome of the Rock before I went there. It is the third holiest site in Islam, the first two being in Mecca and Medina in Saudi Arabia. It houses a boulder there with the footprint of Prophet Muhammad ﷺ embedded in it. It is the place he mounted *Buraq* (a winged horse) and ascended to the highest heavens in a journey called *Israa* and *Miraj*. The masjid itself has a beautiful dome of gold that makes it the dominant feature in any photo of the old city of Jerusalem. In the cool dimness of that masjid, I saw the boulder and the footprint. In Jerusalem, I also walked the path of Jesus to the crucifixion and visited the Church of the Holy Sepulchre to see the relics stored there. These experiences held no apparent religious or spiritual significance to me, just curiosity. I asked myself, *Could these things be true? What kind of people believes these stories? What kind of faith do they have?*

Mount Sinai is in the Negev Desert near Sharm El Sheik. Israel took this territory in 1967 and returned it to Egypt in the 1980s. In 1976, I am blessed with the opportunity to climb the mountain where Moses (a.s.) received the Ten Commandments. That ascent is much more than just a physical climb. It is a step to a higher level in my spiritual journey, an awakening.

A desert is like no other place on earth. By day, it is scorching hot and filled with undulating sand dunes that stretch to infinity. At night, temperatures drop below freezing. But the desert sky at night is magnificent. In the pitch-black darkness, the stars almost touch the ground. They are the brightest, most beautiful stars I've ever seen. I gaze my fill before being put to bed in the monks' hostel at the foot of the mountain.

Our group is awakened in the middle of the night to start our climb. We want to watch the sunrise from the summit. We begin the ascent, which is gradual most of the way and just a bit steep toward the end. Many of the rocks are naturally terraced and make for an easy climb. It is exhilarating nevertheless. A peace descends on us as we climb, and I feel that holiness I am always searching for. It is truly a sacred place, the hallowed ground that Moses (a.s.) ascended. All of Palestine is the land of the prophets and truly a destination of pilgrims from Judaism, Christianity, and Islam, but this climb in Moses's footsteps is a once in a lifetime experience. And so is the view. The expression *purple mountains' majesty* becomes clear. The black peaks of the night turn purple as the first light of dawn appears, streaking the sky in orange, pink, and purple.

The view from the summit is unforgettable. Smaller desert hills and sand dunes stretch out in all directions around the massive rock that is Sinai. The Christian monks have built a very small shrine at the top, big enough for one person at a time to enter, sit, and reflect. We each take our turn, exhausted and sweaty but victorious because we've made it to the top. I have no words, only awe and wonder, as I gaze out on the sunrise and feel connected, once again, to the mysterious Whole.

> *For he was specially chosen,*
> *And he was an apostle*
> *And a prophet.*
> *And We called him from the right side*
> *Of Mount (Sinai) and made*
> *Him draw near to Us*
> *For mystic (converse)*
> *(S. Maryam, v.51-52)*

CHAPTER 12

College Days

1977

In adulthood, I've understood that one can feel alone, even in a room full of people. This is just part of the existential human condition. I didn't understand this when I was an adolescent and a young adult, although I certainly experienced the angst of it many times. Then again, there are times when I crave solitude. It's always hard to strike a balance, and balance is one of things Allah tells us to pray for. In every prayer of *Surah Fatiha*, we say *Show us the straight path.* "Straight" does not translate the Arabic word *istaqama* adequately, because *istaqama* also carries connotations of balance and uprightness. The straight path has more than two dimensions. I spent my adolescence and young adulthood searching for that path, taking many detours along the way.

I return from Israel refreshed and recharged. In the fall of 1976, my parents drive me to upstate New York to Kirkland College, the private liberal arts school for women I've chosen for its small size and innovative structure. It's also new, having been established in 1968. It is the sister school to Hamilton College, a traditional, all–male college established in Clinton, New York in 1812. Clinton is a small sleepy town that derives most of its revenue from the college.

Courses can be taken on either campus. While Hamilton has a traditional grading system, Kirkland courses have pass/fail options. Hamilton has traditional lectures. Kirkland's courses are mostly seminars. I take French, art history, and philosophy courses at Hamilton and sociology, anthropology, and ceramics at Kirkland. I take literature classes on both campuses. I also take a class in the Old Testament. I want to somehow keep my budding spiritual experience at Mt. Sinai alive. The course is mostly history. I read about the wrathful God of the Jewish people, but I see no resemblance in Him to my spiritual experience at Mount Sinai or the mystical force I felt through transcendental meditation, or even among the spiritual entities I'd met while studying William Blake's poems in high school. I do not pursue this type of religious study beyond the one Old Testament course. However, during my sophomore year I develop an interest in Zen Buddhism as it's represented in Asian art. In general, I enjoy my studies and do well in college.

After experiencing several different living situations on campus, I apply for a place in the Co-op for my sophomore year. This dorm has a cooperative living arrangement that reminds me of life on the *kibbutz*. The residents are responsible for purchasing and cooking their own food with the food allowance being taken out of everyone's collective room and board payments. We have our own dining room and take turns preparing, serving, and cleaning up meals. With forty-five residents in the Co-op, I can always find people around to hang out with, especially in the dining room and kitchen. Living in the Co-op staves off some of the loneliness I feel living so far from home and civilization as I know it.

One Co-op job is baking fresh bread. I'm in awe of the students who have mastered this art, so I sign up to assist in the process. Fresh bread is baked in the early morning hours once the yeast has risen overnight. Nothing is as delicious as that fresh, warm bread still steaming from the oven. I spread it with butter and have a cup of herbal tea, another Co-op favorite with many varieties of loose tea available in the kitchen, forever steeping in pots and cups and strainers.

Between my studies and my responsibilities at the Co-op, I enjoy the two campuses and their beautiful natural surroundings. Hamilton, true to its tradition, has a well-kept garden with a hedge maze and labeled floral areas. Kirkland, true to its wilder nature, has the Glen. The Glen is a wooded forest that has been kept as part of the college grounds. It's wild and free, and that's how I feel when I walk there. It only takes me a few moments to feel totally at home in the woods. As I walk, I become part of the streams and the trees. It's a relaxing, serene experience. Sometimes these walks carry a slight element of danger to them, too, especially if I get lost. One afternoon while walking in the glen, a sudden rain storm erupts. The sky darkens and the wind howls ominously as the rain starts falling in big, fat drops. There's rumbling thunder and even a few bolts of lightning. There's nowhere to seek shelter, so I just have to keep walking. I quicken my pace and break into a run once I can clearly see the end of the path. As I return to the artificial, man-made world of dorms and the campus, the storm peters out I am drenched from head to toe. My sneakers are waterlogged. But I am also exhilarated—in the Glen, during that wild rain storm, I was temporarily absorbed into the mystical Wholeness. It's a sacred secret I've discovered. I do not call it God, though it brings me the peace and tranquility I need to balance out the emotional upheavals caused by my social relationships at school.

Hamilton/Kirkland has some strange social dynamics going on, and this sometimes serves to deepen my sense of isolation and meaninglessness.

Hamilton attracts mostly preppie, wealthy boys from conservative families. One of my male friends is the heir to the Woolworth fortune. Kirkland, meanwhile, is progressive and liberal, so it attracts artistic, creative, divergently thinking girls who prefer to be called women. These two archetypes don't always mix well together. There is a certain tension that doesn't make for good male-female relationships. There is also a large contingent of lesbian and bisexual women on Kirkland's campus. I have my first exposure to the gay lifestyle when one of my friends invites me to her Massachusetts home and tries to sleep with me. I am uncomfortable with her advances and cut the visit short.

I have several relationships with men at college, but none of them are as deep and meaningful as I want them to be. Gary even comes to visit me at Kirkland, but we fail to repair the rift that separation caused in our relationship. We've both changed in a year. I experience loneliness, heartache, and misery as I watch some of my peers get involved in serious relationships that sometimes lead to living together or even marriage.

There are as many adolescents searching for their identity at Hamilton/Kirkland as on any other college campus in America. However, the administrative bodies of the two campuses decide they cannot co-exist. In 1978, the liberal arts experiment that is Kirkland closes its doors. Female students can choose to be assimilated into the Hamilton student body, now co-ed, or they may choose to transfer somewhere else. I choose the second option.

In upstate New York, it snows and snows for at least four months of the year. The glistening landscape of snowy pathways that sparkle like diamonds quickly turns slushy and gray. When the walkways are plowed, they form walls of snow as high as eight feet on either side and one has to walk through these tunnels to get to class. The long sunless winters depress me. I even get frostbite! I am down the hill from school taking a pottery class as part of my winter internship. I've worn sneakers to walk down the hill in the morning. While I wait for the bus back to campus in the late afternoon, it starts to snow. Light flurries escalate into a small blizzard. The bus is late, and my feet get soaked as they sink further into the wet snow. By the time I reach campus, I cannot feel my toes. It takes several hours before the circulation to my extremities returns to normal. To this day, I need two pairs of socks in the winter or the toes on my right foot become painful, then numb.

Winter is rough in upstate New York. I yearn to be back in the city. Sophomore year I do my winter internship at the Sotheby Parke-Bernet auction house in Manhattan. Uncle Murray and Aunt Pixie host me on their sofa bed. I learn the basics of cooking from my uncle and the delights of Jane Austen and the New York Times crossword puzzle from my aunt. They give me plenty of freedom to come and go as I please and I'm very happy there.

I love the sophistication of the auction house world. It reminds me of my childhood, though now I am a young adult navigating this familiar territory from the other side of the auctioneer's gavel, so to speak. It is a comfort and a pleasure to be back in the art scene. I start to think about declaring a major in art history. And what better place to do this than the city itself? Even in winter, it's a lively and interesting metropolis.

I decide to transfer to New York University for my junior and senior years at college. I plan to live in Greenwich Village. This decision heralds another dramatic change of direction in my life. Sometimes the straight path isn't straight at all!

> *The Prophet said, "The vessels of your Lord are the hearts of His right-eous slaves, and the most beloved to Him are the softest and most tender ones."*
> —*Hadith of Prophet Muhammad* ☙

CHAPTER 13

The Eye of the Heart

With my mother in 1979

By 1979, I'd transferred to N.Y.U. and was living in the heart of Greenwich Village. The first apartment I shared with a struggling opera singer was a short-lived venture. After I ate some of her food and let a friend sleep over in her bed, she asked me to leave. I had obviously spent too long living on the *kibbutz* and in the Co-op! Turns out I had a lot to learn about being a roommate in the city.

My next apartment is in a luxury building with a doorman on the west side of Fourteenth Street. I share it with Kathy, also an NYU student. Our fathers are footing the bill. My seventeenth-floor bedroom faces the needled tip of the Empire State Building. No taller buildings block my first-row view of the best light show in town. The tower's lights change in a dazzling display for each season: yellow and orange in autumn; green and red at Christmas; and red, white, and blue for the Fourth of July. It's beautiful and comforting to enjoy those lights each night before I close my eyes to sleep.

At NYU, I briefly consider a major in art therapy, an up-and-coming field that involves psychology and art. I take a course that has each student observe an art class in a NYC public school. At the class I attend, the teacher points out one girl in particular who paints everything red, the color of aggression. Expression through the arts is being promoted as a way for children to reveal what may be the difficult, troubling, or just plain dangerous circumstances of their lives. A career in art therapy would be an interesting and creative way to help children. But if I major in art therapy, I'll need to take several psychology classes, and that will mean more time in school. Besides, my parents reason, "It's a new field. What if there are no jobs when you finish your degree?" They aren't particularly supportive, and I don't really want to spend more time in school, so I declare a major in art history instead.

It seems like the logical thing to do. My art-collecting parents raised me to appreciate and love art. I see a glamorous future for myself in the gallery and museum world of Manhattan. I get a paid internship in an art gallery on Fifty-Seventh Street, commuting on foot or by subway from NYU to the gallery several days a week, dressed my best in stylish suits and heels.

Meanwhile, my search for a faith to believe in continues. At Kirkland, I had developed an academic interest in Zen Buddhism and its relationship to Asian art, but I never considered Buddhism as a spiritual choice because it doesn't include the concept of God the way I understand it. There's a Jewish temple near my apartment. If I'm going to seriously consider becoming religious, I should first take another look at Judaism. Maybe the conservative temple—more traditional than the Reform temple of my childhood—has something to offer me. I sign up for classes, and once again, I'm learning about the Jewish people and why they were chosen by

73

God. The message is the same old one I learned in Hebrew school, and it doesn't hold my interest for very long.

Between classes and work, I spend time in Washington Square Park adjacent to the NYU campus. I love that seedy park with its historic arch and defunct fountain. There's always something happening there. I love the impromptu songs performed by an *a cappella group* of men who moonlight as drug dealers.

"Do you believe in God?"

A handsome African American guy asks me this question as I stand with the small crowd enjoying the music. I'm caught off-guard. His eyes are such a deep brown and his expression so welcoming that I respond truthfully. "I'd have to think about that. No one has asked me that question in a very long time." I'm reminded of Grandma and Missy Cheply, the neighbor who loved me enough to want me to get baptized. Something about this man makes me want to know more.

A relationship grows from this encounter in the park, an attraction that's more than physical. "It's not about me," Abdullah says. Yet, in the beginning it certainly is about him, as far as I'm concerned. He's a handsome gentleman and the first black man I've ever gotten to know well. He treats me like a fine lady, and soon I'm following him everywhere—to New York nightclubs, cozy dim-lit restaurants, and even seedy hotels.

"It's not about me," he keeps telling me. But then, who is it about? Late in the afternoon, Abdullah washes up and prays in my apartment. He has a rug he carries with him, and he lays it down at an angle, facing northeast. I see him stand, bow, then put his forehead to the ground. When he's done, he smiles and seems at peace. He describes a warmth that comes over him when he prays, and points to the middle of his chest, at his heart. I don't understand, but I keep asking questions.

"How do you *know* there's a God? How can you be so sure about it?"

"Just look around. The universe is full of signs that point to God's existence. Who created all this beautiful world?"

While Abdul was wonderful to be with, he often disappeared without a trace for days on end. And I knew very little about his life outside of Washington Square Park. On these occasions, alone and feeling lonely, the gnawing anxiety and disconnected emptiness returned. I had lived with these feelings since adolescence and had always wondered: *What is missing? Why do I feel so alone in this world? I have a good life. Why is it not enough?*

One cold and dismal afternoon I go home to my apartment and light a candle. I know candles are important in most religions, including Judaism, though I don't know why. I stare into the flame and make a sincere and earnest request: "God, if you exist, prove it. Show Yourself to me. "

The candle flame barely flickers. After staring at it for some time, expecting who knows what, I feel foolish and blow it out.

If My servants ask you about Me, I am near. I answer the call of the caller when he calls upon Me. They should, therefore, respond to Me and believe in Me so that hopefully they will be rightly guided. (S. Baqara, v.186)

Over the next few weeks, I suddenly become more observant than I was before. I begin to look at the natural world more deeply, more intensely, perhaps as I had in childhood. While walking through the city, I notice the colors of the sky in their infinite variations. I observe how the sky changes from minute to minute—clouds changing shape and texture; sunrays blazing down or gently peeking through the clouds; shades of pink and orange bleeding to red and indigo as the sun sets, before becoming the blue-black starry night. How marvelous when you stop and truly look! No human artist could work with a canvas so vast or colors so transmutable as the progression from day to night or autumn to winter, spring, and summer. This is not human artistry at work but Something much greater performed by Someone with a plan!

I notice the flowers, how their petals are arranged in perfect symmetry around a central point and how their colors represent every subtle shade in the rainbow and beyond. Flowers come in infinite varieties, as do insects, birds and other living things. I had studied evolution, had even wanted to be an anthropologist. But random mutation would not have created so orderly, precise, and symmetrical a world as earth, would it? And what about the planets? The first Voyager space shuttle photos in the newspaper show the perfect gas rings of Saturn. I know they've been designed and formed, not haphazardly thrown together, rather perfectly planned by a master planner. He is the One, and now I know! The inner eye of my heart begins to open, as it had been open in the innocence of childhood, and I begin to perceive the essence of all I see: the inner beauty that comes from Allah, the Creator.

I want to know more. I'm hungry for knowledge and full of curiosity. I begin bombarding Abdullah with questions he can't answer, so he says, "The Quran is the open book of the universe. Get a Quran and start reading." Yes, reading has never failed me in the pursuit of knowledge. It will be easy for me to learn from a book. NYU's Tisch Library seems the perfect place to start. I search the many Quran translations on the shelves, surprised to find them so different from each other. I'm confused about which one to select but finally settle on one with beautiful red leather binding and gilt-edged pages. It has been translated at the turn of the century by a man named George Sales.

Abdullah had suggested I open the book at random and see what any particular verse might offer. Full of hopeful anticipation, I close my eyes, flip through the pages and put my finger down:

"If you see a Jew behind a tree, you must kill him."

A mixture of revulsion and rage overtakes me. I slam the book shut and throw it down on the table. I rush out of the library and into the park to find Abdul.

"What kind of crap is this Quran you told me to read?!" I accost him angrily. "All it talks about is hate—See a Jew and kill him—and all my family are Jewish. It's ridiculous!"

Abdul smiles at my anger, which upsets me even more.

"What kind of Quran did you get?" he asks calmly.

I describe the book and the translator.

"No, no," he says. "That isn't the real Quran, just a false translation by someone who wanted to prevent the spread of the religion. George Sales was a missionary who wanted to spread Christianity among the Muslims. So he deliberately misinterpreted and included false statements in his translation. God would never say that. Look at all the prophets He sent to the Jews. You need to go to a mosque and get a real Quran. There's a mosque in the East Village."

So I continue my quest. I must have the answers I seek, and I need a proper Quran. By now, I know a little bit about modesty in the Muslim religion, so I put on a long, Indian-style dress and drape a shawl around my shoulders, thinking to use it as a head cover if needed. I walk ten blocks east across town to a seedy, rough looking neighborhood and stop at the address I'd been given. A large, African-American man stands on the sidewalk with arms folded across his chest. Except for his white robes, beard, and turban, he could have been a bouncer at a night club.

"Is this the *masjid*?"

"Yeah, you have business here?"

"I want to get a Quran."

"Women don't come here. You Muslim? Muslim women cover their heads, outta respect."

I take the shawl from my shoulders and drape it over my head. That passes his inspection.

"You married? Muslim women supposed to be married."

Putting on what I hope is a tough girl face, I reply, "I'm not a Muslim, and I don't want to get married. I'm just here for a Quran. Can I go in and get one now?"

"Lemme see," He steps inside the door and returns a moment later.

"Yeah, go on in. The *imam* will see you. "

His muscular arm swings the heavy door open. I step down into another world, cool and green and dimly lit. A young bearded man gestures toward my feet and I quickly remove my shoes. Then he beckons me to kneel down on the carpet. After I do so, he himself sits down gracefully across from me.

"What brings you here, Sister?"

"I want to read the Quran in English."

"There are many translations, but the Arabic is the true word of God."

"I can't read or understand Arabic."

"In that case, I recommend Yusuf Ali's translation. We have them for sale here."

He goes away and comes back with a thick green and gold book, a Quran translated by Yusuf Ali. He tells me the price, which is fifteen dollars. I gladly pay, thank him, and leave without saying much to the bouncer outside.

This Quran is not an easy book to read. There is no consistent storyline. The phrases that most catch my eye are the ones about nature. The trees, the birds, and the earth's landscape are beautifully described. Before or after each description, God says, *"Do you not see?"* or *"In this is a sign for people who reflect."* The verse about killing Jews behind trees is nowhere in this book, though there are verses about fighting and slaying non-believers if they prevent Muslims from practicing their faith.

Abdul is pleased I've gotten the book, and he tells me to keep reading, even if I just open it to any random page and let it speak to me, or ask questions about a problem and see what it offers in return. I do not really have the faith to do that. After all, I'm just starting to recognize the proof of God's existence. I don't yet realize that I can actually have a personal relationship with Him.

I talk to Abdul about many, many things, including loneliness. Since late childhood, I've continued to experience a certain void, a well of meaninglessness that nothing and nobody can help me fill. I've tried to fill the void with friends and lovers, partying and drugs, even transcendental meditation, but all of those were temporary fixes that didn't last. With regard to men, I've thought each love affair would provide the missing link to my happiness. And yet, the whole time I've been with him, Abdul has been telling me, "It's not about me." He's been trying to make me understand that true happiness and peace does not come from another person. It comes from within.

One day he tells me, "Stef, you're never really alone. You just think you are."

"No, Abdul, I know I am. I feel lonely most of the time. And you are not much company, either!"

He looks at me tenderly and says, "You know, there's a way to be with God whenever you feel lonely."

"How?" I'm very eager to know this secret.

"You can call his hotline number."

"Oh, come on Abdul! Hotlines are for suicide cases, not calling God."

"Stef, I'm not kidding."

"Ok, what is the number? I'll write it down." I grab a pen to play along with his little joke.

"It's 33, 33, 34."

"Ok. Now what do I do, dial it on the phone?" Abdul ignores my sarcasm.

"No, you say '*Subhanallah*' thirty-three times, '*Alhamdulillah*' thirty-three times, and '*Allahu Akbar*' thirty-four times. That makes a hundred."

I repeat it haltingly after him. "What does it mean?"

"Glory be to Allah, All praise is to Allah, and Allah is the Greatest."

Abdul smiles with satisfaction, knowing he's finally made some headway with this stubborn white girl and her attitude. "You try it Stef, and see if it makes a difference."

I know from my previous meditation experience that repeating a phrase over and over again does affect the brain in interesting ways, so I decide to try Abdul's "hotline number." By now, I actually believe there is a God who has created the universe and everything in it, including me. But can I really connect with Him and feel His presence in my life by repeating a formula?

I feel some strange comfort in repeating those phrases and thinking about their meaning. They become familiar and necessary to me. Some part of my brain is reacting, making me want to say these Arabic words. Those God-conscious neurons that were my birthright are not dead after all. They have withered through disuse and sustained damage from the lifestyle choices I've made, but maybe they can be revived. That is the role of *zikr*, of remembrance, to keep our connection to God vibrantly alive! I begin feeling God's presence in my life and realize that He has always been there, even if I haven't recognized His existence. As I walk to and from work, I add the hotline number to the rhythm of my footsteps. I feel blessed and protected. And I know, beyond a shadow of doubt, that I am not alone. He has been with me since He sent me into this world at birth and He will be with me for eternity, *"the most trustworthy hand-hold that never breaks."* (S. Baqara, v. 256)

Abdul was a messenger and belief in Allah (SWT) was the message. The time soon came to separate the man from the message, however. It came in the form of a petite black woman who caught up with me in the park, grabbed me by the arm and said, 'Don't be messin' with my man, white girl. It may be a feather in his cap for you to become a Muslim, but stay away, 'cause he's got a family to take care of.'

I was caught completely by surprise. I didn't say a word but thought, *I had no idea he was married! Yes, I will stay away.* Abdul (though this woman called him Mike) was a married man! I was stunned into silence as the woman stalked away. This was the first time in my life I had encountered such a situation, and I was afraid and ashamed—afraid of this fierce woman who could easily beat me in a fight and ashamed that I'd been so naïve and gullible.

It took me months to recover from my relationship with Abdul. I thought I'd never find another man like him. He had always said, "It's not about me," and in the end, he was right. The most important part of our relationship was the blessing that remained: It is true that we are put on this earth to help each other and to urge each other constantly forward in the pursuit of spiritual growth and development. But ultimately, the only Pure Existence is Him. People are born and they die. There's a mixture of good and evil in every one of us. I've learned to take the bad with the good because no person or situation is all one way or the other. Allah (SWT) tests us in all kinds of relationships and circumstances. These trials and tribulations are what make us grow in spirit.

A few years later, married with a child, I had the urge to go back to the park and find Abdul. I wanted him to know of the progress I'd made as a Muslim and to thank him for helping me take the first steps. Indeed, I found him there, in the same place and in the same condition, a bit older and more frayed around the edges. He needed financial help, so I urged him to go to that masjid on Eleventh Street. There was nothing else I could do. I had to leave him in his place and time and move on with my life. I went home and cried, both for the losses and the gains.

Allah Ta'ala declared in a Hadith Qudsi, "Neither My Earth nor my Heavens can contain Me, but the heart of a Believing Servant can."
—Imam Ghazali, Ihya Uloom ud Deen

CHAPTER 14

My Iranians

The night of my Shahadah, fall, 1980. Farzaneh is to my right.

Abdul was out of my life, but his message remained. I firmly believed
that Allah existed. He was my Creator, and I had a relationship with Him
that surpassed all earthly relationships. I was still at NYU, attending my
classes downtown, and working part time in the art gallery. I lived with
Stacey, my new roommate, in our apartment on Twenty-Fourth Street,
midway between work and school. The location allowed me to walk to my
job or to class when the weather was nice—it beat the sweaty smells of the
subway!

My walks had a higher purpose now. They showed me God's beautiful
sky painted with a different palette each morning. They afforded me time
to think about what I was reading in the Quran and to recite my remembrance, *Subhaanallah, Alhamdulilah, Allahu Akbar!* All praise is to God,

God is great! As I walked, I felt sheltered and protected under the vastness of the sky amidst the bustle of the city.

On November 4, 1979, a group of Iranian students take over the American embassy in Tehran and hold the residents hostage. This is an earth-shattering event that lasts 444 days. No one has ever dared touch an American on any soil. We are the richest, most powerful, most democratic nation on earth. *How dare anyone mess with us?* I am outraged, along with all my countrymen and women. I agree when presidential candidate Ronald Reagan calls the Iranian people "barbarians." *Who do these people think they are, anyway?* Like most Americans, I don't know much about Iran. In high school social studies, I'd learned that all countries in the Middle East are the enemies of Israel, the one true democracy in the region. Arabs were made to seem very foreign, while Israelis were just like us. One of my teachers had even once told my class that Allah was a different god than the one many Americans worshipped.

Now, however, after a few months of reading and studying the Quran, I know with certainty that Allah is the one and only God, the same God worshipped by the Jews, and that Islam is the religion of most Iranians and Middle Easterners. NYU has a Muslim Students' Association (MSA). I visit their booth at the Student Activities Fair in search of more information about the religion.

When I approach the booth, I realize the people standing there are all foreign-looking men. I ask which countries they come from. A few are from the Gulf states, but the majority are from Iran. *Iran! That traitor state that is holding our people hostage and blindfolded!* Anger rises in my throat but I swallow it and speak directly, "I think your politics suck… But tell me about your religion." A couple of the guys chuckle softly to themselves, but one of them smiles warmly and says, "What would you like to know?"

I have many questions, and get the opportunity to ask all of them over the next few weeks. The Muslim "brothers," as they call themselves, invite me to dinner in the school cafeteria and to political rallies uptown at Columbia University. I quickly learn all about the Iranian revolution, Khomeini, and his call for an Islamic revival.

Iran is a predominantly Shi'a country. Shi'a groups exist in most Muslim countries, though the majority populations are Sunni. Both branches of the faith are part of Islam, but unfortunately do not always recognize each other that way. Political Islam has shed much blood over the differences between the Shi'a and Sunni sects. If the Muslims at N.Y.U. had shown that kind of political infighting to me, I would not have respected them or their religion. But the M.S.A. represented a cross-section of the international Muslim community. The Iranian students at N.Y.U. were all Shi'a but their imam was a Sunni Muslim from Iraq. He had recently married a Shi'a girl from Iran. To their credit, these students made me feel none of the sectarian differences between the Shi'a and Sunni.

Although they are young, dark, and handsome, these guys, who are actually practicing their religion here in the West, are different from American guys in some important ways. They do not try to have a relationship with me, and they are very polite and respectful. They don't conform to the stereotype of the hot-headed, hot-blooded Middle Eastern man I'd been conditioned to expect. No matter what difficult questions I ask them, nobody loses their temper or becomes impolite in any way. To avoid having too much interaction with a member of the opposite sex and to help me learn more about Islam, they introduce me to the Muslim women in the group: their wives, sisters, and fellow students. I find that the women at NYU and Columbia are as fervent about Islam and Imam Khomeini as the men. I also see that they do not flirt with the guys in their group, at least not openly, like American women would. Men are not the main issue on their minds. These women are serious students and political activists: strong, fearless young women who believe wholeheartedly in their cause and support it, even from inside "enemy territory." They support the revolution in Iran because they believe it will bring Islam back to the people. Under the Shah's regime they were not free to practice their religion. Khomeini has given that freedom back to them. I reflect on the modest way they dress, in long, loose-fitting tops, tunics, and headscarves. Of course, I'm not one of them and don't have to adhere to their rules. Still, I like the confident self-assurance they possess, and I want some of that for myself.

There's a bond of sisterhood between these women that reminds me of my happy days at camp. One of them takes an almost motherly interest in me. Farzaneh comes to know that I live in my own apartment with a roommate and go out on the weekends to parties and other gatherings featuring drugs, alcohol, and the whole range of what is available on the NYC social scene. She is concerned about my involvement in these activities and asks me to come to her apartment in Queens on weekends instead. I'm curious about how this Muslim woman lives, so I go for a visit.

Farzaneh's apartment is neat, clean, and sparsely furnished. I leave my shoes at the door, as is customary in a Muslim home. I feel as if I'm stepping into a sacred space, a place removed from the grimy world outside its windows, a place to worship. I cannot place my finger on what makes her place so special, but I make a mental note to find out.

Farzaneh greets me with a welcoming smile. She lives alone and is clearly comfortable with that. Iranian students from NYU and Columbia University often gather at her place for meals and meetings. There are no tables or chairs in the living room. A clean white tablecloth on the floor suffices for their meals and fiery, intense discussions about the new Islamic Republic and what it means for their beloved homeland. When her friends leave, Farzaneh is careful to vacuum up every crumb that may have strayed to the carpet.

I learn about the basic practices of Islam from Farzaneh: how to pray; how to cleanse myself for prayer; and the difference between *haram* and *halal* food, drink, and relationships. I can talk to her about the womanly things I wouldn't have mentioned to the men in the group. Farzaneh is literally a godsend. When I look back on this time in my life, I can see exactly how Allah (SWT) was holding my hand every step of the way through the people He put in my path.

I do not go to Farzaneh's every weekend. In fact, the more seriously I think about becoming a Muslim, the more I also wish for a final, last fling; a last opportunity to enjoy sinning before I take a leap of faith.

That opportunity presents itself around Halloween. My roommate Stacey and I have planned a costume party at our apartment. We invite college friends and others to come and have a good time. Stacey doesn't yet know it will be my last fling, and I don't yet know exactly how momentous an occasion it will prove to be.

The last hurrah, the Halloween party of the decade, if not the century, is planned and carried out. I dress up as a pirate in tight blue spandex pants with a big blousy shirt belted over the top. I carry a plastic dagger at my hip and wear a pirate hat with an eye patch to complete the effect. We party with abandon all night. Alcohol and drugs flow freely so everyone can choose their preference.

Afterward, I feel some guilty regrets. I brush them away by turning to my study of Islam with even greater intensity. I even mention my interest in the religion to my parents. My dad tells me, "I would have been just as upset if you had decided to be an Orthodox Jew." He has long been an atheist, or at least an agnostic, so I understand where he's coming from. My confession raises a red flag for my parents: I'm moving away from my Jewish roots. I'm sure they hope it's only a fad, like transcendental meditation had been in high school.

In December, I realize my period is late and I begin to worry about the consequences of my wild Halloween night. So far, I have kept the party a secret from Farzaneh and my other Muslim friends. But now I am scared, and I confide in Farzaneh. She listens carefully, with great concern etched on her face. Then she urges me:

"Now is your time to pray. Pray to Him and ask His forgiveness. Tell Him your heart. You need to take *shahadah* (witness God's oneness) now. What are you waiting for?"

Farzaneh wants me to see the seriousness of my actions and the possible consequences in this world and the next. No one has ever pointed the consequence of sin out to me before. And she is right. I could die tomorrow in a state of sinfulness and disbelief. None of us can control the time of our birth or the time of our death. I wash, cover my head, and pray:

Oh Allah, I have wronged myself. I may even be pregnant. But this time, no matter what happens, I will submit myself to you. I know abortion is wrong. If you have put life inside of me, no matter what the circumstances, I will keep the baby and you will help me to raise it. If I am not pregnant, so be it. I will still submit to You, because now I understand that it's what I must do.

When I finish this prayer, a sense of peace—the peace that surpasses all understanding—washes over me. I know Allah will help me no matter what the outcome because I've sincerely submitted myself to His will in the prayer position of *sujud*, where we put our foreheads to the ground. Behind the forehead is the forebrain, a structure involved in planning, analysis, and willpower. *Sujud* represents the submission of my will to Allah. I'm ready to formally declare myself a Muslim now. I tell Farzaneh I will say *shahadah* in front of witnesses at the next opportunity. Farzaneh embraces me, her eyes shining with happiness and also relief. She makes arrangements for a gathering the following week at her apartment with the leader of the group and other members of the MSA. Meanwhile, I discover I'm not pregnant and breathe a huge sigh of relief. The *shahadah* will go on as planned, however. The pregnancy scare was just a test. I need and want to be a Muslim as soon as possible.

The night of my *shahadah* is the happiest in my life. One of the sisters has sewn me a blue headscarf that I wear. I choose an Arabic name for myself, *Sommieh*. It means *elevated*. The first Sommieh in Islam was a lady who was martyred for the faith after seeing her son and husband killed before her. I want a name with a good meaning that also begins with an S, like Stephanie: a new name for my new identity. I sit in the circle of believers, the men to one side and the women to the other. I repeat the words of the *shahadah*, bearing witness:

Ashadu an la ilaha il Allah.
Wa ashadu anna Mohammad ur rasool Allah.
I bear witness that there is no God worthy of worship except God.
And I bear witness that Muhammad is the messenger of God.

I cannot stop smiling. I feel a wonderful lightness of spirit. I've been unburdened and washed clean, as I had felt years ago in the temple, but this time the euphoric feeling remains with me over time. Allah is giving me a fresh start in my new life.

I truly thought I'd revolutionized myself and was born again as a new, sinless being. True, as a new Muslim, I *was* sinless and could start my spiritual life as if I'd been reborn. But old selves never really die. They might go into hiding for a while, only to re-emerge in new guises and re-assert their qualities at any time. The genetic code of our *fitrah* is a powerful influence but so is our upbringing and our environment. The whole of our lives on earth are a drama as nature and nurture fight for balance in the tug of war that is our internal *jihad,* our inner struggle.

Do men think that they will be left alone on saying, "We believe," and that they will not be tested? We did test those before them, and Allah will certainly know those who are true from those who are false. (S. Al Ankabut, v. 2-3)

CHAPTER 15

The Blue Headscarf

My first hijab, 1980

I had gone with one of my Iranian sisters to a fabric store and chosen a dusty blue cotton material for a headscarf. She had sewn it into a square and showed me how to fold a triangle and pin it under my chin with a simple safety pin. Even before taking my shahadah, my Iranian sisters had carefully explained the Muslim dress code to me. The key word here was modesty. Besides covering my head, I was expected to cover my arms and legs down the wrists and ankles. Also, clothing had to be loose-fitting so as not to reveal the body's silhouette in any way. The Muslim women at Columbia and NYU usually dressed according to their ethnic styles, ranging from *abayas* and *jilbabs* on the Arabs, to *shalwar kameez* on the South Asians, to long tunic tops over loose-fitting jeans for the Iranian women.

I gradually acquire a collection of outfits in all these styles, though jeans and long tops are the easiest to adapt from my own wardrobe. Overnight, I go from being a stylish art gallery assistant dressed in heels and business suits to a Muslim woman in a headscarf, tunic, and baggy pants. Imagine my boss's consternation! She asks me what it's all about. When I explain, she looks at me with uncomprehending eyes, tactfully removes me from the showroom floor, and relegates me to the backroom for the remainder of my employment.

I can do modest! In fact, I actually welcome the hijab, or Muslim way of dress. It represents freedom from a lifetime of fashion dilemmas and issues with body image. For as long as I can remember, style and fashion have played a key role in my life. My maternal grandparents were in the clothing business, so when it came to quality fashion, the women in our family always had the best of everything. Having the best and the nicest clothing in school conformed to my distorted view of myself and my family as some sort of aristocracy among the peasantry of West Islip.

In my parents' childhoods, both their mothers had cooked with chicken fat, a staple of Jewish cooking in Eastern Europe for generations. My brother and I benefited from the high-fat foibles of our ancestors. Worries over heart disease and high cholesterol drove my mom to learn about whole grains, veggies, and fiber. Early in my childhood we stopped going to McDonalds and began eating whole grains instead of Wonderbread. Mom read *Diet for a Small Planet,* a ground-breaking book promoting whole grains and healthy eating. No question, she was way ahead of her time.

There was a positive and a negative side to all this focus on health and thinness, though. My parents were dieting all the time. I remember the Metrecal Diet, the one where dieters would eat dietetic cookies. And how about the grapefruit diet or the Atkins diet? My parents tried them all with varying degrees of success. My father lost substantial bulk with a combination of diet and exercise in his thirties. Mom wasn't fat, though she did have a belly due to lack of exercise. The point is, she thought she was fat and never appreciated her beautiful body. She couldn't enjoy her food because she worried incessantly about the number of calories it contained. Eating was a guilty pleasure and one that made her physically sick at times.

From a young age, I learned that being beautiful meant having an excellent figure and a perfect weight. Those were objectives worth pursuing because they affect other peoples' perceptions of you. I can remember appearing before an aunt of mine wearing a hot pink midriff top and white jeans. My flat stomach was tanned and my long, lustrous hair was in two pony tails tied with pom-pom elastics. I was about thirteen or fourteen-years old. My aunt looked me over and exclaimed, "Wow, you are turning into such a woman. What a beautiful figure you have!" I blushed but also beamed with pride at such a compliment. Looking grown up, mature, and sexy was the key to success and I had it. I learned to use it for all it was worth over the next ten years. But there was always the anxiety of weight gain, of flab creeping on to my belly and hips like some unpopular girls I knew. I avoided such imperfections at all cost.

I spent my high school years making lists of every mouthful of food I ate, trying to keep it under 1000 calories per day and berating myself if I failed to achieve my goal. I'd sneak cake from the freezer to binge on in the middle of the night, then vomit it all up. I was bulimic and nobody knew. The only thing that probably stopped me from full-blown anorexia was visiting a friend who had it.

I spent the summer between my junior and senior years at Phillips-Exeter in a prep school program designed to help me get into a good college. There, I became friendly with a girl who was even more obsessed with her weight than I was. At night, we'd compete to see who could swim the most laps in the pool, thus swimming off the calories we had consumed that day. After the summer, we parted ways, but a few months into my senior year, her mom called and begged me to visit her daughter, who was down to 68 lbs., but still believed she was fat. She had been in and out of the hospital and was a gaunt skeleton, a shadow of her former self when I visited her. "If she doesn't start eating," her mother cried, "she will eventually die." The experience of visiting her at home and seeing what she had become scared me straight. I gave up binging and purging, though I continued to struggle with weight issues until I became a Muslim.

Near my job on Fifty-Seventh Street there's a construction site where the workers have hung an effigy of Imam Khomeini with a sign listing the number of days the hostages have been held, already more than four hundred! That event astonishes me. Even though I am now a Muslim and have some understanding of the meaning behind the Iranian students' actions, I'm still an American with a sense of patriotism, and like everyone else in 1980, I want the hostage crisis to end. Although I'm a Democrat, I consider voting for Reagan, who promises to bring our ambassadors home!

As soon as I begin wearing Islamic dress, the catcalls from the construction workers at the site stop. Non-Muslims often pity Muslim women for being oppressed by their coverings. However, I think *hijab* is actually liberating. It prevents people from judging a woman solely on the basis of her physical appearance. A covered woman is much less of a sex object than an uncovered one, though the mystery of what is undercover is also alluring. Hijab offers me protection from others as well as from myself. It helps me see my body as a gift from God that is worth protecting. Eating a balanced diet becomes part of the way I respect myself, as well. Wearing *hijab* effectively removes my obsession with body fat.

Over the years, it's been interesting to gauge people's reactions to the clothing I wear, especially the headscarf. People often assume I'm a foreigner. "But you speak English so well!" they say, perplexed by my New York accent. One rude woman in a restaurant once told my Muslim friends and I to go back to where we came from. I quickly replied, "I'm from New York!" The funniest reaction, however, came from a group of Italian-American men. They were congregated on the sidewalk of my Jersey City neighborhood when I walked by them with my daughter in her stroller. In my blue and white ensemble, I looked like a nun and they greeted me politely with "Good morning, sister." As I passed by, they must have realized I was pregnant. Their polite smiles turned to looks of astonished confusion. I smiled to myself and walked on as I heard one of them exclaim, "Sister!" They must have wondered what the Catholic Church was coming to.

Now, however, when it comes to the implications of how I'm dressed, it's my parents that concern me. If my boss's response had been difficult, how would it be for my parents? I pray to Allah to make it easy, but I know that seeing me in *hijab* for the first time will be a shocking experience for Mom and Dad.

> *O Prophet, tell your wives and your daughters and the women of the believers to draw their cloaks close round them (when they go abroad). That will be better, so that they may be recognized and not annoyed. Allah is ever Forgiving, Merciful. (S. Ahzab, v. 59).*

CHAPTER 16

So That You May
Know One Another

Islamic Center of Jersey City, newsletter staff, c. 1981

At this time, my parents are renting an apartment in the city. They drive in from Long Island on a Thursday or Friday night and stay for the weekend. We usually meet for dinner once a week. Soon after taking my *shahadah* and donning the scarf, I'm to meet them at the Hunan Balcony, our favorite Chinese restaurant. I arrive wearing my blue headscarf. As I sit down, my parents look me over. Dad, trying to be diplomatic and calm, comments, "That's an interesting looking thing you have on your head.

What does it mean?" When I don't answer right away, Mom jumps in, already upset. "I'll tell you what it means. It means she's a Muslim. I saw it in my dream the other night!" This isn't the first or the last of her prophetic dreams concerning me. Around this occasion when she dreamt of me, I must have been reciting the *kalima*: *There is no god except God and Muhammad is His messenger.*

Clearly, nobody has an interest in dinner so we leave the restaurant, walking and talking for many blocks. "Have you been brainwashed? What kind of cult is this? What are you planning to do next?" These are some of the fears my parents express. I try my best to calm them, but this monumental decision of mine is a bombshell. Years later, my father will tell my son, "Your mother was a bigger rebel than you will ever be." He must have been thinking of this night and the months that followed.

My extended family kicks in their support behind my parents, of course. Over the next few weeks, relatives call to try and assess the extent of my "brainwashing." Some of them think a cult has gotten hold of me. Reverend Sun Myung Moon, leader of the Moonies, had recently been exposed on TV. Isn't this similar? Cults were targeting American youth and turning them away from their families and their religions. My parents viewed this conversion as a rejection of their value system and the way they'd raised me.

My relatives try to convince me I've done wrong in causing my parents to worry, and that I am going against my own people and siding with our enemy, the Arabs. My younger cousin asks me if I'll now start wearing a muu muu and let myself become a fat, sloppy housewife!

In spite of their fears, I am happy with my decision. I answer them all as rationally as I can. I hadn't been brainwashed. I'd done a lot of reading and thinking and had asked many questions. It wasn't a sudden decision, but one I'd arrived at after many years of searching for the truth. Allah had shown me the answers through His signs, and I had submitted to His will. Luckily, I have my new Muslim friends for support. And eventually time would help my family realize this was a self-induced change, not a case of brainwashing at all.

I take my neo-Islamic identity so seriously that I get rid of all my pre-*hijabi* clothing. I give my entire designer wardrobe of career suits, slacks, skirts, and jackets away to a friend in Manhattan. When my mother finds out about this, she insists I try to get the clothing back, but my friend had promptly altered everything to fit her tiny size-three body. The damage is irreversible.

I learn that people don't react well when those close to them make major lifestyle changes. Unbeknownst to me, my mother has called my friend Lisa and begged her to talk some sense into me regarding my conversion to Islam. We've both been away at school and need to catch up, so we meet for lunch. When Lisa arrives at the restaurant she finds this new Muslim, Sommieh. She is shocked, not just by the new look, but by the fact that she hadn't known a thing about it. She keeps saying, "I guess I don't really know you anymore." After an awkward meal, we part ways for a time, although I do attend her wedding two years later.

New friends supplant old ones. My sisters in Islam are a feisty group of women from all over the globe. They are mostly students at N.Y.U. and Columbia University. I begin attending a study group that meets on Saturdays at Columbia. I meet Egyptian, Pakistani, and Sudanese women. Sometimes, Farzaneh and the other Iranian women attend, as well as other American converts—black, white, and Latina. I enjoy getting to know this group of women with their diverse traditions of dress, food, language, and religious practices. My worldview widens through my association with women whose native cultures are so different than my own.

We call our group *Sisters in Islam,* and we are truly sisters to each other. In Islam, men and women often have separate yet parallel social worlds. There is no dating in the western sense, but courtship and marriage instead, and the family plays a large role in the choice of a life partner. Without the pressure of attracting guys, women can really value their female friendships in a way that had been previously lacking in my life. I become very close to one other American in this group, a woman named Debbie. Debbie was brought up in the Church of Christ, Scientist. She and her whole family were devout believers until their mother died of cancer. It was a slow, painful death at home because her mom believed illness was a matter of spirit. She didn't seek help from doctors or take medicine. After watching her mother die, Debbie rejected Christian Science. She left her home in the Midwest on a motorbike and eventually ended up in New York City where she met her husband and embraced Islam. She's married to an imam, one of the community's religious leaders, and is living the life of a parson's wife, so to speak, serving incessant cups of tea and a home-cooked meal to guests of all kinds who seek her husband's help and counsel. Her husband is especially interested in meeting converts, so she invites me to their home in Jersey City.

I usually say my prayers at home or on campus, but one day, I decide to return to the masjid in the East Village. It is time for the Friday prayer, and I want to join the congregation and hear the *khutbah* (sermon). The Thirteenth Street Masjid is really just a storefront consisting of a few rooms. It was initially established by taxi drivers and restaurant workers from Bangladesh and Egypt.

I get there early because I want to be sure I have a place to sit in the women's section. When I arrive, the man in charge seems surprised to see me. He takes me to the door of the women's room but asks me to wait. He goes around the room shaking what appear to be large bundles of cloth and whispering to them. When one of the bundles stands up, I realize there are men sleeping in all four corners of the room. Prayer room by day, homeless shelter by night. Women aren't really expected at this bachelor masjid. In fact, I am the only woman in this empty room when the prayer begins. I listen to the *khutbah* and then follow along with the prayer on the loud speaker. When I finish, I turn around to find one other woman there with me. I find out her name is Latifah, and she's also a convert from a formerly Jewish background, though she's been Muslim longer than I have. I ask her a question that's been on my mind. "Why do women have to sit in separate rows behind the men when we pray?" She answers frankly, "Would you be comfortable knowing a man might be looking at your backside while you knelt in prayer?" I hadn't thought of that. Allah has a good reason for everything!

At one point during these first few months as a Muslim, I have an out of body experience. Nothing like this had ever happened to me before, and it proves to be a one-time event. I'm lying on my bed in my apartment when my jaw suddenly locks. I literally cannot open my mouth. At the same time, I feel my essence rise swiftly from my physical body as if my spirit wants to leave. I hear some beautiful, soft music, the tinkling of bells. My spirit is very excited. *Let's go, Let's go*, I hear myself say inside my head. As soon as I say those words, the answer comes back, *Not yet*, and my spirit swiftly drops back into my body on the bed. I am disappointed but later realize it just means I have *miles to go before I sleep** and so much more to learn.

*Excerpt from the poem *Stopping by Woods on a Snowy Evening* by Robert Frost

Cloud Nine,
New Muslim Mind

First visit to Mom and Dad with Mohammed, 1981

Many single, immigrant men lived in the New York-New jersey metro-politan area. One of the imam's jobs was to help them find wives, especially American ones. Marrying an American citizen would make it easier for the men to gain permanent status in the United States. For us converts, the issue was different. When we took our *shahadahs*, we were told that we were now as pure as newborn babies. Any sins we had committed prior to entering Islam were now erased from our book of deeds. Having relations with the opposite sex outside of the bonds of marriage is a sin in Islam. For a practicing Muslim woman, the only reason to meet men is with the intention of marriage.

In the best-case scenario, the American wife would learn a lot about Islam from her Muslim husband. The men, on the other hand, were away from their homes and their family social circles. They needed to find women to marry, preferably Muslim women or those who had the potential to convert, and raise their children as Muslims. The immigrant community helped fulfill the role of the family and many intercultural marriages were arranged as a result.

My first marriage lasted twenty-five years and included many struggles, especially during its final decade. I finally got divorced in 2005. My ex-husband was one of my first and best teachers. I learned the basics of the faith from him and the people he knew. I was very fortunate to have married a man who was actually practicing the religion. There were many situations where women were asked to convert by men who wanted to marry them but did not really practice Islam themselves. It was more difficult for those women than it was for me. My marital struggles were more cultural than religious.

I take the PATH train to Jersey City, New Jersey to visit Debbie and Sheikh Hanooti (may Allah be pleased with him). He is older than Debbie by more than ten years and is well known and respected in the community as a scholar and religious leader (hence the title sheikh before his name). Debbie, a warm and gracious hostess, serves us tea in tiny glasses—the Arab way—and the three of us start talking about the many difficulties of changing one's faith and lifestyle. The sheikh also wants to know if I'm interested in marriage. I've just turned twenty-two. I've had plenty of experience with men pre-Islam and feel ready to settle down and start a family with someone. I had always thought I'd marry someone from a different culture, so the idea of marrying a foreigner doesn't bother me. The Muslim men I've met so far know how to treat a woman with respect and dignity, so when the sheikh asks me if I'd like to meet someone, I agree. He describes a few single men he knows in the Jersey City community. I've recently read a *hadith* (saying of Prophet Muhammad ﷺ) about marriage which states that the best reason to marry a woman is for her piety, not her wealth or beauty. I think of this hadith and naively apply it to the men the sheikh is describing. One of them is a young brother who works with Sheikh Hanooti in the masjid. I think to myself, *if he works with the imam, he must be the most pious.* I agree to meet that brother and the meeting is arranged for the following weekend.

During the week leading up to the meeting, I try to prepare myself mentally for the interview. Other Muslim sisters advise me to ask questions. I have a short list ready in my head. When I arrive at her home, Debbie lends me one of her most beautiful scarves so I will look my best. She sits with me in the living room as we wait for Brother Mohammed Aftab Uddin to arrive with the sheikh. The first thing I notice about the brother is his smile. His teeth are very white in contrast to his skin color, which is a tawny brown. He is from Bangladesh. The extent of my knowledge about his homeland is that the Beatles performed a charity concert for the Bangladeshis in 1971. It was the first benefit rock concert!

"Are you planning to stay in the US?" is the first question I ask the brother. I've heard stories of women who had to go overseas with their husbands and adjust to life in another country far from home. I don't want that kind of life.

"I plan to stay in the US, *Inshallah* (if Allah wills)." He answers most of my questions and asks a few of his own. We have tea and then the interview is over. Now I have to let Debbie know if I'm interested in seeing him again. I like his honesty, sincerity, and simplicity. His smile is somehow reassuring, so I say *yes.*

Aftab and I spend a few weeks getting to know each other. I start calling him Mohammed, not realizing that it is not his first name, but is used as a term of respect before a man's first name in South Asian culture. We always go out in public, so we won't be alone together. We eat dinner in the city and talk on the phone quite a bit. He's a very calm and peaceful person. He answers my many questions about the religion in a straightforward way and always ends an issue with *Inshallah.* I have many worries, many what ifs, and his *Inshallahs* make me realize everything is in Allah's hands, not ours.

I am a new Muslim, a baby in my faith, and I accept everything at face value. This state is a sort of bliss, a cloud nine existence. *I have found Allah.*

I will never be completely alone again. Anything and anyone Allah sends me will be just what I need. It is in this frame of mind that I agree to marry Mohammed. He is pious and good. His innocence touches me He doesn't seem strong enough to hurt me or break my heart, which has been broken many times before. I feel safe with him.

I have to let my parents know. So I hit them with the second shocker of the year: "I'm planning to marry this Muslim man I met." At this point, they've hardly gotten over my conversion. Now I want to marry one of them. I guess they can no longer think of it as just a phase I'm going through. Initially, they agree to meet Mohammed. But then they decide they aren't emotionally ready for such an encounter. So my Aunt Pixie and Uncle Murray step in and invite us to their New York City apartment for dinner. It's an awkward meal to say the least.

My uncle tries to draw parallels between orthodox Judaism and Islam. He feels I'll be going backward in time by getting involved with "all of that religiosity." Mohammed is polite and respectful, and therefore doesn't say much. As we leave in a taxi, we reflect on the meeting. It had been very awkward, but Mohammed had done his best to be polite and respectful to people with whom he had virtually nothing in common. That's a point in his favor with me. I let him hold my hand briefly before we part. "Everything will work out, *Inshallah*" he says reassuringly. "Don't worry about it."

After the dinner with my relatives, I realize it's quite far-fetched to expect anyone in my family to support my idea to marry Mohammed. This thought is confirmed by the sheikh and my new Muslim friends who tell me not to wait for my family's approval because I won't get it. Instead, I speak with another Muslim woman in the community who had met Mohammed but married someone else. She gives him a glowing recommendation, saying she did not choose him because she thought the cultural differences would be too much for her to accept. I dismiss that red flag as not applying to me. I think myself worldly and sophisticated, enough so not to care about cultural differences but, in fact, to embrace them! Easier said than done, as I will soon learn.

The following week, Mohammed prepares a wonderful dinner for Debbie, her husband, and me. I'm very impressed by his abilities as a cook, especially since I myself don't have much confidence or experience in the kitchen. Everything from the soup to the curried meat he serves is expertly seasoned; his culinary skills are another point in his favor.

I arrive for dinner with a sense of anticipation and excitement because I've already decided to accept Mohammed's proposal of marriage! Sometime after the lentil soup and before the evening prayers, I suggest that we get married that very evening. He eagerly agrees.

I have never been big on ceremonies, and I know my family will not approve in any case, so we all go next door to Sheikh Hanooti's office. Someone grabs two witnesses from the masjid and Debbie acts as the third as her husband pronounces our marriage vows. Later that week we get an actual license at city hall, which makes us married both civilly and Islamically.

Anas ibn Malik reported the Messenger of Allah, peace and blessings be upon him, said, "Whoever Allah provides with a righteous wife, then he has fulfilled half of his religion. Let him fear Allah regarding the second half." (Hadith)

CHAPTER 18

The Best of Planners

1981

What had I done? I leapt before I looked, that's for sure. Mohammed and I eloped in February of 1981. I moved from my New York apartment on Twenty-Fourth Street to the rooms Mohammed lived in at the masjid. In Jersey City, the main mosque had two buildings, a winter house and a summer one. The building on Park Street was so large that it could not be heated in the winter because the community couldn't afford its heating bill. The masjid also owned a two-story house where guests could stay, and people could pray downstairs, especially in the winter. Mohammed lived in the guest quarters upstairs, and I moved right in there with him. The old-fashioned rooms were spacious compared to my NYC apartments.

But there was no privacy. There were men coming in and out of the building day and night. Sometimes, men who didn't yet know Mohammed was married came into our room, unannounced. This meant I had to wear my *hijab* at all times, even in my own room. The large kitchen downstairs was also a community place. The brothers were used to coming in and out, making their tea, etc. I could hardly think of it as my own kitchen. There were little messes everywhere, as most of the brothers didn't clean up after themselves. I tried my best to be patient. I was a new wife and a new Muslim, unsure of others' expectations in either capacity.

When I first move into the house, some of my boxes are accidentally placed in the kitchen, one of which contains some photos of mine, an album from my days in Israel. Some of the brothers from the community see the album and take a look, out of curiosity. In a few of the pictures, I'm standing with a group of Israeli soldiers in uniform. I'm posing with my arms around one of them, and there's a big, teasing grin on my face. Well, this is wrong on many levels. First, I'm wearing jeans and a t-shirt. My long brown, *uncovered* hair is cascading over my shoulders for all the world to see. I'm obviously flirting with soldiers, and what kind of woman does that? On top of that, they are Israeli soldiers, and my new brothers are mainly Palestinians and Egyptians. What must they be thinking about Br. Aftab's new wife? *Maybe she's a spy?*

One of the African-American Muslim brothers, a convert, saves me from undue embarrassment. He takes the box from the kitchen and brings it to our upstairs room. He tells me what has happened and explains that he's told the brothers the pictures were none of their business. I'm grateful for this, and for some later occasions when this same brother leads me or my family out of trouble. May God bless Br. Zaid and keep him close in *jennah* (paradise). Eventually, I get rid of the offensive material, saving only those photos that won't raise eyebrows.

Photos can be destroyed, but what about the memories of my life before Islam? New Muslims are told that once they say *shahadah*, they're considered brand new people. Any sins they have committed before embracing Islam are forgotten. A new Muslim has been "born again" in that sense. But our brains and hearts still carry the memories of the past. Our personalities have been molded from those experiences, and they cannot simply be erased. The past shapes the present, no matter how much we might wish otherwise. We are made of what we came from, and we take that with us, transforming it for the good as we go, *Inshallah*. Only in this way can we be complete, whole, and genuine. I know that now, in hindsight.

American women marrying Muslim men from overseas are advised that it would be best not to talk about past relationships, that the immigrant husband would not be able to understand or accept the fact that there might have been other men before him. In my case, I could not expect a young man from Bangladesh to accept and understand my liberal Long Island upbringing. Significant areas of my early life would remain a secret from my husband. But such attempts are doomed to fail. Secrecy, in one form or another, had always been a theme in my life. My mother had been high-strung and easily upset, so I'd learned not to tell her things that would upset or aggravate her. In fact, my father had advised me not to upset her on more than one occasion. However, in relationships, secrecy blocks intimacy. It creates walls that grow thicker and more insurmountable as time goes by.

When we first marry, I convince myself that the socio-cultural differences between Mohammed and me won't matter much. After all, I am ready to change my whole lifestyle, revolutionizing myself from the inside out as a Muslim. Of course, my husband should be a totally different kind of man than my father, brother, or uncles are. To my cloud-nine, new-Muslim mind, the vast differences in education, economic status, and upbringing are not enough to outweigh the goal of reinventing myself as a Muslim. I have married Mohammed for his piety, and he is as humble and self-effacing as my father is self-confident and proud. The fact that I am a product of my family and society doesn't faze me at all.

On the face of it, I was a New Yorker, born and bred, and he was from a village in the jungles of Bangladesh. *What was she thinking?* must have been the question on everybody's mind.

The truth is, I'm not thinking. Rationality didn't play a big role in my decision to marry Mohammed. I am a new Muslim. Converting was the best decision I ever made in my life. I'm in euphoric state; swept up and led along in this whole new way of life. Arranged marriages, set up by people who know the both of you sound ideal. But really, how well does anyone in my new-found community know *me*? I don't even know myself anymore. In the beginning of my life as a Muslim I think I have revolutionized myself. Later, I will realize that becoming a Muslim is an evolutionary process, not a revolutionary one.

At times, the differences between Mohammed and I seem insurmountable. I have married a man who comes from a poor, Third World country. Our ideas about proper standards of living don't align. During that first month, I buy him a shirt as a present. It costs about fourteen dollars, yet he tells me I've paid too much. Pre-Islam, I had a designer wardrobe worth thousands of dollars. Now my husband tells me a fourteen-dollar shirt is too expensive.

He tells me there had been a time in his life when he had only one shirt and had to go without to wash it. He tells me many stories about his life in a village in Bangladesh. How he would grow bananas and take them to the market to sell. How only his older brother had received a good education. How his father had died of tuberculosis before he himself was ten. How his mother had raised six boys and a girl. How his sister had died shortly after her own marriage. His brother's first wife had died, too, when a bolt of lightning came through the window of their home and killed her on the spot. These stories are exotic and heartbreaking to me. They give me a glimpse into Mohammed's former life. If I can't relate, at least I can empathize. When I finally go to Bangladesh some years later, I'm better able to visualize his childhood and adolescence.

For now, though, I try my best to understand the man I've married. It's a struggle for us to find common interests and common ground, except in Islam itself. Mohammed has come to the States to earn a living and help his family back home. He's had various jobs in the city. He's seen many men from back home lose their Muslim identity in America, too, yet thankfully, he's not one of them. *Alhamdulillah* (All praise is to God).

In the early days of Islam, men who were not rich in material wealth were encouraged to offer their knowledge of the faith as dowries for their wives. In a similar sense, Mohammed becomes my teacher in matters of the faith. After high school, his main area of study had been Islam. When he came to the US, eventually finding work at the masjid in Jersey City, he had the chance to study with scholars from the Middle East. One of his prize possessions is a red, leather bound Quran given to him by Dr. Sulieman Dunya, an Egyptian sheikh. This Quran shows the English translation by Yusuf Ali side by side with the Arabic and has wonderful footnotes and appendices. It's the first Quran I read from start to finish.

I learn the basics of the religion and its practice from Mohammed and the people he knows. He's a sincere man who always practices what he preaches. One of the reasons he works for the masjid is so he can practice his faith freely. During our marriage, he'll also run a series of small businesses—he prefers working for himself to working for anyone else. I admire him for his dedication and commitment to the faith. He's as eager to teach me as I am to learn. I also teach him a few things, like how to drive a car. I help him to obtain his green card and eventual citizenship, a much easier process in pre-9/11 days.

About six weeks into our marriage, I begin feeling very tired and sick to my stomach. At first I think I'm just depressed. I've taken Mohammed to meet my parents. We don't tell them we've gotten married, but by the end of the visit, they've guessed the truth. My father is very angry. Not only have I become a Muslim, but I've deceived my whole family by marrying behind their backs. The result is that my father decides not to talk to me. This has never happened before. In our close-knit family, we might have occasional arguments, but we have never cut off communication from one another for more than a few hours or days. This is a clear indication of the wrong that I've committed in marrying someone from such a different background than my own. I begin to feel both guilty and trapped in my situation, though I've obviously brought it upon myself.

I have to get out of this mess and get back to my family. I put together a basic escape plan. I will run away to Madison, Wisconsin, where my brother is enrolled at the university. I will somehow start a new life for myself there, where nobody will know me. I tell no one of my secret plan, not even Andrew. I just assume he'll be willing to help me, even though he and I have not talked since he went away to school. He only knows of my conversion and marriage secondhand.

Meanwhile, my period is late and I feel sick enough to go to the doctor. I tell Mohammed I think I might be pregnant. He is surprised and upset that it's happened so soon, especially when I tell him I don't love him. Neither one of us is really ready to believe I'm pregnant until a doctor confirms the news. It's important to find a female doctor, for the sake of modesty. We go to an OB/GYN that someone in the community recommends, an Indian Muslim woman. I find her very cold, clinical and somewhat stern, not at all like the doctors my parents had taken me to as a child. She confirms that I am six weeks pregnant and prescribes the usual prenatal vitamins and monthly checkups.

Mohammed had wanted us to have more time together before we had a child, but that is no longer an option. Over the next few months he adjusts to the idea of fatherhood. I am quite happy with this news, secretly thrilled. It is a game changer. Now I have a reason to stay in my marriage. Full of emotion, I put my head on the ground in *sujud,* the most humble posture of prayer, and submit to God's will. *Oh Allah, You've given me a reason to stay in this marriage, a sign, the blessing of a child. I will do my best to make this marriage work.*

"Do you think you can grow to love me?" Mohammed asks with hope and trepidation. I answer *"yes,"* because our baby is a sign of the potential for love to grow between us. Pregnancy is the glue that holds our marriage together that first year. It also brings my parents back to me. First, my mother begins talking to me to find out how I'm feeling. Then my father sends me a card and some money when he learns that his first grandchild is on the way.

The urge to up and leave my marriage had been assuaged by the impending birth of my first child. But the tendency to escape trouble by exploring a new horizon would remain a pattern in my life.

But they plan and Allah plans. And Allah is the best of planners (S. Al Anfal, v. 30).

CHAPTER 19

Salt is Bismillah

There were many firsts in my first year of my marriage and Islam. One of them was *Ramadan,* the month of fasting. Yom Kippur, the one day of fasting of the Jewish faith, is easy compared to fasting for twenty-nine to thirty days in the heat of August and pregnant besides. No one told me I didn't have to fast. Although it's not required of pregnant women or nursing women, my friends told me it was better to fast than to have to make up the days in some other month later. I was living amongst stalwart Egyptian and Bengali women, and I was strong and healthy so I tried my best to fast.

Pregnant and overheated in long, polyester tent dresses, I walk to the masjid with Mohammed for morning prayers. That's the coolest time of the day in midsummer, right before dawn, at about 4:00 am. We've eaten our *suhoor*, or pre-dawn meal, prepared on a hot plate in our upstairs kitchenette. My Bengali husband wants to eat leftover curry and rice in the middle of the night, a choice that causes me to shake my head in bewilderment and scorn. I can barely manage a bowl of cereal at that hour, and he wants dinner. This routine of early morning food preparation is made much worse one morning when a poor, unsuspecting mouse accidently gets fried on the hot plate. Try dealing with that on a pregnant, nauseous stomach.

I soon learn that if I don't eat more, the day will just be too long for me to complete the fast. As it is, I collapse in tears in front of the air conditioner from about 6:00 pm to 9:00 pm when the sun goes down, and we break our fast. It is hard. Allah does not test a soul with more than it can bear, but I feel He is certainly stretching me as far as I can go. I even have the stretch marks of pregnancy to prove it.

Mohammed and I both enjoy our early morning walks to the masjid. A new day is dawning and all things are possible. As we walk, Mohammed helps me memorize short chapters of the Quran with something that approximates correct pronunciation of the Arabic words. Prayers in the mosque early in the morning are very holy. One can feel the presence of angels and the power of the prayer itself. The uncrowded space resonates with the prayers of prior supplicants.

Paradoxically, Ramadan, in addition to fasting, is also about socializing and eating. On one of the first days of the fast, Mohammed and I walk to the masjid for a community dinner. I am hot and famished, desirous of water and the fruit salad already set out in little bowls, colorful and refreshing. I can think of nothing else except how good that fruit salad will taste. I notice it has little dark specks on it. *Cinnamon. What a nice touch.*

Finally, the call to prayer is made and I get a bowl of fruit salad and dig in greedily. After a moment, I notice my mouth is burning. Pepper! The dark specks are not cinnamon, they're pepper. Now I'm angry. "Who would put pepper on fruit salad?" I comment with disgust. "Pakistani people do," says someone standing nearby. "Well, they should warn the rest of us. What a dumb thing to do!" I can hardly contain myself over the ruined fruit.

Food, its preparation, and service are a big issue during that first year of marriage and beyond. I've been raised on broiled meat and plain vegetables. Salt was practically the only seasoning my mother used, and that in great moderation. Mohammed has been raised on spicy food, served daily with rice. So right there, I must make a big adjustment. My mother has given me a copy of *The Joy of Cooking*, the bible of western-style meals. I resolve to try as many recipes as I can. But whatever I cook is not to Mohammed's liking. He'll eat a little bit and then leave the rest, without saying anything at all. I know the practice of the Holy Prophet ﷺ. He would never criticize food he didn't like. He just wouldn't eat it. I take offense, especially after spending long hours cooking from *The Joy of Cooking*. I lack confidence in the kitchen, but I'm an adventurous eater and like a varied diet. My parents had encouraged me to taste everything at least once when I was a child. I can't understand why Mohammed doesn't want to try new things, too, only preferring what is more familiar from his childhood. Out of necessity, he begins to teach me a few simple Bengali dishes and also does some of the cooking himself. He salts his food before even tasting it. "Salt is *Bismillah*," he explains, "like a blessing for the food. "

I want to learn these new recipes, too. My mother had never entertained much at home. Cocktails and hors d'oeuvres in the living room and extended family dinners for holidays was basically all the home cooking she could manage for guests. Our family went out to eat several times a week. As a pregnant newlywed, though, I am now part of a community where people host or attend dinner parties at home every weekend. Naturally, I have to reciprocate, even if I'm not up to the task. I also want to feed people what they like, so I gather recipes from the Egyptian and Bengali ladies who host us, trying to carefully record the amount of each ingredient, although they themselves never measure. But my approximations never turn out the way their dishes do. The chicken curry is bland and undercooked, and the rice is mushy. The chocolate chips are not supposed to melt in the pudding, and the grape leaves won't stay rolled. Unfamiliar ethnic dishes prepared by a novice cook for first time guests is a risky business. I cause myself unnecessary stress and even panic when the recipes don't turn out as they should.

At the same time, I know the house should be spotlessly clean, as my mother's had been when my parents' guests arrived. The bathrooms, especially, must be clean. Mohammed makes fun of me for worrying about this. "Why do Americans spend so much time cleaning their bathrooms, as if their toilets were thrones?" he inquires. "Don't worry so much about how things look. Just make the people feel comfortable in your home. They won't care what they eat. Why are you making such a big deal about it?"

But it *is* a big deal to me. I'm sure these women, nice as they are, will certainly judge me inadequate as a homemaker and wife, a job for which I have not been properly trained. The first time I have people to dinner, I nearly break down in a nervous fit. Mohammed wonders what kind of mess he's gotten himself into. As it turns out, our guests are very nice, of course. They praise both the food and the house, just as I had done in their homes. I'm taking my new role as a Muslim wife and expectant mother much too seriously. My perfectionistic attitude adds undue stress to my life and my marriage.

> *On no soul does God place a burden greater than it can bear. It gets every good that it earns and it suffers every ill that it earns. "Our Lord! Condemn us not if we forget or fall into error; our Lord! Lay not on us a burden like that which You did lay on those before us. Our Lord, lay not on us a burden greater than we have the strength to bear..."*
> *(S. Baqara, v. 286)*

CHAPTER 20

Muslim in America

With Andrew, Tahera, and my cousin Patty, 1982

In classes for new Muslims, fellow converts and I were asked to draw a clear line between life before and life after converting to Islam. We were encouraged to assume whole new identities. So far, the transformation had been little more than skin deep. I'd changed my clothes and covered my head, learned the postures of prayer, and even memorized some verses of Quran—but I didn't yet understand the real meaning of submission to Allah (SWT).

Many aspects of my prior life don't fit in well with my new religion, like music, art, and the whole New York cultural scene. Before Islam, I spent a good portion of my leisure time visiting art museums and going to concerts and theatrical performances. After all, I had majored in art history and lived in Manhattan, a mecca of culture. I'd been raised by art collectors. Growing up, my family and I spent our weekends in art galleries, at antique shows, and visiting museums. Broadway shows, Lincoln Center opera and ballet, Carnegie Hall concerts: these were regular family activities. Then there were the rock concerts and sporting events at Madison Square Garden with my friends. New Yorkers with money know how to have fun.

My parents' marriage had been built on the pleasures they enjoyed together: collecting art, attending concerts and the theater, and dining out together and with the family. By converting to Islam, I have to give most of this up, and I just don't feel ready to do so. I cry many tears over these sacrifices during these first months. I also wonder what I will build my marriage upon.

The answer comes back: *faith*.

But still I am worried. Can the common bond of Islam really be enough to make the marriage Mohammed and I share a success?

As a single, young Muslim I might have given up some of my pleasures gradually or found a way to incorporate them into my new lifestyle. But now I am married and need to also take my husband's likes and dislikes into consideration. He has no experience with and little interest in art museums and concerts. If he participates, it's only to please me. Even I can recognize that most of these activities have un-Islamic aspects to them. Museums have nude sculptures and other representations of the human form, considered *haram* in Islam. My new husband is embarrassed to look at what I have been raised to consider the beauty of the human body. Concerts and plays are not scheduled to accommodate prayer times, and besides, there are no designated prayer areas at Lincoln Center or Carnegie Hall. Some friends of my parents once see us leaving in the middle of a concert to perform our prayers. My husband is trying to make me understand a new set of priorities, but I am torn between my old life and this new one. The beaches I grew up on are, of course, full of bikini-clad bodies and are therefore unsuitable places for practicing Muslims to spend their time. *But, what is summer without the beach?* I lament to myself.

On an intellectual level, I understand that my prior recreational activities do not fit into my new religion. And yet, it is very hard to give up all that I once enjoyed. What is there to take the place of these activities? I don't see anything satisfying on the horizon. I resent my husband's black/white, *halal/haram* thinking. I want to rationalize and compromise—to go to a concert and still find a way to pray on time. I don't want my Islam to be so limiting, so oppressive. I need time to develop my views, develop an Islamic perspective I can live with. In the meantime, I let my husband, the more knowledgeable of us in the *deen*, take the lead. Though his general education has been limited, he has knowledge about Islam and he is a sincere believer. I have much to learn from him.

Through my husband, I meet many good people. As the *moathen*, the caller to prayer at the Islamic center, he's known and appreciated by everyone in the community. My social circle grows to include his friends' wives from Egypt, Palestine, Pakistan, and Bangladesh. He is closest to the people of his own country, and I get to know and love them and their families.

Shara is a simple and beautiful Bengali sister. Her love of God and her fellow human beings, Allah's *bandi* (slaves in Bengali) as she calls them, bubbles out of her at every turn. There is always something to learn in her presence, and her deep spirituality is contagious. She and her husband, Ali, live with eight children in a lower-income housing project. Ali works hard in a Jersey City factory—hard enough that he is eventually able to retire and buy Shara a big house in Dacca, Bangladesh, where she continues her mission of helping fellow Muslims in need. The first time Shara visits me in my Jersey City apartment, she must be appalled at my shorts and t-shirt, because within a week, she has made me a *shalwar-kameez* outfit with baggy turquoise pants and a printed tunic top. Meanwhile, an Egyptian sister makes me a dress of dotted Swiss polyester. It is huge and hot, but that is the style in Egypt in the 1980s. It completely hides the fact that I'm pregnant.

Shara introduces me to the Tablighi Jamaat, a Muslim group that focuses on the proper practice of Islam by stressing six points: belief, prayer, remembrance, service to humanity, sincerity, and *da'wah* (propagation of the faith). There are meetings where we sit in a circle and listen to stories and advice. I learn a *hadith* (saying or tradition of the Prophet ﷺ), which says that in meetings where Allah (SWT) is mentioned, the angels come to sit and record what the people are doing. They then bring that information back to Allah (SWT) who blesses and praises those people, forgiving any sins they may have committed. After the Tabligh meetings, I do in fact have a special sense of being spiritually cleansed. In these early days, I am only just starting to believe in the more unseen or mystical aspects of faith, such as angels.

At one particular meeting advice is given about how to be sincere and focused in prayer. When I go home, I visualize what I'd heard. I imagine the Kaaba in Mecca in front of me, the angel of death behind me, Hell to my left, and Heaven to my right. I imagine standing on the bridge of *Siraat,* the one we must all cross over to get to our afterlife. As I'm praying and visualizing with sincerity, I see a light stretching out in front of me. I become very warm, as if heated from inside. I feel that I am no longer in the room. I'm standing on my prayer rug, but I'm in a different dimension. I can see my husband as he enters the doorway to the bedroom, but that space seems to be far away from where I am.

The moment passes, but a strange premonition remains. I was able, for a very brief time to transcend my place in the room and exist somewhere else, in another dimension. It was clear that Mohammed could not follow me to that place. I somehow understood from this experience that at some point in life, our paths would diverge.

My unspoken goal, however, is to develop a close relationship with my husband and to somehow bridge the religious/social/cultural/economic divide between him and my family. I had eloped without the presence or blessing of any family members, so introducing Mohammed to relatives for the first time is awkward to say the least. We've been married just a few months when my cousin Patty announces her engagement and upcoming marriage. She and I are quite close, only six months apart in age. We've grown up together, often dressing like twins in the matching Danskin outfits our mothers had bought us. Following the announcement, Mohammad and I drive to her parents' home for a family dinner. Patty and I are so excited to discuss our new statuses in life that I simply forget about my husband, leaving him alone to fend for himself in the living room. When I return, my uncle is trying to explain chopped liver to him by comparing it to pâté. Talk about cultural relativity. To his credit, Mohammed is always polite and respectful to my relatives, greeting them with a smile and a handshake. The first time my grandma meets him, she says, "You should always wear light colors so your skin doesn't look so dark." Instead of getting upset or reacting negatively, he just smiles wider, flashing his extra white teeth, and thanks her for the advice. To me, she says sadly, "Stephy, you cheated me out of dancing at your wedding."

On another occasion, my mom asks him, "Mohammed, why do you make Stephy cover her head with that *shamatte* (rag in Yiddish)?" He answers calmly, "I don't make her, Mom. She does it because she wants to." Family is everything in Bengali culture, and Mohammed is particularly nice to mine.

I was to be a bridesmaid at my cousin's wedding, but now I'll be an expectant matron of honor. My paternal aunt Dotty, Patty's mother, is the most understanding and accepting person in our family regarding my conversion. On her hall table, there is a plaque with the famous quote by Henry David Thoreau: *"If a man does not keep pace with his companions, perhaps it is because he hears a different drummer. Let him step to the music he hears no matter however measured or far away."* She is a wonderful hostess who always makes me feel accepted and at home, no matter how different I appear to be in my Muslim garb. I think she understands I am basically the same person they know on the inside, even if I am dressed a little differently on the outside. Most of my relatives have at least a distant cousin who is an observant Jew and more on the conservative side, so maybe my appearance isn't all that strange. Also, my cousins, Patty and Robert, both adopted, had given my aunt enough to worry about as we were growing up, so maybe my conversion to Islam doesn't seem so awful by comparison.

Aunt Dotty takes it in stride when I say I need to cover my head as well as my arms for the wedding. We pick out a high-necked baby blue gown in the bridal shop, double the sleeves, and get a turban made of the same fabric. I've honestly never looked good in that color, but baby blue is the color my cousin has chosen, so at least I'll fit in even though my mother says I look like a cancer patient with that baby blue turban.

It's a typical Jewish wedding with lots of delicious food, enough to drink, a band, and dancing, of course. I have always loved to dance, so when the *hora*, a traditional Jewish circle dance begins, I start tapping my feet and clapping. I really want to get up and join the joyous circle and celebrate with my family, but Mohammed holds me back.

"I don't think so. It's not right. Muslim women can't dance in public with men," he reminds me.

"But they're my family!"

I can't believe he's stopping me from doing this. It's the most natural thing in the world for me to dance at my cousin's wedding.

"They're not all family, so you can't hold hands and dance with them. Besides, the music is too loud for me, and it's time to pray, so we need to go now."

He gets up and I have no choice but to follow him. I certainly do not want to make a scene. Tears sting my eyes as I reluctantly leave the wedding hall. We go outside to pray on the grass. Tears of frustration drop from my eyes as I recite the words of a new *surah* I've learned:

Didn't we find you an orphan and support you?
Didn't we find you wandering and guide you?
(S. Dhuha, v. 6-7)

About halfway through the prayer, my mood changes. Allah (SWT) is talking directly to me, reminding me how He has led me to His religion and how, even if I don't understand quite how, it will be enough to carry me through all these small frustrations. In *sujud,* I submit to God once more, and I smile through my tears.

CHAPTER 21

Married with Children

Our little family, Mohammed, Tahera and Imran, 1984

Mohammed and I had four beautiful babies together over a period of eleven years. The mixture of Eastern European and Bengali DNA resulted in children with creamy, tan skin tones, lustrous dark hair, and big brown eyes. Our middle child, Safiyeh, has incredible hazel eyes that become greener or bluer depending on what they are reflecting. In that, she takes after some of her Bengali cousins who are quite striking with their hazel eyes and tawny skin tones. Intercultural marriages often produce beautiful children, and ours are gorgeous, if I do say so myself!

I tackle my first pregnancy by reading up on natural childbirth. I will have my baby in the hospital, but without anesthesia, and my husband will be my birth coach. In traditional Bengali culture, men do not get involved in human childbirth. It is strictly in the women's realm of affairs. But Mohammed has helped animals give birth and therefore isn't afraid or unaware of the process. There is also no extended family of women in New Jersey to help me. I convince Mohammed that he has to attend the birth and also make him go to Lamaze classes with me. It's an education for us both. The common goal of preparing for our baby's birth helps us bond as a couple

My labor is smooth and easy. I'd been taking a homeopathic muscle relaxant during pregnancy, and I think it's made a difference. There have been some strange new sensations going on in my body for a day and a half, but neither of us are sure I'm really in labor. When we call our doctor she says, "First babies rarely come on time, but you can go to the hospital and check." By the time, I'm examined I've already dilated six centimeters, so they admit me. The labor progresses for the next few hours. At some point an epidural is given, but I feel too tired to push. Dr. Khaliq gets tough with me, so I give it my all and push my daughter out.

Tahera is born on November 1, 1981. Though the doctor said first babies rarely come on time, she arrives nine months to the night Mohammed and I eloped. Her birth is a sign of Allah's perfect plan. She couldn't have been the person she was destined to be without His timing.

I expect to hold my baby right away, as I've seen happen in the movies. As they plunge her into the metal basin and wash her, I hear a strong cry and see one little hand reaching out. Then they wrap her up, but will not give her to me. They whisk her away to the nursery, instead, telling me I'll see her later.

I spend a few hours in an agony of anticipation. I'm supposed to rest, but I can do no such thing until I hold my child in my arms. How could the hospital staff not care about that critical bonding time? Mohammed is able to see her through the nursery window but doesn't get to hold her until the next morning.

I will never forget the moment I finally do hold her for the first time. She is all wrapped up in a receiving blanket, with only her fuzzy black hair peeping out from the top end. I stand near the window with her in my arms and look down at her in the moonlight. A baby has never been more beautiful or more precious. We name her Tahera, which is one of the nicknames Prophet Muhammad ﷺ had for his first wife, Khadija. It means pure, as in physical and spiritual purity.

I perceive Tahera's conception and birth as an absolute sign from Allah that Mohammed and I, no matter how unlikely a pair, had to come together to produce this child and her future siblings. This beautiful baby girl has wispy black hair so long that the baby nurse brings a little pink comb and brush to my bedside. This tiny girl with porcelain skin and shining eyes is so perfect-looking that people mistake her for a china doll.

In time, this child would begin reciting Quran as soon as she could talk. Her Arabic would one day be so beautiful she would become the poster child for our local Islamic school: "This child's parents are American and Bengali. They do not even speak Arabic. Do you hear her beautiful recitation? Send your children to our school and see how successful they will be."

Only Mohammed and I know that I had listened to the entire Quran in English and Arabic on audiotapes while pregnant with Tahera. She'd been hearing Quran since she was conscious in the womb, so it must have already seemed familiar to her when she starts memorizing it at age two.

I am the proud mother of a beautiful baby girl and life has changed irrevocably. For one thing, she has colic and fusses for hours at a time. Mohammed can't stand to hear her cry. He discovers the trick of rocking her swiftly back and forth in his arms to calm her and sometimes it works. We limit our travel because Mohammed will not drive if she starts to cry. He actually pulls over on the side of the road so I can nurse her or find some other way to soothe her. I spend hours reading in the middle of the night as I pat her to sleep on my shoulder. A Palestinian friend shows me how to wrap her up securely in a receiving blanket, and that seems to calm her down.

I'm a complete novice when it comes to babies, just as I had been with cooking. I try to get help from my mother: "Ma, I need to give the baby a bath. Can you come and help me?" She readily agrees, and my father drives her over from Manhattan.

Mom and Dad come to visit often, bringing new toys and clothing for Tahera. They are utterly smitten by their first grandchild. We fill the tub with warm water we've tested with our elbows and leave it in the kitchen sink. We undress Tahera and lay her on a towel. We both look down at this adorable wriggling infant, squirming on the towel, waving her fat little arms and legs. "Ok, Ma, so what do I do next?" "I don't remember," she says with a giggle. Both of us are too afraid to hold on to a slippery little baby in a tub, so we take a damp washcloth and give her a little sponge bath, and that is that!

Tahera loves my milk and later loves her bottle, but does not have much interest in food, not even the food I make myself in the simple baby food grinder I've bought. I want her to appreciate my efforts, but at most she just plays with her food or falls asleep over it. Our pediatrician assures me that she is growing normally but will probably always be petite since South Asians like Mohammed are of generally small stature, and nobody in my family is taller than 5'8." Tahera resembles her father in most of her features, from her hair to her eyes. Her complexion is a few shades lighter than his but still much darker than mine. She looks Bengali through and through.

Life settles into the routine of caring for Tahera. Mohammed's job at the masjid can't pay him enough to support a growing family, so he starts thinking about opening a business. He decides to go into partnership with a friend in a small neighborhood pizzeria. That is the first of his small businesses. He names it *Tahara Pizza*, after his daughter. He learns how to make excellent pizza and does well. As Tahera gets older, she waits for him to come home and stands up in her crib calling *"ba ba ba"* to get his attention. A pizza business generates lots of small change and dollar bills. Tahera loves to play with this money, throwing it in heaps around her crib. Mohammed and I delight in her cuteness.

Since he no longer works for the masjid, we move out of our rooms there and into an apartment in another part of town. It's near the park, a big plus for me as my children mature. The park has a good-sized playground with all the usual equipment. I keep Tahera happily occupied there for several hours at a time.

At this point in our marriage, I have not yet met any of Mohammed's immediate family members. Four of his five brothers and his mom still live in their village in Bangladesh. He wants to take me there to meet them, but by the time we can arrange a trip, I am pregnant again. It seems risky to travel to Bangladesh, an underdeveloped country, with a toddler and while pregnant, so we decide to meet some of his family in Great Britain instead. Mohammed has a half-brother in West Bromwich and some cousins living in London. We would meet them there and I would remain with them for the summer while Mohammed went on to Bangladesh.

Rich and varied travel experiences with and without my family had given me certain expectations about going abroad. To me, travel meant exploration and adventure, staying in hotels, eating new foods in restaurants and seeing cultural landmarks and local sites.

I get a Fodor's guide to England and begin reading up on places to visit in London and Birmingham, near where Mohammed's brother lives. On my list are the zoo and the Regents Park Masjid, as well as museums and Buckingham Palace. I've never travelled to visit family before, but I think perhaps they'll enjoy sightseeing with us.

For Mohammed, the purpose of the trip is to see his family, not the sights. This creates a conflict of interest and causes frustration for us both soon after we arrive. He tries to please me by taking me to the zoo. We go there straight from the airport and have to drag our luggage! We are both too inexperienced to know any better but he holds this against me by saying, "Seeing animals is more important to you than seeing people? I just can't understand!" I quickly grow frustrated just sitting at home while in England. We stay with his family in London and in the countryside. They are lovely people, most friendly and welcoming, but the women don't speak English, and I don't speak Bengali at all. Conversation is very limited. I had hoped Mohammed could translate for both sides, but he is usually with the men, and Tahera and I are with the women, as is appropriate in Bengali culture. Besides, translating conversations is a more tedious and difficult job than one might imagine. I know that now, in hindsight, but at the time I blamed him for putting me in a situation where my child and I were basically on display to a group of smiling, well-meaning women chatting together in a language we couldn't understand.

It is all very well to say you want to marry a foreigner and learn about his culture. That was something I had known about myself since I was in high school. However, I was naïve. I didn't realize how difficult all the differences, big and small, would be, and how much I would have to swallow my feelings, try not to cry, and just go along with whatever situations presented themselves. I had many preconceived notions about how things should be and the reality just didn't live up to my expectations.

I stay in West Bromwich for a few weeks after Mohammed leaves for Bangladesh. Eventually, I learn to relax and be a lazy pregnant woman as Tahera is showered with attention from her aunts, uncles, and cousins. Noor, my oldest brother-in-law, does speak English and occasionally arranges an outing for the family so that I'm not stuck at home all the time. I also enjoy little walks in their suburban English neighborhood where many people have beautiful flower and vegetable gardens.

I travel back to the States without Mohammed, who spends another two months in Bangladesh. Tahera is eighteen months old, and I'm five months pregnant. On the return flight, she is eager to walk up and down the aisles of the plane. At one point, I fall asleep and wake to find her missing from her seat. A momentary panic sets in before I realize there is really no way for her to get lost. It's not likely that she's left the plane. I soon find her a few seats away, sitting next to a pretty, blonde woman. She's watching intently as the woman applies her make-up. The woman graciously thanks my happy, chatty daughter for keeping her company, and we return to our seats.

In those pre-email days, Mohammed and I actually write letters back and forth from the United States to Bangladesh until he returns. Absence does make the heart grow fonder, as our love letters attest. When Mohammed gets home, I'm delighted to see him and we rush into each other's arms. Tahera, on the other hand, is not happy. It's as if she's angry at her father for leaving her with no apparent explanation. She refuses to look at or talk to him for a few hours, but then she gives way and forgives him. By the next day, they are playmates once again, laughing together as Mohammed marvels at how her vocabulary has increased while he's been away. He teaches her a few Bengali words and phrases, and this one song about a little bird's nest that all of his children remember even to this day.

After the trauma of not being allowed to hold Tahera until hours after her birth, I want to give birth to my new baby at home with a midwife, as two of my friends have done. I was there at both their deliveries and had marveled at the sacred miracle of life. Mohammed is happy to have the baby born at home. In Bangladesh, homebirths are still the norm. The hospital is a last resort when a caesarian birth is required or other complications arise.

The midwife we all know lives in Brooklyn and has no phone or car, but that is a minor drawback compared to the wonderful opportunity of a homebirth with family and friends in attendance. She also states upfront that she cannot do an episiotomy or stitch any minor tears that could occur, two other details I carelessly overlook. I read up on homebirths, as I always do on anything that keenly interests me. By the time the baby is due, I am ready.

But I have been spoiled by Tahera who came right on schedule. This baby is late... two weeks late. Of course, only God knows the exact time in the womb, but this one just does not want to come out! I engage in all kinds of physical activity during those two weeks, from scrubbing the floor to re-arranging the furniture. I walk all the way to the supermarket carrying Tahera and pushing a heavy shopping cart back. Then I swallow some castor oil, which produces some awful gastric distress, but no baby.

When labor finally does begin, I know more or less what to expect. Eighteen-month-old Tahera is sent down the hall to a neighbor's apartment. Debbie comes over to help. Mohammed drives to Brooklyn to pick up the midwife. After many hours of pushing, sweating, and grunting, our son Imran is born. His name is the family name of the prophets from Moses to Jesus. He is born right in our bed, taken off to the bathroom sink to be cleansed and then put directly into my waiting arms. It's a holy moment when his father calls the *athan* loudly to proclaim his birth. I nurse him till he sleeps and then eat a big bowl of Wheaties because I'm starving.

God bless the women throughout history who have taken on the role of midwife or birth coach. Our midwife, Sayyidah, is a saintly woman with a beautiful, serene smile, and almond-shaped eyes. She has a long, long list of babies to her credit. Some of them have turned into very fine people, like my son, Imran. *Masha'Allah.*

Tahera comes back down the hall with the neighbor, takes one look at her new brother in the bassinet and says she's "hoppy, hoppy," hopping up and down and running back and forth to prove it. Then she runs off to play with something more interesting. Looking back at pictures, one can see the jealousy in her face, but it's nothing out of the ordinary for a first child. She and Imran become fast friends as they grow.

I am now the busy mom of two children. Imran is an easy baby compared to his sister, as he doesn't have colic and sleeps soon after he's fed. But maybe it's also that Mohammed and I now have some experience. Imran eats everything I give him; that is, until he can walk. Then he spends several years running away from the table.

I'm the mother of two babies, but I can't quite accept the idea of being *only* a mother. My generation has been raised to believe we can have a career *and* a family and that we can handle it all because we are superwomen. But my new religion says it's best to stay home and nurture the family, especially when the children are young. Environmental conditioning plays its role in telling me I should be doing more with my life than just watching Sesame Street with my children. Like many young mothers, I feel tied down by my kids and want to be out in the world more. Because I bug my husband so much about this and seem so depressed over not doing more with my life, he acquiesces. "Ok, please go ahead and look for a job, if you think it will make you happy." My parents also encourage me to work outside my home.

There is a small Islamic school in the neighborhood that needs teachers' aides. Tahera is two and a half, almost old enough for their preschool class. Imran is young enough to just come along to school with me. Other teachers bring their babies as well. I begin working a few mornings a week at the school. Tahera is happy there and begins learning to recite the Quran.

I can only keep this job for a few months because Imran develops pneumonia and has to be hospitalized. Any parent with a child in the hospital knows what a trauma it is to see your child sick and scared in a strange bed. Although he recuperates well, I've realized the considerable challenges working mothers with young children face, and I don't think about going to work again until Imran is a preschooler.

Otherwise, those early years are a mostly happy blur of babies and family life. Mohammed and I have our occasional clashes, though probably not more so than most families. The children are a blessing, and their welfare is our shared interest and concern. Their needs outweigh my desire to enjoy the pleasures of my former life.

Tahera and Imran soon grow old enough to start school. In addition, my friends and I try to keep our kids occupied with trips to local parks, story hours at the library, and visits to each other's homes. The summers, though, seem long, as the kids are full of energy and often difficult to keep fully occupied. I had always gone to camp as a child, but in inner-city Jersey City, finding a camp that is appropriate for young Muslims proves impossible. With no other alternative, my friend Amal and I take matters into our own hands and start our own program—*Summer Fun Day Camp* is born. We each have two children of our own, and there are some other interested families in our community, so we end up with twelve kids attending. We take them to the lake, the beach, and to libraries and museums for weekly field trips. It's on one of these trips that I acquire my first gray hairs.

A parent's worst nightmare is losing their child. Growing up in the seventies I had seen plenty of afterschool movie specials about lost, stolen, and abused children. The true story of the kidnapping and murder of Adam Walsh on July 27, 1981 had been made into a movie that I had seen in 1983, the year Imran was born. The gory details of the kidnapping and torture of a six-year-old boy were simmering somewhere in my subconscious on the day we took our little campers to the Brooklyn Children's Museum.

It is a long drive from Jersey City to Brooklyn and the children, aged three to seven, are hungry. We disembark at the park situated one block from the museum itself and take out the picnic lunch. After eating, the children enjoy the large playground until it's time to go to the museum. Amal and I take the youngest children by the hand and have the older ones hold on to their buddies as we walk up the block.

The museum is for children, so it's full of interactive exhibits that keep them occupied. About half an hour into our visit, I take a head count and realize we have only eleven children. Who is missing? My five-year-old son Imran is not in the room with us. He must have stopped in front of one of the other exhibits. I ask Amal to watch the others as I retrace our steps to the room we have just left, and the room before that, and even the first room we entered. No Imran. Panic is already rising in my chest as I speak to the nearest docent.

"Excuse me, have you seen a five-year-old boy? He is wearing a red shirt and blue shorts and is about this tall," I say as I estimate Imran's height with my hand.

"No ma'am, I don't think so," she's says politely. I look around me and realize the museum has filled up with hundreds of children, many of whom seem to be wearing red and blue. How will I find Imran?

"Please notify the other docents and the guards at the door. My child is missing!"

I go back to Amal, who is now sitting down in a valiant effort to keep the other eleven children in one place. She looks at me quizzically. "You haven't found him?"

I run to the main door and ask the guard there if a child of Imran's description was seen exiting the building. He confirms that he hasn't seen a child of that description, either alone or with an adult. Now I am frantic.

"Close down all the entrances and exits, right now. My child has been stolen!"

I don't stop to make a prayer at this point, or maybe I am muttering one under my breath the whole time—I don't know. I run blindly out of the museum, half-screaming, half calling Imran's name out over and over. People are looking at me, this lady with a scarf, running down the block, looking for her kid. Some of them begin looking around for a lost boy too, calling his name in their various accents.

I run to the park and to the playground, and that's when I see him, standing near the swings, looking around him, calm as can be.

"Imran!" I rush to him, grabbing him in a bone-crushing hug of pure relief. My child is safe, *Alhamdulillah*. I squeeze him as hard as I can until he says, "Ma, you're hurting me, ouch." Then I push him away from me, and, at arm's length, let go with a forceful slap across his face. Tears well in his eyes, as if to say, "What did I do?"

"Never, never, ever do that again! How could you leave the museum without me!?" I am beside myself. "Did someone take you?" I look around quickly for a likely suspect.

His lower lip is trembling now. "No, Mama, but, but I wanted to go on the swings."

He wanted to go on the swings. Well, I was done for the day, maybe even the week. We end the field trip early and go home. The next day, I'm sure I can count some new gray hairs on my head that weren't there the previous morning.

We have enjoined on man kindness to his parents. In pain did his mother bear him and in pain did she give him birth (S. Al Ahqaf, v. 15).

Your worldly good and your children are but a trial and a temptation, whereas with God there is a tremendous reward (S. Taghabun, v. 15).

CHAPTER 22

Educators and Education

With Uncle Murray and Aunt Pixie, mid-1980s

I never thought I would be a teacher. My mother was a teacher, and my father had been one before becoming an attorney. My great Uncle Murray was a wonderful teacher at the High School of Performing Arts in Manhattan. The "teaching gene" was obviously part of my DNA, so why did I think I'd escape it? I'd majored in art history at NYU and had no formal training in education. Teaching was not part of my career plan, until suddenly, it was.

It all starts when Tahera is about three years old and Imran is just starting to walk. We are living in Jersey City, where our Muslim community is composed of Egyptians, Palestinians, Pakistanis, Bengalis, African Americans, Latinos, and a handful of white, mostly female, converts. Everyone has young children and many parents are concerned about having to send their kids to the inner city public schools. There is great concern for preserving faith, culture, and language, especially Arabic, the language of the Quran. A meeting is held in the Islamic center to discuss the possibility of opening a school there.

I am in attendance that day by chance, having come to the masjid for some other reason. Tahera and Imran aren't with me, but I realize that soon they will be going to school, so I sit down and try to listen to the discussion. There are two women next to me and they're talking in Arabic the whole time. I ask them to please be quiet because I want to hear what the men up front are saying. They pretty much ignore me. Imagine my surprise when, later on, one of these women becomes the principal of the new school we're going to establish. The two of us really start off on the wrong foot with my shushing her in public.

As a product of public school education, myself, I know there is much benefit to gain from that whole system, at least in middle-class suburban neighborhoods. But we're living in a small, inner city where the public schools don't have a good reputation. I also know that the local public schools will not help us Muslims to raise children of faith. Our children will not learn about God in school, and whatever information they do pick up will probably revolve around Christmas and Easter celebrations. Public schools cannot and will not help a child develop his or her consciousness of God because their mission is to provide a secular education to all students, regardless of their particular faith tradition. The awareness that we are all part of God's unity and Oneness, is key to living a meaningful and productive life. I want my children to have that, and so I want to be part of the new school's development.

I am warmly welcomed, but not for the right reasonns. As one Egyptian puts it, "You speak English. Please come and teach at our school!" My college degree was in art history, and I had vowed never to be a teacher, but here I suddenly found myself, helping to plan a school and then to teach the first grade.

The first thing I do is seek help. Some friends and I locate a real teacher, an older Muslim lady who has taught for years in the New York City public school system and is now retired. She helps us decide how to set up the rooms, what kind of furniture to buy, and what textbooks and supplies we need. She is also our first kindergarten teacher. Sr. Bilquis is a godsend.

The school will be housed in the building of the Islamic Center of Jersey City, a huge Gothic-looking edifice in the middle of a very poor neighborhood. In its past life, it had been a Masonic Temple. There is already a Sunday school there. With a little renovation, the Sunday school rooms can be made into fulltime classrooms. The large social hall in the center of the first floor will function as a gym and lunchroom. The parking lot will have to double as a playground. As the school population grows, we add a modular unit and continue remodeling the spacious interior of the building to better serve our needs.

We opened Al Ghazaly School in February, 1984. When I look back, I realize we knew nothing. We did not screen our students, but accepted anyone that first year, and thus had to deal with some crazy situations. For example, in my first-grade classroom of fourteen students, I had a six-year-old boy and his eight-year-old sister. Something should have made me realize the eight-year-old didn't belong in my class, especially when she would not talk. Not only that, but anytime anyone would raise their voice, she'd dive under her desk. Eventually, we had to let her parents know that we thought she needed special education of some kind. But just imagine, here I am, an art history major who happens to be a native speaker of English in a mainly immigrant community. And I'm teaching first grade. The only thing I know about teaching reading is to tell the child to sound out the words. And classroom management? All I know how to do is raise my voice or flick the light switch on and off.

Being in that school is like being in a whirlwind. By June, I know that if I want to maximize my opportunity to do the job right, I need to go back to school and get a teaching certificate. In fact, the board recommends I do so. So I enroll at Jersey City State College and launch my new career in education.

Nowadays, if you have an undergraduate degree, you can enter a master's in teaching program and get both the state certificate and the master's degree. When I applied thirty years ago, I was told I'd need to do a whole second B.A. in elementary education, but that it would only take two years, including my student teaching. So I forge ahead. I love being back in school and doing something with my mind. Fortunately, there is a good babysitter available for Imran, a wonderful Bengali woman who loves my son as if he is her own. Tahera is already enrolled in preschool.

I quickly see that having children of my own will make me a better educator. The limited classroom experience I've already had helps me to distinguish educational theories from practices that might actually work in a classroom. I learn that when it comes to teaching reading, there's a war going on between the proponents of whole language and the supporters of phonics first. My experience tells me a balance of both is needed. Not all children learn the same way.

I come back to Al Ghazaly two years later with some credentials under my belt. Though many of the teachers there are uncertified, they're among the most dedicated individuals I've ever known. They look at teaching as an *amana*, a trust from God. Parents entrust teachers with a significant role in the upbringing of their children. We teachers will be answerable before God for the benefit or harm we have done to our students. How well have we fulfilled our trust?

During my twelve years at Al Ghazaly, I teach English and social studies in every grade, from first to twelfth. Of course, teaching is an education in itself. Nobody learns more than the teacher, especially if she is a lifelong learner. With the younger students, I try out all the innovative methods I've learned in college, such as invented spelling, the five-step writing process, and roleplaying simulations.

Sometimes the principal disagrees with my methods. *She may be in charge, but she's no more qualified than I am,* is what I think whenever I am questioned about my methods in the classroom. In truth, I am a bit jealous of the principal of Al Ghazaly. She has a teaching degree, but that is all. The fact that her family members are major financial contributors to the school gives her an advantage that I don't appreciate. Although I don't have money, I am putting in a lot of sweat equity and dedication. I make it a future goal to one day hold a position of power and influence of my own in school administration.

My favorite students are the high school girls. We have very small classes in high school, and they are run like seminars. We have stimulating roundtable discussions about literature. I am a real taskmaster, assigning too much reading and writing. When I teach AP English to the best and the brightest, I have to stay up late at night reading Shakespearian analyses so that I will be prepared for class. I certainly learn as much as the students, and the hard work pays off. One girl comes back to Ghazaly after her first semester at New York University to say that her professor held up her paper in front of hundreds of other students and said, "I don't know where the rest of you went to school, but this girl can write!" She had been my student for most of four years in high school, so I think I can take some of the credit, even if she is otherwise a genius. This young woman is now a doctor of political science and a national spokesperson on Egyptian and Muslim affairs.

When I think of where some of my former students are now—at the U.N., working for the best law firms in Manhattan, or as doctors and engineers, etc.—I realize that a ragtag bunch of would-be school founders actually accomplished something through hard work, determination, and faith. I'm delighted that so many Al Ghazaly girls have become teachers, too. They include my own daughter Tahera and an inordinately large group of her friends, who are now busily raising their own families. Even so, they're still giving back to their communities, either by teaching, administrating, or establishing their own new Islamic schools throughout the US and Canada.

Seek knowledge even though it be in China.
The ink of the scholar is more sacred than the blood of the martyr.
Seek knowledge from the cradle to the grave.
—Hadith of Prophet Muhammad

CHAPTER 23

The Struggle Within

1990

I worked very hard at Al Ghazaly and throughout my thirty-year teaching and administrative career in the United States. All of us pioneers in Islamic education worked hard. We were trying to establish schools of quality education for our children and grandchildren. Mohammed also worked at the school for some time as a bus driver and sold food and toys there on Fridays after prayer. At this point in our marriage, we were a team, working hand in hand with our community to raise children with a strong foundation in faith. In helping to establish and develop the school, we'd found a common goal. In many ways, those years at Al Ghazaly were the strongest years of our marriage.

As the school grows—we add a new grade every year—so do my responsibilities. Work and family life are often out of balance. I depend on Mohammed to pick up the slack at home. He's always been the better cook, so he assumes that responsibility. If I have to attend a meeting or give a presentation, he stays home with the kids. He is a supportive accommodating spouse. He enjoys spending time with the children, and doesn't balk at changing diapers or preparing meals. As Imran grows older, he often accompanies his father to the masjid for prayers.

And yet, despite all his efforts, I am not satisfied. I begin to spend more and more time at school with my fellow teachers and administrators. I crave the intellectual conversations I can have at school with colleagues but can't have at home with my husband. I respect and admire some of the brothers I work with to an inordinate degree and begin to feel emotional attachments to them that are in conflict with the way I feel about my own husband. I feel guilty about this, but am unable to change my behavior or my feelings.

Meanwhile, Mohammed and I continue to have our intercultural struggles at home. In 1989, my mother-in-law arrives from Bangladesh. She's going to stay with us for one year. This will be enough time for her to get a green card and apply for visas for her four sons back home. We also plan to travel to Mecca for the *Hajj* (pilgrimage) with her later in the year.

Gulap Jan is a tiny middle-aged woman and is dressed in a traditional Bengali sari and sandals when I first meet her. She wears the *niqab*, or face veil, and has done so all of her adult life. My mother-in-law has only a fifth-grade education but has had religious training and knows Arabic well enough to say all her prayers. She raised seven children alone in the village where Mohammed grew up after her husband died. Gulap Jan inherited her husband's agricultural land and a house, but had to hire manpower to farm it since the children were too small at the time. Life was a struggle for her. The Bangladesh War for Independence took place from March to December of 1971, bringing violence and more hardship into her life. Sometimes there was not enough food or clothing. Some of her sons had to work so that the others could go to school. She's had a difficult life and its challenges show in her wrinkled face, work-worn hands, and unhappy demeanor.

I greet her at the airport with *Ami tu mai balobashi,* "I love you" in Bengali. I'm sure she doesn't know what to make of that, or perhaps she hasn't even heard or understood my mangled Bengali, but it is one of the few phrases my husband has taught me. Mohammed is not a great communicator and can do little to help us connect. Word-for-word translation in the middle of a conversation is a skill he does not possess. I don't know how to establish a relationship with my mother-in-law. My very presence and manner seem to intimidate her. Is she afraid of me? Compared to a soft spoken Bengali daughter-in-law, I am loud and rough. I yell at my children when they don't cooperate, and I rush around like crazy, multi-tasking as all American mothers must learn to do.

She remains a timid, almost ghost-like presence in my house. Alone all day when we are at work or school, I find her standing by the window, peering through the curtains when we come home. It must be a very lonely time for her. She shows some affection to Tahera and Imran and will speak a little bit to her son, but mostly she just sits. Everything is strange to her, and most of all, I am a stranger. It's quite an uncomfortable situation, one that's ripe for conflict and miscommunication.

There is a Shoprite directly across a busy highway near our subdivision in Jersey City. I decide to take my mother-in-law to see it, knowing she's never been in a supermarket before. She wanders up and down the aisles with me but is especially interested in the vast array of fruits and vegetables. Bengali bazaars are open air markets. Every village has its fruit and vegetable stands. They sell strictly what's in season. The produce comes daily from local farmers, so, of course, it is fresh. That is the main difference between food consumption in the US and more agricultural countries—their food is fresh and ours is not. You need only to taste the difference to know.

In planning this supermarket fieldtrip, I have not thought about how we will cross the highway on foot. Gulap Jan has never walked across a highway and is not used to cars, traffic, honking horns, and flashing lights. She is definitely afraid of attempting the crossing, and I don't blame her.

I've actually had similar, though not as intensely frightening, experiences trying to cross the street in Dacca, where there are no lights and cars are whizzing around a circle while you try to cross. I must grab her hand and drag her across, both coming and going to the supermarket.

About three months before *Hajj*, Mohammed puts his mother through some basic training for the rigors of the pilgrimage. He buys her a pair of sneakers and takes the family to a running track in the local park. It is smart of him to do this, because *Hajj* does entail a lot of walking, some of it quite rapid. He and I are both in good shape, but we aren't sure about Gulap Jan. After a few laps around the track, we find out she can hold her own. After all, walking is her main form of transport back home.

Escalators are another matter. Someone has advised Mohammed to get his mother used to them by taking her to the mall. But the plan backfires. She is afraid to step on the moving stairway at the mall and never uses the escalators in Saudi Arabia. Her fear leads to our climbing lots of stairs in Mecca.

There is one incident in our home that forges a tenuous connection between my mother-in-law and me. It happens shortly before we go to *Hajj*. The tension in the house has become so thick you can cut it with a knife. Mohammed must be feeling it most of all as he has to listen to all my worries about taking care of his mother en route. She also has her concerns to discuss with him, however brief those discussions are. One day, he just explodes and starts yelling at us both. He even tries to threaten me with a belt, but his mother stops him. Then I intervene to make sure he doesn't hit her by accident. We each defend the other against him. After that, we both sit down in Tahera's room and cry. Mohammed has never shown that kind of anger to me before. Gulap Jan and I have a sort of conversation using hand gestures and very few words. I guess that she is concerned about not wearing her veil. She nods to affirm this. We have been trying to get her to go without it since it isn't allowed at *Hajj*. I hold her hand and try to explain a bit more, but it's clearly the experience we've been through, not my words, that make the difference.

Ibrahim ibn Abi 'Ablah said to some people who had just returned from a military campaign: "You have returned from the lesser jihad. But what have you done about the greater jihad?" They asked: "What is the greater jihad?" He replied: "Jihad of the heart."

CHAPTER 24

Hajjah

Aerial view of pilgrims at the Kaaba in Mecca

I made my first pilgrimage to Mecca in 1989 with Mohammed and his mother. The trip was arranged by the Islamic Center of Jersey City. It was planned for June and July, which was Hajj season that year. Tahera and Imran would stay with Jehan, the kindergarten teacher from Al Ghazaly, until school was out, then my parents would take them on a vacation to New Hampshire for the remainder of our trip.

Taking my mother-in-law to Hajj was a trip in itself. Before 1989, Gulap Jan had never left her village. All of a sudden, she was whisked off to England, the US, and Saudi Arabia, all in one year. How's that for culture shock?

We board the plane at Newark International Airport surrounded by people from our own Jersey City community. *Hajj* is said to begin as soon as the pilgrim makes his intention to go. In that case, the three months I just spent with my mother-in-law at home have definitely been part of my *Hajj* struggle. And there is more to come, starting on the plane ride to Saudi Arabia.

After a short time in the air, I start having allergy symptoms. Since I am only allergic to cats, I am puzzled. There couldn't be cats on the plane, could there? When I get up to use the bathroom, I glance at the seat behind mine and find a middle-aged couple. There is a cage on the seat between them and in that cage is a cat. I call the stewardess.

"Miss, why is there a cat in the main cabin?"

"Ma'am, this couple is traveling to Saudi Arabia for work, and they are taking their pet with them."

"Ok, but why is the cat on a seat?"

"Ma'am, they requested a seat for their cat."

"But I am allergic to cats. Please remove it from this area."

"I cannot do that at this time, ma'am."

"Well, then you have to move my seat. It's either move the cat or move me!"

"I'll see what I can do, ma'am."

I'm growing impatient. I just can't believe a cat is being given priority over my allergies. Finally, the stewardess comes back. She has found an empty seat for me in first class, so I move there, leaving Mohammad with his mother for the remainder of the trip.

Entry into Saudi Arabia and the pilgrimage sites requires many passport checks. Every time we move from place to place, Saudi personnel board our bus and check everyone's passports. Only one person in our group does not have an American passport and that is my mother-in-law. This usually causes a few minutes of extra checking and questions that Mohammed must answer. However, it occasionally leads to being separated from the group and made to go through a different line. One time in Madinah, the Saudis actually confiscate Gulap Jan's passport and Mohammed's as well, when he raises his voice to them in protest. He and another Jersey City man have to go searching all over town for the right agency to get these all-important documents back.

Our Jersey City Islamic Center travel companions are mostly elders and they prefer to speak Arabic. This means I will be left out of most conversations, but since I live in an immigrant community, I have grown accustomed to this. In Mecca, the women share hotel rooms equipped with bunk beds. The ladies all scramble for the lower bunks, leaving only the upper ones for my mother-in-law and me. I do not think it appropriate to make her climb. I have to ask our tour guide leader to intervene on our behalf. He scolds the women until one of them gives up her lower bunk for my mother-in-law.

The first stop at *Hajj* is the *Kaaba,* the large stone cube located inside the *haram,* or sacred precinct. The first time I see it, it takes my breath away. It is majestic but also intimidating as hordes of pilgrims circle it in a never-ending cycle called *tawwaf.* Many of the pilgrims are elderly people who have saved for a lifetime to make this journey. Tears come to my eyes as my own parents come to mind. I wish they would become Muslims. I want them to share my belief in Allah (SWT) and the Oneness of God with them. We join the *tawwaf,* circumambulating the Kaaba seven times, performing the first rite of *Hajj.* Then we walk quickly between the two hills of Safaa and Marwa seven times to symbolize the running of Hajar between these two hills when she was searching for water for her son, Prophet Ismail (a.s.). This holy water, known as *Zam Zam,* still gushes from the same spring and is available to all pilgrims in Mecca and Madinah. It is known to cure illness and disease. As I take my first sips of *Zam Zam,* I ask Allah (SWT) to cure a skin problem I have developed on my fingertips. *Alhamdulillah,* He grants this *du'a* and the problem doesn't return.

This is my first *Hajj.* I feel too young in my faith to be making this pilgrimage. However, it is the right time for Mohammed and his mother. I've done my best to learn some of the Arabic prayers that one should recite at the various landmarks, but I have only memorized words. I haven't internalized the full meaning of what I recite. I sometimes wonder if such an imperfect *Hajj* could count in the eyes of God. Then I stop myself. Of course it counts. It takes me from where I am in my spiritual development and brings me to the next station of faith. It's a rite of passage.

Hajj requires tremendous patience, a virtue I struggle with. There can be no fighting, arguing, or cursing at Hajj. One cannot even kill an insect. Allah (SWT) tests my patience and many times I fall short. For example, what do I do when a grizzled old man, who has been hacking all over the floor of the bus, asks to drink from my canteen? I give him the drink. I have to, but I also give him the canteen because I'm disgusted by the thought of his germs all over it. His cough sounds tubercular to me. Good intention? Bad? Ulterior motive? Not exactly treating my brother as myself.

And how do I feel when my husband is sick on the floor of the bus? I blame my mother-in-law for needing to eat rice in the heat of the desert just because that is the food she's accustomed to. He had eaten it with her, then climbed a hill in the noonday sun. He got overheated from the climb, drank a bottle of cold tamarind juice and then became sick. We are traveling on a bus that will take many hours to reach our destination, and he needs medical care. I am not very patient with this situation, if truth be told.

Before leaving on this trip, I had discussed some of my concerns with Iman and Sheikh Hanooti. I am well aware of my arrogance in often thinking I am better than my husband in education, upbringing, and intelligence. I wondered whether I was ready to go to *Hajj* with those feelings. Iman, who has already been to *Hajj* assures me, "Don't worry Sommieh, the heat of the plain of Arafat will burn those feelings right out of you!" And it is on this very plain that Allah blesses me with a vision, a signpost to mark the significance of my *Hajj*. Arafat is a dusty, barren desert plain. It is mentioned in the Quran as the place where all our souls were gathered at Creation to bow before our Lord. It's the place where our Prophet Muhammad ﷺ made his final speech before his death in 710 A.D. It is a place to ask forgiveness for all sins. One is supposed to stand and beg forgiveness in the time between the afternoon and sunset prayer. The men are outside, but the women in our group have been placed in a very large room with noisy fans running to keep us cool. The afternoon sun is baking down on the concrete building, making it very hot. The droning sound of noisy fans combined with the heat that radiates in the room causes me to doze off and dream. I awake with a start and clearly remember: I was standing in a doorway to a room. In the room was the Prophet ﷺ, seated with a group of people whose faces I could not see. He looks up and sees me there. He smiles, and I am reassured.

A Declaration at Hajj

Oh Muslim!
When you ask Allah to change you,
You must work to change yourself.
Try to uphold your part of the bargain.
Are you sincere?
You've begged Allah to change you
Now work to change yourself.
Show some effort!
You must strive and sweat
Teeth clenched against your own desires.
Frustration mounts
Tears fall often
Try to shed them only for Allah
And not in the presence of men
When you fall short of the mark
*(And you **will** fall short!)*
Then sigh out
And cry out
"Forgive me, Allah!"
"Help me, Allah"

Your duas coincide with your pain.

Though the struggle is unending
Strength seems ever at an end

To Allah belongs the lifeline
You founder and fumble
Only inches from the fire
To Allah belongs the lifeline
Oh Muslim!
Just try to climb up!

—*S. Flower (written at Hajj, July 21, 1989)*

And hold fast to the rope of Allah, all together, and be not divided...
(S. Al Imran, v. 103)

CHAPTER 25

The Second Generation

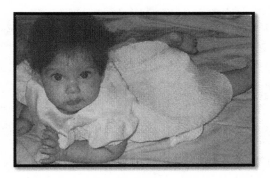

Safiyeh, 1990

My daughter Safiyeh was conceived in Medina, the city of the Holy Prophet, Muhammad ﷺ. Maybe this explains her lovely green eyes— the Prophet's favorite color—eyes that seem to encompass the world. They look, as Allah says in the Holy Quran, until they get tired because they can see no fault. They take in everything. Her birth was another kind of adventure all together, an emergency caesarian, the key word being *emergency*. Here's what happened.

It is the end of my pregnancy; it's Ramadan, 1990. So I'm fasting. I did it with my first two pregnancies, so why not this one? Besides, it's too hard to think of making up all those days. So I fast and work fulltime as the fourth-grade teacher at Al Ghazaly School. My brilliant students have written an original play based on an old Chinese Muslim folk tale, *Cheng Ho's Voyage*. It is to be presented during the Ramadan Fundraising Dinner. I'm director, but Allah has another performance planned for that night.

My water has never broken before, so I'm not sure what that should feel like. It doesn't feel wet, which is strange. There is just some kind of weird pinching inside me that goes on all night. I plan to mention it at my upcoming doctor's appointment the next day, but I never get the chance.

The nurse does the usual sonogram then asks me to wait, which I do, for a long time, while quite hungry from fasting. I want to get home and prepare dinner for everyone. But I wait until my young female doctor bustles in and starts talking about the dehydrated amniotic sac and possible danger to the baby. She says, "We're going to have this baby now." It is two weeks early, but apparently, it's time. They call my husband to meet us upstairs in the hospital. He's not allowed in the room this time because I'm having a Caesarian, and there will be too much blood. I'm scared when I hear this, but I immediately start praying silently to Allah (SWT) for a good outcome and a healthy baby.

Pediatric ICU is prepared for a newborn, and Dr. Leonetti decides to make two cuts across my belly, one at the bikini line and another interior cut down my belly, vertically, but on the inside. My inexperienced doctor seems a bit over cautious in doing this procedure, but she really must believe the baby's life is in danger. With two incisions, they can get the distressed baby out more easily.

But she isn't distressed in the end, *Alhamdulillah*. She is perfectly fine and beautiful, a little dry and scrawny at first, but that changes within a few hours. From then on, she is just gorgeous, with beautiful blue/gray/green eyes. She looks like some of my own baby pictures and, in fact, becomes the child who is most like me in many ways. We name her Safiyeh and call her Safi for short. The named means war booty, but it carries a beautiful story with it. Before Prophet Muhammed ﷺ married his young wife, Aisha, he had seen her in a dream, wrapped up in a piece of white cloth usually intended to hold war booty, and that cloth was called the *saf*.

After her dramatic entrance into the world, Safiyeh quickly becomes the crankiest baby on Earth. She cannot be awakened from a nap unless you want a tantrum to ensue. So I learn to wait and to stay home when necessary, sending Mohammed and the kids out while I enjoy the peace with my sleeping child. She also throws tantrums when she wants candy or doesn't want to leave a place she wants to stay in, or, just in general, if anyone dares to say no to her, though few brave souls do! Her lip quivers and she starts that tearless whining Tahera and Imran learn to recognize as a fake right away. "You don't even have tears," they say, and then attempt not to give her what she wants, until they really just want her to shut up. Baby spoiled, for sure. It's the eyes that do it. The comment of one family friend is, "the product is improving," meaning this child is more beautiful than her older siblings. In our mostly immigrant Muslim community, fair skin and light eyes are considered more desirable than darker hues. Age-old prejudices die hard.

Tahera is ten when Safi is born. She becomes a very willing big sister. She even asks to have Safi move into her room when the next baby comes along. I stay happily snuggled in bed on Saturday mornings when I hear Safi wake her sister up for "ceo and meo" (cereal and milk). Imran and Tahera develop a hatred for Barney, the purple dinosaur so beloved by their sister. They sing "I hate you, you hate me" until their baby sister comes crying to me that they aren't singing it right. When she is eleven, Tahera writes a story for school that she calls "Neverland." I laugh when I read it and realize that her "Neverland" is a place with no little sisters where you can do whatever you want.

Imran is the only boy of the bunch, and he desperately wants a brother. He even runs away from home when he hears that a *third* girl is going to be born. Another little sister. He only goes around the block to his buddy Ahmed's house, to commiserate because Ahmed has three sisters too.

Sajdah, my youngest child, is also born by Caesarian section in 1992. At least this time it is planned. She arrives easily to the world, and I get a few days of rest in the hospital. Sajdah is a good baby and a happy child who follows her sister Safi everywhere. They become the best of friends. I like to eavesdrop on their imaginative games where Safi is usually saving Sajdah from all kinds of danger. Safi pretends that a pile of laundry on the basement floor is a mountain. "Come on honey," she tells her little sister, "I will keep you safe. We just have to get over this mountain, and then we'll be home." As children, they look very much alike except for their eye colors. Sajdah's eyes are a deep, beautiful brown like Tahera's, while Safi's are hazel green. When they're pre-teens, Safi becomes the shy one, depending on Sajdah to do the talking for her in the library or other public places.

The name *Sajdah* means "prostration." When we pray, the position of making *sajdah* is when our foreheads hit the floor in *sujud*. The part of the brain behind the forehead is the *naseya* in Arabic, or forebrain. It is the part that does all our planning, scheming, and rationalizing. If we do not submit it to Allah, then it can become the "devil's playground" as negative intentions sabotage our thoughts and pull us in unhealthy directions. That is why submission to Allah is so important.

Mohammed and I have two generations of children together. They grow up in different environments and circumstances. As adolescents, Imran and Tahera would say we were not as strict with their younger sisters as we were when they were small. Maybe we learned a few things along the way, or maybe we just got tired. Imran and Tahera spent their childhoods in New Jersey, while Safi and Sajdah spent theirs in Michigan. The Muslim communities and Islamic schools in suburban Michigan were wealthier and more liberal than the more conservative, inner-city community in New Jersey. Our family circumstances were different, too, and so was my job status and salary. The two different generations, places, and times sometimes lead to differences of opinion that cause them to distance themselves from each other. But I want and need my children to remain close as they get older and start families of their own.

> *Oh mankind! Reverence your Guardian-Lord, who created you from a single person, created, of like nature, his mate, and from them twain scattered (like seeds) countless men and women; reverence God through whom ye demand your mutual rights and reverence the wombs that bore you: for God ever watches over you. (S. Nisaa, v. 1)*

CHAPTER 26

The Center Does Not Hold

Mohammed with Safi and Sajdah, 1992

At first, it was the children themselves that kept our marriage together. Then it was our common goal to provide them with a good education. Both Mohammed and I worked to build Al Ghazaly School and were both an integral part of the Jersey City Muslim community. I worked at Al Ghazaly for twelve years as a teacher and as chair of the English department. Mohammad worked as the transportation supervisor for about five years, but he was always a key figure in the Islamic Center. He had been the *moathen* when we first met and then later sold candy and food there after Friday prayers. We were a couple whose marital identity was tied to the community. In the eyes of our neighbors, our marriage was an intercultural success story.

Beyond the eyes of Al Ghazaly and the Islamic Center, we struggled with intercultural and financial issues. My father provided a financial safety net that let us live beyond our own means. Mohammed started his first business, Tahara Pizzeria, with money I inherited from my grandmother. Some years later, my father loaned him money to set up a butcher business, a short-lived venture. Dad bought us our Jersey City home and used the rent money to pay the mortgage. When that home was sold, we turned the profit into the down payment on our home in Michigan. My parents had an apartment in Manhattan where they spent their weekends so we would visit at least once a month, and Dad would always take us out to dinner. He and Mom took the children to museums in the city, nurturing their cultural development. During the summer, we would join them for a week at their favorite resort, or we would send the children, so we could have some time to ourselves. My father financed the college education of my four children, including medical school for my son. He gave us yearly gifts that bought us cars and took us on all-expense-paid vacations.

All this financial assistance let us maintain a lifestyle that was comfortable enough so that we were not living in poverty, and we were not struggling. Mohammed could remain self-employed and therefore be able to completely fulfill his religious obligations without worrying about the demands of a boss. We did not have to pay interest on a homeowner's loan or college tuition loans. Dad's incomparable generosity made our lives much easier than the lives of the working class and professional people in our faith community.

But all this financial ease was not necessarily good for our marriage. Mohammed and I didn't have to depend on each other for economic survival. I'm not sure what would have happened if we did. Would it have brought us closer to each other, or would it have caused us to fight about money and lead to a divorce sooner rather than later? Knowing my husband's temperament and my own, I suspect it would have been the latter, but only God knows for sure. We could have said, "No, please keep your money, we will make it on our own," but we took the easy way out.

During our time in Jersey City, I acquire plenty of teaching experience at Al Ghazaly and develop close relationships with my colleagues there.

Some of them are also American converts married to Arabs or South Asians. Many of us have non-Muslim family members with whom values sometimes come into conflict. One of my friends takes care of her invalid parents at home and tries her best to get them to embrace Islam. Shortly after her mother dies in her sleep, I attend the funeral. I arrive early at the funeral home and am in the chapel alone with her mother's casket for a few moments. Suddenly I hear her mom speaking. She says, "Pammy was right," using her daughter's pet name to finally acknowledge the truth of Islam, even in death. This makes me worry for my own parents, but I am never successful in my discussions of religion with them. For my dad, Islam is too wrapped up in politics and news reports for him to separate the faith from the hype.

Meanwhile, I generally enjoy my teaching career. There's great satisfaction in seeing my students make progress, and I like collaborating with colleagues on curriculum projects. But I often disagree with the board over employment policies. Salaries in Islamic schools are notoriously low, especially when compared to public schools. There are some years when we have no medical insurance or summer pay, and there is no pension plan whatsoever. I had tendered my resignation several times over the twelve years I worked at Al Ghazaly, but it had never been accepted by the board. Most of the time, I had resigned in a fit of temper or over a disagreement with the board or administration. They would talk me out of it by reminding me how much the school needed me and offering me a small salary increase or some other perk. Free or discounted tuition for our children had always been part of the benefits package I received at Al Ghazaly and at the four schools I worked in after leaving Jersey City. Once, I wrote a heartfelt letter to the board on behalf of all the teachers. I wrote, "we shop at the same stores you do and need to buy the same boxes of pampers. According to the hadith of Prophet Muhammad ﷺ, 'A Muslim wants for his brother what he wants for himself,' so why won't you give us a decent salary?"

After I'm on staff for about five years, I become the chair of the English department. This position gives me some of the administrative responsibility I've been seeking. But at the same time, the school has hired a principal that doesn't speak English. The language of our teachers' meetings has suddenly switched to Arabic with a translation for those of us who don't understand it, along with suggestions that we must learn the language. Although this principal's employment is short-lived and untenable, an event in 1994 leads to my final resignation from Al Ghazaly: a single male teacher and a high school student get engaged.

This event upsets me very much. The school had an established policy of not allowing single males to teach the high school girls. But they broke the school's policy in order to allow this one man to teach computer science, and now he is marrying a student. To me, this means our girls, including my own daughter, have perhaps been this young man's prey. He may have had the ulterior motive of marriage the moment he entered the classroom. This outrages me. It is our job as parents and teachers to protect our children from harm. The board has violated their own policy, and this is the result. The principal's and board's position is that the teacher and student have done nothing wrong since he has followed proper Islamic guidelines by going to her parents and asking their permission to marry their daughter. My position is that they've violated their own policy of hiring a single male teacher, thus potentially endangering all of our daughters. I boycott the teacher's class by refusing to let my daughter attend and by submitting my letter of resignation.

The board of the school, an all-male body at the time, are in disagreement with my action and are especially taken aback by my attitude, which is one of angry defiance. In a heated argument with one of the board members, I compare my outrage with that of a mother bear who would kill in order to protect her cubs! They have seen my assertiveness and anger before over other issues, such as pay raises, adequate day care facilities, and students' rights. They decide I have cried wolf one too many times and therefore accept my offer to resign. In the ensuing years, I will continue to clash with all-male school boards. I will have to learn the hard way that any show of anger in the workplace can be construed as unprofessional. As a school administrator, I will face even bigger challenges in dealing with men who want to micromanage and control the way I do my job.

And the Book (of deeds) will be placed (open) and you will see the wrong-doers fearful of that which is (inscribed) within it. And they will say, 'Woe is us! What kind of a book is this that leaves out neither the small nor the great but has enumerated (everything)?" And they will find what they did, present before them, and your Lord will wrong no one. (S. Kahf, v. 49)

CHAPTER 27

Fanning the Flames

Al Ghazaly School and the Islamic Center of Jersey City

Leaving Al Ghazaly marked the end of an era. My friends and colleagues threw me a party and gifted me with a beautiful gold bracelet crafted from Egyptian gold. The school gave me a plaque to commemorate my twelve years of dedication and service. I chose not to mention the elaborately engraved misspelling of my name. Mohammed and I had been pillars in the school, and the school had been a pillar of stability in our marriage. No one could have predicted the nature of events that would follow.

I leave Al Ghazaly at the end of the school year in 1994 and quickly find a brand-new school to work at in Queens, New York. Our family friends Hassan and Lara Ariani have asked me to join their community in establishing an elementary school. They offer me a teaching position scheduled to begin in the fall. The three of us spend the summer working together, planning the curriculum, ordering books and supplies, and writing the staff handbook. My years of experience at Al Ghazaly help us complete the job over the summer months. The plan is to carpool and commute daily from New Jersey to Queens to work at the new school. My youngest daughters, Safi and Sajdah, will attend kindergarten and pre-school classes there. Tahera will continue to attend Al Ghazaly High School, while Imran will remain a student in the public-school system in Jersey City. Although the situation has improved, in the early years of Islamic education, schools like Al Ghazaly couldn't offer enough in the way of sports and extracurricular activities to satisfy male students once they reached the middle school grades. Imran's academic performance at Al Ghazaly was adequate, but his behavior, which included fighting with teachers and running away from school, indicated he was not willing to be there. He was better off in a public-school setting. Mohammed, meanwhile, is running a beverage distribution business from our home, driving a private transport van for Tahera's school, and selling home-cooked food and toys at the masjid on Fridays.

The Arianis and I have set ourselves up for a very long commute. To get from New Jersey to Queens, we have to go through the Holland Tunnel, cross Manhattan on Canal Street, then cross a bridge into Queens. On Friday afternoons when people are leaving the city the roads remain jammed with traffic for hours. Safi and Sajdah fall asleep in our laps coming and going to school. In the mornings, I actually take them straight from their beds in pajamas and dress, wash, and groom them at school. We try to leave early enough to beat the morning rush, but it's still a challenge.

The Arianis are excellent conversationalists. The time spent commuting passes enjoyably and quickly in their company. Like Mohammed and I, they are an intercultural couple. But unlike us, they are well matched in terms of educational backgrounds. They had met at a Midwestern university when they were both students. Both husband and wife have masters' degrees and are highly educated.

Hassan, Lara, and I spend many hours together throughout the summer and school year. I begin to compare Hassan and Mohammed in terms of education and outlook on life. I also compare Hassan and Lara's marital relationship with my own relationship with Mohammed. This couple share many academic interests with one another, including a love of linguistics and poetry. I first learn about Jalaluddin Rumi through the Arianis, and I'm immediately captivated by his poetry.

I am also becoming emotionally attached to Hassan Ariani and he to me. Inspired by Rumi, we begin sharing poetry with each other, the first poetry I've written since high school. We both know we are headed in the wrong direction but are too embroiled with our emotions to push away. We spend hours together in the car and at work, more time than we actually spend at home with our families. We confess our feelings to each other. It's such a relief to express them. We talk about the problems in our marriages. Hassan asks, "How in the world did you end up married to him in the first place? Nothing matches. You are from two different worlds." His matter-of-fact statement of the issue makes the reality even starker, but I feel relieved to know someone understands my situation.

We agree that there will be no physical component to our relationship. If we can contain ourselves physically, we will not cross over the line into infidelity. The punishment for adultery in Islam is being stoned to death. If the punishment is not carried out in this world, then a worse punishment awaits in the Hereafter. We also don't want to devastate our families. But we are just fooling ourselves, trying to rationalize what we find irresistible. Our long, soul-baring conversations have already marked us as emotionally unfaithful to our spouses.

Mohammed finds a romantic note I've written to Hassan Ariani. How could I have so carelessly left it lying about? It's as if I wanted to get caught. Unfortunately, Imran was at home when Mohammed read the note. Some years later, he described his father's reaction to me. "Baba let out a howl of pain. It didn't even sound human. He howled like an animal in pain."

This, apparently, is all out of the blue to Mohammed. He didn't like me spending so much time with the Arianis and especially did not like our long commute to Queens, but he did not expect this kind of betrayal. He confronts me, and I have to admit that I have feelings for my co-worker. He demands that I quit my job at the new school immediately. We have a trip to Bangladesh planned for December, just a few weeks away from this fateful disclosure; I will stay home till we leave the country. I do not return to Queens and neither do the girls. The school scrambles to replace me. I do not try to contact Hassan or Lara.

I am quite shaken by the reality of what I've done. I've been emotionally unfaithful to my husband by confiding in another man. I had confided in male colleagues before, but not to the extent of developing romantic feelings for them, and not to the extent where I had actually contemplated divorce. Since a man could have more than one wife in Islam, I had actually contemplated marrying Hassan Ariani and had even discussed this possibility with Lara, who seemed open to the idea, at least in theory.

Mohammed consults Sheikh Hanooti, and on his advice, treats me as though I had a mental breakdown and need rest. He casts Hassan Ariani as an evil man who has lead me astray. He explains as much to Tahera and Imran, to the extent necessary to help them understand that something is dramatically wrong with Mama. I am certainly a wreck. I spend my time crying on the couch. At some point, Lara Ariani calls and says she doesn't understand what's going on. I can't begin to explain it to her. I pray desperately to Allah to forgive the wrong that I've committed. I even cry out loud in the masjid on one miserable, rainy afternoon.

What were the losses? What were the gains? In my friendship with Hassan Ariani, I rediscovered the poet in me. I realized that one could still be a Muslim and appreciate the arts of music and poetry. A part of me that had lain dormant more than twenty years was jolted back to life once more. I started writing incessantly in my journals. It was the only way I found to process the murky mix of negative emotions I so deeply felt.

I had found and lost a best friend, someone who connected with me and understood me in ways my husband did not. That was the hardest thing to give up. In one of my letters to Hassan, I wrote that the ending of our relationship was like the sacrifice of Ismail. Abraham was asked to sacrifice his beloved son for Allah. We were required to sacrifice our love and friendship for our faith. It was a mark of our relationship that we always tried to stay within the bounds of Islam to whatever extent we could. We were not completely successful. If we had been, all contact would have ended much sooner than it actually did.

The losses were obviously much greater than the gains. I had lost my bearings on the straight path. I'd caused irreparable harm to an already shaky marriage. My children were old enough to understand what was going on, and they were therefore confused, hurt, and worried. The repercussions of my actions must have had some negative effect on their own views toward love and marriage.

Rumi and other Sufi philosophers say a heart must be broken to be ready to accept God's love and mercy. If that is true, then this episode caused my heart to break. But now the journey forward could proceed.

The Guest House

This being human is a guest house.
Every morning a new arrival
A joy, a depression, a meanness,
some momentary awareness comes
As an unexpected visitor.

Welcome and entertain them all!
Even if they're a crowd of sorrows,
who violently sweep your house
empty of its furniture,
still treat each guest honorably.
He may be clearing you out
for some new delight.
—Jalaluddin Rumi (translated by Coleman Barks)

CHAPTER 28

Dousing the Fire

Beanibazar, Bangadesh 1988

The trip to Bangladesh was supposed to wash away the past and be a new start, but I was miserable the whole time we were there. I kept writing to Hassan in my journal. In fact, I spent the next few years writing down the pain and the passion of that relationship, blaming myself for willfully having gone so completely astray. Allah knows us better than we know our own selves. He knows our weaknesses and how easily we can be influenced to do the wrong thing if we think we will gain some temporary satisfaction from it. This is why He sets clear guidelines for men and women regarding how we should relate to each other. Looking for emotional satisfaction outside of my marriage left me very vulnerable to the whispers of evil.

In December 1996, my family and I travel to Bangladesh for the second time. We now have four children with us instead of two. I met most of the family the first time around, so we aren't strangers, and I am familiar with the landscape and culture so it isn't so much of a shock to see rice paddies underwater or car ferries crossing rivers. We spend a bit more time in the capital city of Dacca on this trip. In fact, we get stuck there because of a taxi strike and spend most of our time in the hotel and at a very nice Chinese restaurant we could walk to. I've loved Chinese food since childhood but had avoided it as a Muslim because the meat was not halal. So it is a pleasure for me to find it in Bangladesh.

The children have a wonderful time with their cousins in the village. Safi and Sajdah chase chicks and see newborn puppies for the first time. Safi loves the chicks so much she literally squeezes one to death. One minute she is cuddling it and the next minute, it is dead. It's a sobering lesson for a five-year-old. Imran is given a baby goat so he can start his own flock. Once it mates, he will have more goats. Once we are back in the states, we actually keep track of how many he has for a while. Tahera bonds with her many female cousins, establishing ties that will last until they reunite in New Jersey a few years later.

As always, we are very careful about what we eat and drink while in Bangladesh. The lack of clean water is a tremendous problem there, as in most of the developing world. I make sure anything we drink comes from a sealed bottle. But Imran is twelve during this trip, and he likes to hang out with a pack of his cousins. One day I ask him where he'd been and if he'd had a good time and he said, "Yeah, ma. Oh, by the way, I drank the water out of the sink at some people's house, but I think it was okay." My heart sinks. I pray for no repercussions, but we aren't that lucky. Back in the States, Imran becomes ill with diarrhea. When the usual remedies fail, I know he has probably picked up a parasite in Bangladesh. He is losing weight and cannot attend school. It isn't until I take him to a Manhattan clinic that specializes in tropical diseases that the right antibiotic is found and he starts to recover.

The next school year I am back in New Jersey teaching English and Language Arts at *Nur ul Iman School* in South Brunswick, NJ, commuting from Jersey City with Safi and Sajdah in tow. I am taking action on my long-term plan to be a school administrator by working on my master's degree in curriculum and administration. At this point, I've had more than ten years teaching experience to draw from for my research papers. There is a new requirement in my graduate program: all work has to be done via computer. As unbelievable as it may sound to younger readers, before the 1990s, college students still used typewriters for their coursework. I have to master a new skill set in order to complete my graduate program. Fortunately, I do know how to type, so it is just a matter of mastering the other aspects of the computer. After some initial frustrations, I manage to learn how to use computers, mostly by trial and error, and by asking younger people to help me. This is a humbling experience and the first time in my adult life when I realize I am becoming part of the "older generation!"

Nur ul Iman means "light of faith." While Al Ghazaly's founders had been immigrants to the US, Nur ul Iman was established primarily by American-born Muslims. That makes the school's philosophy of education more progressive than many Islamic schools of the time. Safi and Sajdah both thrive there. I use my time at Nur ul Iman to recuperate from the recent trauma of my marital difficulties. The commute is long, but we car pool with a younger teacher from Jersey City, and I bribe the girls with McDonald's fries when they get hungry on the way home.

Our first year there, Safi is in first grade and Sajdah in preschool. Safi writes and illustrates long, detailed stories. When she is given a worksheet, she races through it and then turns it over to draw fascinating pictures. She goes through a phase of drawing girls in matching, color-coordinated outfits that she sketches in great detail for someone her age. She is beginning to show the artistic temperament that will one day lead to her majoring in fashion design. The preschool teacher at Nur ul Iman is Montessori-trained. That particular approach to education proves to be very beneficial to Sajdah. It helps her become a confident, industrious, and self-directed learner.

Meanwhile at home, Mohammed and I continue to struggle. I'm guilt-ridden over my past misbehavior and can barely look my husband in the eye. For his part, he tries to get our relationship back to where it was before the catastrophe. He does not discuss the incident, other than to try and find out information from me. I remain silent to his questioning. Only once does he remind me, "If we were in Bangladesh, you could be killed for something like this, so at least try to be nice to me." My heart is not in the relationship. I am extremely depressed. The only outlet for my feelings is my journal, where I write incessantly, totally absorbed in creating songs and poems to express my inner turmoil:

> *Maybe someday, love will be like a gentle stream,*
> *caressing our hearts,*
> *Maybe someday laughter and love will return once again, but I don't*
> *know when.*
> *'Cause right now love is an ocean.*
> *Deep and stormy and wide*
> *and I'm tossed by waves of emotion*
> *there's no-where, no place to hide.*
> *I'm drowning inside.*

I keep my writing secret from everyone, especially Mohammed, and this only increases his suspicions of me. Our verbal arguments escalate. They are about everything from money to how to raise the children. My tendency to plunge into my work and neglect my home life has not abated. And now I have added graduate school courses to my load. Mohammed has built up a soda distribution business that is based at home, so he spends more time there than I do. He also does most of the cooking and watches the kids when I attend my evening classes.

In the earlier years of our marriage, I complained that we never went out without the children and never had any fun together. In an effort to try and dissipate some of the distance that exists between us, Mohammad starts planning date nights. He asks our upstairs neighbor to watch the kids and takes me out dinner, the movies, or for a walk in the park. It feels like too little, too late to me. My heart is just not in it. When he asks me if I have grown tired of him, I don't respond. On one of our walks, he laments, "Now that you have four children from me, you just want to throw me out, like an old shoe." It's a pathetic expression. I feel pity and I feel guilt, but that is all the feeling I can muster; my heart is as dry as a desert. We attend a few counseling sessions with Sheikh Hanooti, Sheikh Shaker, and even a certified marriage counselor. I also attend therapy on my own for a time. I say that I'll try to improve, and Mohammad says the same. He acts on his promises by trying to make me happy with small presents and flowers. But at one point, I implore him, "Please, don't ask me about the condition of my heart." Life is very difficult. We have moved our bedroom downstairs to give our former room to Safi and Sajdah to share. But there are many nights when I just curl up with my youngest child and cry myself to sleep.

There are other days when anger gets the better of one or both of us. One evening, we're in the kitchen together, arguing over some petty little thing. We each have our own ideas about how the kitchen should be organized, even about how to place the dishes in the dish rack. He says something (now forgotten) that makes me so angry I actually hit him with the frying pan that's in my hand. This is the first time I've actually hit my husband, and it scares me. *This is really the end. I have to get out of here.* The next day I walk down the block and put one month's rent on a small studio apartment. I plan to move there. *This way, I'll be out of the house but still close enough to be with the kids,* I reason. I even bring Safiyeh, who is not more than five years old down there to show her the apartment and explain "Mommy will be right here and will take you to school every day, just like I do now. And maybe you can come and sleep here sometimes, too." Somehow the storm blows over and I do not move out of the house, though I do lose my nonrefundable deposit.

Nothing good comes to you except it is from Allah, and nothing evil comes to you except that it is from yourself. (S. An- Nisaa, v. 79)

Part III.

Evolving

Wings to Follow the Compass of the Heart

My belly is the bane of my existence
Always wanting something,
Turning my thoughts to the next morsel,
Savoring its taste long before it reaches my lips,
Always thinking of food, my lower self's desire.

Birds too have a belly.
They peck and peck for nourishment.
He has scattered their food far and wide and their job is to find it.
But He's given them wings!
Where are mine?

With wings, we can leave this petty and pitiful place
But how far can they take us?
Insects have wings.
They flutter and hover
I want to go higher.
Not like the butterfly
Who exists for her beauty
The peacock is proud of his feathers so he stays on the
ground, pecking and preening.
We do the same.
There are all kinds of birds.
Some will fly a great distance with effort.
Their wing span is short but their muscles grow strong
with their flapping.

Mine have grown flabby of late.

Deep in my prayers
I imagine my wings
Iridescently feathered and strong
With a strength not my own.
Open to energized air.
Close with a powerful thrust.
Bank to the right, bank to the left
Decline the mundane and search for the Truth
Follow the currents and reach for the goal

Birds know The Truth by their instinct
Am I more poorly equipped than a bird?
Or is there a human advantage
Which only Eternity knows?
—S. Flower, September 2016

Have they not seen the birds above them spreading their wings
and closing them? Nothing holds them up but the Universally
Merciful. Truly He is the Seer of all things.
(S. Mulk, v. 19)

CHAPTER 29

Journeying On

Canton, Michigan, 2006

I know people who've salvaged their marriages from the worst of infidelities, violence, alcoholism, and drugs. If both parties are willing, it can be done. But the truth is, by that point, I didn't want to fix my marriage. I wanted a way out. Looking back, I can see that I always sought out emotional connections and satisfactions outside of the bonds of matrimony. I would find colleagues with similar interests and intelligence to have long conversations with. I could not stop comparing my husband to these other men. I would willingly spend hours of my time on my teaching responsibilities to avoid spending time with my husband.

It seemed that, for all the changes I'd made in my life, I was still looking for a marriage that was more like the one my parents had: a marriage based on common interests. I developed emotional attachments to colleagues who shared my interests in education, literature, and the arts. I placed Mohammed firmly outside of this circle. The more my attachments grew, the more guilt I felt toward my husband. Initially, we'd had a good physical relationship, but that had begun to deteriorate as well. I began to disconnect from my body so that I would not really be involved in the proceedings. The psychological cost of disassociating was very high, and I would regularly stay depressed for days as a result.

Mohammed and I started our marriage from two very different positions. He had been a Muslim his entire life. I was a convert. He grew up in a poor village in Bangladesh and had a religious education. I was an upper middle class New Yorker with a degree in secular education. He was very humble. I was too proud. Neither of us were great communicators, and that just added to our problems. We tried a few counseling sessions, but they got us nowhere. We certainly grew and changed, but mostly we grew apart. There were many small events that added up to our distancing ourselves from one another, alienation, and a lack of understanding on both our parts. There were some large, dramatic events and inner shifts of consciousness that eventually led me to one stark conclusion: *I have to leave this marriage.*

I complete my masters and begin applying for administrative positions. Some friends call to tell me about an Islamic school they've founded in Michigan. They are searching for a new principal and want me to apply for the job. I fly out there for an interview and am offered the position, which I accept. I'm going to be a school principal. One of my important career goals has been met. But I'm also going to leave Mohammed behind, thus achieving a marital separation in a very natural way. Mohammed has to stay in New Jersey for two important reasons. First, Tahera wants to finish her senior year at Al Ghazaly High School. She's been there since kindergarten and flatly refuses to leave before she graduates. Second, Mohammed's brothers' visas have come through. They are due to arrive from Bangladesh and need a place to live. The Jersey City house can eventually be sold if he comes to Michigan, but for now it's needed to accommodate his brothers, their wives, and their children.

Safi and Sajdah will attend Huda School and Montessori tuition free as part of my principal's contract. Imran can attend an excellent public high school, much better than what is available to him in New Jersey. If Tahera gets into the University of Michigan, then Mohammed could come to Michigan in a year as well. It's a good plan.

I let Mohammed help us move. We all like the beautiful townhouse apartment our friends have rented for us in Auburn Hills, Michigan, a relatively affluent suburb. It's a welcome change from Jersey City. There are many children in the neighborhood playing together outside, largely unsupervised, something that was unsafe to do in Jersey City. There is a nice pool in the complex for summer use.

I don't even mention the word separation until Mohammed and Tahera come for a visit. I stay in a motel to emphasize the point that we are now separated, as far as I'm concerned. Mohammed is shocked and insulted. "See how she welcomes us?" he says angrily to Tahera. My eldest daughter certainly has mixed feelings about what is going on with our family at this point. She has been living with her father and has had to hear his feelings of loss and betrayal. I often think the worst part of estrangement and divorce is what the children have to go through, especially if the parents speak ill of each other in front of them. When I drive them back to the airport, as we're standing at the ticket counter, Mohammed begins to speak.

"It's finally over. You can get rid of me."

"I didn't say that," I protest weakly.

"But I know the truth." There's a hard glimmer in his eyes. Was it the bitter realization of my true feelings that made him speak so directly, or had he actually read my journal? "This is what you've planned all along, isn't it?"

I really can't deny the fact.

Well-intentioned friends begin calling from New Jersey, urging me to come back to my husband. "What you are doing is not good for the marriage or the children," they reason. "You are being very selfish." I consider their advice but do not heed it. I try to explain my decision to Safiyeh, who is nine years old now. Her reaction is absolutely heart-rending. "If the family is not together, then we aren't a family anymore" she says frankly. I try to reassure her with the example of a friend whose parents are divorced. "She sees her father every weekend, I explain, though our situation of being in two different states is not the same and she knows it. I am happy as a single parent in Michigan. I'm emotionally reprieved from the burden of my marriage and my guilt, and I'm happy with that, at least for now.

Safi and Sajdah adapt quickly, though they miss their father and older sister. Imran is older and not as flexible. He's used to Jersey City life with its ease of transportation and proximity to Manhattan. He's annoyed to find out that most of the high school kids have been driving since age fourteen and a half, and he is already fifteen. So he gets a bike for basic transportation and starts driving lessons right away. He also gets a job and begins classes at a new high school. He has decided to turn over a new leaf and starts to do very well in school, *Alhamdulillah*. But he is not happy to be all the way out in the suburbs with no public transportation and not much to do. The banged-up walls of our new apartment attest to his restless anger. When we move two years later, he has to learn to spackle and paint just to cover up the damages. I'm sure most of his anger is a reaction to me dividing the family and uprooting him from his childhood home and friends.

I miss Tahera. She has been my biggest helper, my beautiful, dutiful eldest daughter. But more than that, ever since her birth, she has been my *sakinah*, my peace of mind. I miss her companionship, the easy give and take of our relationship, the daily dose of pride and joy she gives me when I hear her read Quran. We talk on the phone, but of course it's not the same. I'm glad she stayed at Al Ghazaly for her final year, but I worry about her having to cope when her father is upset and with the possible comments from family, friends, and teachers regarding our separation.

When Imran, the girls, and I move from New Jersey I decide to leave our old TV behind. It isn't worth the trouble of moving it. Safiyeh has become obsessed with watching everything from cartoons to reality shows, and I don't want to spend my time policing her, so we try life without TV. It works out very well. Imran focuses his efforts on school, Safi becomes a voracious reader, as I had been as a child, and Sajdah is not far behind. I have always preferred reading to television, so it isn't a problem for me. As the kids get older, they begin watching everything online anyway. With so many different options available, a television set seems superfluous.

I am delighted to finally be a principal: the new principal of Huda School and Montessori. Every morning when I open the door to my office and read the plaque that says "Principal," I feel the thrill an ego boost provides. I try to do my best to improve the school, as per the board's directive. I find the educational standards higher in Michigan than they were in New Jersey. In the Islamic, schools there is more of a push to make sure all teachers are certified, so there are a higher percentage of non-Muslim teachers than there had been in our New York/New Jersey Islamic schools. The Arabic and Quran program at Huda School is much more advanced than our program in New Jersey. My children needed tutoring to catch up in Arabic, and Sajdah needs further help with reading and math, because the Huda School students are ahead of her.

Until the end of the twentieth century, most North American Islamic schools had foreign-born principals. These individuals rarely held a degree in education. Sometimes they came from the business community. Because they were not native speakers of English with backgrounds in education, the schools would usually have an American-born person in the role of curriculum coordinator. As more and more native-born Muslims and converts earned degrees in education, the two positions of administrator and curriculum coordinator were folded into a single principal's job. That was the position I took at Huda School and then later at Crescent Academy International in Canton, MI. I worked long hours to fulfill the variety of responsibilities these jobs required, from monitoring the parking lot on cold winter mornings to making decisions about hiring staff, implementing curriculum, and disciplining students.

Huda School is located in Bloomfield Hills, a city north of Detroit in Oakland County, one of the wealthiest counties in the United States. The immigrant community that sends their children to Huda are of a higher socioeconomic class than our community in Jersey City. They hold the principal and teachers to a higher standard. I work overtime to acclimate myself to Huda's unique school culture. Meanwhile, I am enjoying my larger paycheck and my new environment. But more trials and tribulations are just around the corner.

Till the end of the twentieth century, and even into the twenty-first century, Islamic school and masjid boards are dominated by immigrant men. American-born-and-raised Muslim men and women were just starting to come into positions of power. Imagine me, a forthright, straight-shooting New York woman coming head to head with a group of Syrian, Egyptian, and South Asian men. I should have been able to more aptly apply the lessons learned from my hot-headed days at Al Ghazaly: 1. These men will not accept expressions of anger from a woman. 2. They are scared of any show of emotion whatsoever. 3. They need to feel that they're in charge at all times.

I survive the first year by relying heavily on advice from a few board members. They seem very happy to help me run the school. One major calamity does occur, however. Huda School is situated in historic Franklin Village. The original structure is a landmark building. Translation: old building, old plumbing. During winter vacation, the weather is especially frigid, and the pipes freeze and burst causing a flood and an expensive repair job. I was supposed to have left the tap running to prevent this, but nobody had told me to do so. Perhaps the former male principal had known, but I didn't. I plead ignorance and am forgiven for this mistake.

My second year at Huda involves a personal trial that affects my job performance in a major way: Lice. They are common enough in schools. The procedure at Huda is for the teachers to do regular inspections of the students' hair, especially after family vacations overseas. If a child is found to have lice, they are sent to the office for the administration to admire their *beautiful hair*—*beautiful hair* being our euphemistic attempt at preserving the child's dignity and self-esteem. From there the parent is called and the family is sent home with instructions for how to handle the problem. The school maintains a "no nits" policy. The parent has to ensure there are no lice eggs snuggled into a child's hair before the child can return to school. In addition to sending the infected child home, the whole class receives a letter stating that lice have been discovered in class and all parents should thoroughly check their children at home. Of course, most parents would ask, "Which of your friends got sent to the office, *habibti?*" thus ruining any chance of preserving the poor, lice-ridden child's anonymity.

I was personally familiar with lice from Tahera and Imran's school days. I had once gone into Imran's preschool and thrown a fit because my son had contracted lice from some dirty child, only to find out when my daughter came home from her school that she was probably the one who had infected her brother. There was another awful situation when we were in Bangladesh, and Safi and Sajdah contracted extremely bad infestations of head lice. I had stood on the balcony of our Dacca hotel dousing their heads with kerosene (the standard lice remedy in Bangladesh) and screaming as I picked large, creepy crawly bugs from their heads and flung them off the balcony. UGHHH.

And now, like my worst nightmare, it's happening again. The children's younger uncle and his wife have arrived from Bangladesh, much to everyone's delight. The girls had gone back to New Jersey to spend some vacation time with Tahera and their cousins. Apparently, the newly arrived aunt found my daughter's hair so beautiful, she just had to style it with her very own comb.

A few weeks after vacation, my youngest child is sent to the office with *beautiful hair.* I am repulsed, but I know what I'm supposed to do. I go to the supermarket and get the standard lice shampoo. I spend a long evening combing nits and lice out of Sajdah's truly beautiful long black hair, and I wash Safi's too, for good measure.

But back at school on Monday, the secretary finds more eggs. I have to take time off to deal with the problem, but these Bengali lice just won't go away. I try all the products on the market. Every few days, Sajdah is back in the office with *beautiful hair*. I get angry, so angry I call the vice principal a "lice Nazi." Finally, someone tactfully suggests that I take my daughter to the Board of Health to get a prescription remedy for this infestation. That's the only thing that finally works. Sajdah is mortified. I am mortified, and I have insulted one of my staff members without just cause. My New York brand of sarcasm has already been labelled as rude in the Midwest. Now I've added fuel to the fire.

There is another major incident in the fateful school year of 1999–2000. It has to do with the board's decision to host a charter school in the building along with our own school. I am opposed to this mainly because the board is not planning to let the parents know about their decision until the new school year begins. I become emotional (mistake!) and mouth off to some parents about this decision. Some of the board members' wives discuss the issue at a social gathering and bring it to the board's attention. A board member comes to the office to discuss the issue with me. At the same time, he reviews the other salient aspects of my professional performance that year. When he tells me not to think about buying a house in the area just yet, I should understand that my job is in jeopardy, but for some reason, I do not take the hint.

My contract is not renewed for the upcoming school year. But instead of telling me directly, the board secretary issues the agenda for the monthly board meeting as usual. Since I am on the board, I get the notice too. Item one on the agenda states "discussion of principal problem."

Now I know I'm a goner. It has been a rough year all around, and I am tired of dealing with the problems myself. Single parenthood has lost its glow. I feel like a failure at Huda, and it's my own fault. Mohammed and I are still married. During our next phone conversation, I cry on his shoulder. He is very sympathetic. We discuss our options. I want to stay in Michigan, and he doesn't mind relocating. Tahera is enrolled at the University of Michigan in Ann Arbor, and Imran will start university the following year. I ask Mohammed to join me in Michigan so that we can try again. He agrees. In fact, he is going to bring his brothers and their families with him and establish them in Detroit. I, meanwhile, begin looking for employment at one of the many Islamic schools in the state.

Whosoever has in his heart, even an atom's weight of pride, he will not enter paradise.
—*Hadith of Prophet Muhammad* ﷺ

CHAPTER 30

They Came by Caravan

Michigan, 2007

The principal's office at Huda was big, roomy, and private. Once I knew I would not be rehired, I spent much of my time behind its closed door working on my own projects. The two secretaries and the vice principal could run the place. Principals at Huda would come and go; the office secretary was a permanent fixture. I performed my job to a bare minimum and concentrated on what pleased me. I had become engrossed in the theory of brain-compatible learning and was reading about and researching the subject for an upcoming presentation I would make at an Islamic Schools Education Conference in April. It would be my first PowerPoint presentation, and I had to master the technology as well as the topic.

When I moved to Michigan in 1998, it was just Imran, Safi, Sajdah, and me. But when Mohammed came in the summer of 2000, he came by caravan. In the interim, two of his brothers and their families emigrated from Bangladesh to the US and were living in our Jersey City townhouse. Now they would also be moving to Michigan. There was a large Bengali community in Hamtramck, a sub-city of Detroit. The plan was to settle them in rented townhomes there.

New Jersey to Michigan is a twelve-hour drive on major interstates like I-75. Mohammed would drive a large U-Haul filled with the household possessions we'd accumulated over nineteen years in New Jersey. Add to that the belongings of his two brothers and their wives and children. Altogether ten people would travel up to Michigan. With Mohammed driving the U-Haul, I'd drive the van; Mohammed's brothers only recently arrived in the country and don't have their drivers' licenses yet.

Packing, packing... what to keep and what to throw away is always a dilemma. At this time in my life, books were non-negotiable. Nowadays, I travel with a Kindle, one of my prize possessions, and much lighter than my boxes of books, but at the turn of this century, it was something that didn't exist yet. Except for the few boxes we gave away to the masjid and public library, most of my books and some beautiful illustrated books my parents had given the children traveled with us. I did my best to sort through the memorabilia of our marriage and the precious mementoes of my children's artwork, first scribbles, and school pictures, not to mention my journals. I had amassed about twenty notebooks and other written documents by this time; the earliest dated back to 1976. Mohammed also had a few boxes of old photos, letters, and important documents from Bangladesh, and a small collection of vintage American and foreign currency. We would be giving some of our older furniture to my brother-in-laws so they could set up their homes in Hamtramck.

Loading the U-Haul takes us a full day. There is a lot of furniture to arrange and rearrange, most of it hand-me-downs from my parents' and grandmother's homes. *Alhamdulillah*, between Mohammad, his brothers, and the boy cousins, everything is made to fit.

It's late afternoon before we finally get on the road. We're driving through the night and are somewhere in the Poconos of Pennsylvania when we stop to say our evening prayers and get some food. After some brief discussion regarding the direction of the *qibla*, my husband and his brothers line up to pray right there on the floor of the rest stop. The boys line up next to them and the women behind. What a strange sight we must have made to the passersby, with the men in their *shalwar kameez* and the women in their black *abayas* and veils with colorful saris peeking out underneath. Our family has never been afraid to pray in public, neither before nor after 9/11.

We drive on through the night. My sisters-in-law and the children, ranging from toddlers to teens, chatter and doze at regular intervals. I'm driving behind the U-Haul when I see it suddenly veer off the road and swerve into a ditch. There is no major damage, thank God, and no one gets hurt. Mohammed was so tired from the two-day pack and drive that he had fallen asleep momentarily at the wheel. There are no relief drivers on this trip, only he and I, and it's exhausting. We pull over to take some rest before moving on.

When we finally get to Auburn Hills, I go to my bedroom and collapse. I am exhausted from the drive and overwhelmed by the thought of taking care of all these family members. So I don't, and I realize nobody expects me to, anyways. I just pull the covers over my head and sleep.

I awake hours later to find my sisters-in-law have cooked a simple meal that we all eat together. Somehow, everyone finds a place to sleep that night. It is nice to have family around, at least for a little while. Over the next few days they all move to Hamtramck where Mohammed has found rooms for rent. He helps them settle in and shows them how to function in their new surroundings. Over the next few months, they find work and otherwise put their lives together.

Enrolling the children in school is the first hurdle. My brothers-in-law are hesitant about sending them, especially the girls. They would prefer to keep them sheltered and safe at home. But we know they need to attend school. Tahera plays a big role in getting the girls registered. She goes with her father to Hamtramck and stands in the doorway of the newly rented home. She and her father tell his two brothers that if they don't hand over the girls' records, they will call the police. I am happy to report their mission was accomplished. All the children go on to finish high school and some attend university.

Nowadays, most of my Bengali nieces and nephews are grown with children of their own. They're spread out, from Hamtramck to Ohio and from Buffalo to Queens. Some of the boys have gone to South Africa and come back with degrees in religious studies. No matter where they live, they have established simple homes that carry the peace of Islam. They read Quran and make *salat*. They teach their children to do the same. They help establish the community masjid and start Islamic Studies classes for women and children. When I enter their homes, I feel that abiding peace that comes from living a righteous life, the same peace I felt so long ago in my friend Farzaneh's home—the same peace I hope others feel when they enter my home.

The (whole) earth has been made a mosque (or a place of prayer) and a means of purification for me, so wherever a man of my ummah may be when the time for prayer comes, let him pray.
—*Hadith of Prophet Muhammad*

A family portrait at The Balsams, New Hampshire

A letter to my father: June 19, 2000

Dear Dad,

When I was 22 and became a Muslim and then married Mohammed, you and mom felt devastated, understandably so. As Mom expressed it to me, you felt as if I was rejecting all your values and everything you stood for, everything you were. At the time, I didn't focus on rejecting as much as on finding something that had been missing from my life. That "something" was a knowledge and recognition of my own relationship with my Creator, Allah (SWT). Not knowing that relationship had caused a palpable void in my life, one that I had felt from early adolescence. When I rediscovered, and actually felt, God's presence in my life, many things changed and I felt happier and more content than I had been before. So it was more of a finding than a rejecting, if you get my meaning.

Marrying Mohammed was a part of the new life that went with the religion. As a new Muslim, I was inexperienced, naïve, and vulnerable. I was unable to see the whole picture of who and what he was. I only saw a very kind, religious person with a warm heart. That is the reason I married him, and, on those grounds, he has never disappointed.

All those qualities I admire in you — your intelligence, honesty, generosity, and your optimism (in the face of Mom's pessimism) are all qualities I have tried to develop in myself. Mohammed has most of these qualities too- they are just couched in a different cultural context. Sometimes I feel lonely in the face of that difference and I know he does too.

Dad, I hope that over the years you have been able to let go of the idea that I rejected you and Mom to be a Muslim and marry Mohammed. I think you can see that the older I get the more I recognize and respect all the good things embodied in you.

All my love,
Stephanie

Dad and Tahera's daughter, Bayan, 2011

CHAPTER 31

Crescent Rising

Crescent Academy International, 2009

It wasn't difficult to find new employment after leaving Huda School. I'd heard through the grapevine that there was an opening for a principal at Crescent Academy International in Canton, a suburb near Ann Arbor, Michigan. I remembered the director there, Dawud Tauhidi (may Allah be pleased with him). He and I had once had a long and fascinating telephone conversation about Islamic education. I gave him a call. He was very receptive. After an interview with the board, I was hired as the principal of CAI, Crescent Academy International.

I would end up spending ten transformative years there. During this time, Safi and Sajdah would attend Crescent from elementary school through eighth grade before moving on to the public high school. Imran would finish high school in just half a year in Canton, then begin his undergraduate degree in Chemistry at the University of Michigan in

Dearborn. Tahera, meanwhile, was already attending the University of Michigan in Ann Arbor, and would eventually graduate with a double major in Education and Islamic Studies.

After Mohammed's family was settled in Hamtramck, we moved to Canton so I could start work at Crescent. We found a temporary townhouse with good storage space for all the stuff we'd moved from New Jersey. When the Jersey City house was sold a few months later, it netted a large profit. My father gave us the difference of $30,000 to apply as a down payment on a house. The house we purchased was on Amber Court in Canton. It was large and airy; the largest house I would live in since my childhood. It had been built in 1995 and had only one previous owner. There was a family room with a high ceiling and a fireplace. A huge picture window looked out on a wooded area of protected wetlands, which gave us a little bit of privacy from our neighbors. It was the upstairs loft and master bedroom that really sold me on the house, though. The huge bedroom would become my own private haven. And I loved the way the loft overlooked the family room. When we added a bookcase and a comfortable recliner, the loft became the perfect place to read. We moved in over the summer before the school year began.

From the beginning of my tenure at Crescent, I feel more comfortable there than I had ever felt at Huda School. It's similar to Nur ul Iman in that it also has an American-born administration, and mostly American-born teachers. Many of the parents at Crescent are also American. Growing up in the US allows for a more unified frame of mind about many aspects of education, since both parents and staff have had similar educational experiences. The CAI community is very supportive of the school's efforts to provide quality education. Parents and community members do not badmouth the school as much as they had done in the Huda School community. The masjid, Muslim Community of the Western Suburbs (M.C.W.S.), and the school share space in a more agreeable manner than I have encountered in other communities. When I join CAI in 2000, the school is in the process of a major expansion. Ground has already been broken for a brand new, seven-million dollar school building. Once completed, it will put Crescent in the forefront of Islamic school facilities in North America. All school personnel work as a united front toward this effort.

CAI director Brother Dawud is himself a convert. He was born in Philadelphia, PA and holds multiple degrees in education and Arabic language. He's a visionary leader. His life's work is the Tarbiyah Project, a curriculum framework for Islamic education. Curriculum development was my master's field of study and of particular interest to me. I had developed a variety of curricula for the Islamic schools I'd previously worked for. Now, as I spend a few days reading through the Tarbiyah Project handbook, I recognize it to be the most comprehensive, fully formed plan for Islamic education in the West that I've ever seen. I'm excited to become a part of Crescent Academy and to work with Br. Dawud on implementing a Tarbiyah curriculum.

The Tarbiyah Project seamlessly integrates Islamic concepts with educational philosophy. As a visual thinker, Br. Dawud produces many beautiful charts and diagrams to elucidate his ideas. His curriculum puts our human relationship with God at its center. All other relationships branch out from the perspective of God's Oneness, or *Tauheed*, a profound word with deep meanings related to the Oneness and Unity of Allah and the impact of that realization on all of creation. The teaching-learning experience proceeds from this God-centered perspective.

As principal at CAI, my job is to ensure that the values and understandings of the Tarbiyah Project are applied to classroom practice. This is a challenging task. Crescent holds intensive summer workshops to familiarize the teachers with the philosophy of the Tarbiyah Project. Br. Dawud explains his ideas and expects all staff members to grasp at least the fundamental concepts. The teachers and I are responsible for using these concepts to develop learning experiences for the students. This is not by-the-book teaching, but creative curriculum development at its best. One of our curriculum projects is called *Children of Charity*. It culminates during the last unit of the school year, which is about service learning. During the school year, each class considers different causes they might want to support in some way through their own service. They vote on the project they will carry out. For example, one year, the third-grade class bought and constructed some much-needed furniture for the Ronald McDonald House. Another year, the kindergarten class collected eyeglasses for Africa. The projects are multi-disciplinary in approach. In other words, while the children learned of the need for eyeglasses in developing countries, they also studied the eye and the way vision works. They grew to appreciate sight as a gift from Allah (SWT). This approach to hands-on charity makes me think about my own views. Charity is not just a matter of donating money. The best charity also involves giving something of one's self. As I will come to learn, the next phase of my life will enable me to implement one-on-one charity in an as yet unforeseen way. Allah is truly the best of planners.

At CAI, the board and administration carefully select teaching candidates who exhibit the potential to teach a thematic, God-centered curriculum. Br. Dawud and I evaluate these teachers from year to year, using a special rubric created at CAI. He, in turn, is my direct supervisor and always expects the utmost in quality, hard work, and dedication. During my first month of employment, I tell him, "No matter how critical of me you may be at times, please remember, I am always more critical of myself than you will ever be." I am trying to get him to realize I am as much of a perfectionist as he is, and in this way, get him to stand back a bit and pressure me less. He gets the point but is not able to change his attitude much. His yearly evaluations are sometimes harsh, though I try to bear them without tears and to use them as springboards for improvement.

He often withholds praise for a job well done, at least with me. One night, after an especially elaborate fundraising dinner, parents are raving about the splendid student performance of a mock *Hajj*. I have worked extremely hard with teachers and students on this performance, and I just want him to recognize my efforts and say thanks. So I keep leaving and then returning to the office, hoping he will get the hint and offer a few words of appreciation. He finally does offer a few words of thanks for my gargantuan efforts, but I feel like a fool for having to resort to such a lame and obvious maneuver.

My experiences at Huda and Crescent affirm that it's not easy being a female administrator. Legions of women in positions of authority attest to this fact every day. When you are assertive, people label you as bossy. Any time I raise my voice, I'm told my tone is aggressive. I'm told to hold the microphone farther away from my mouth or that I don't even need one. It's partly about my being a woman in charge and partly about my being East Coast in the Midwest. A New York attitude is considered downright rude in the Midwest, where sarcasm is undervalued, and superficial courtesy is a way of life. They don't even use their car horns here, whereas in New York and New Jersey, the horn is the language of the road.

I find it easier to deal objectively with children than with the adults who seem to resist female authority figures. I strive to be patient and even-handed with staff members, but it's challenging, especially when my own children are involved. At Huda, it was the lice. At CAI, it is academics. My middle daughter, Safiyeh, goes to CAI for middle school. True to her artistic nature, her school notebooks, much like her bedroom, are haphazardly thrown together at best. We have some excellent middle school teachers who are willing to go the extra mile to help our students succeed, and we regularly enjoy the accolades of praise we hear from the Canton public high school teachers: "Your former students are so responsible! They're the only ones who hand in neat, well-organized work. And they hand it in on time, too!" It is a testament to the fact that we try to emphasize organizational and study skills in our middle school classrooms. But Safiyeh happens to be among the more disorganized members of the class. She is perfectly alright with getting a B without putting in any effort, but when her English grade drops into C territory, I march into class and confront the teacher. Instead of placing the blame squarely on my daughter, I imply that the low grade is the teacher's error. The teacher is justifiably insulted and takes her complaint to the administration. I'm reprimanded for being subjective, heavy-handed, and inappropriate. It's not the first or the last time I have to apologize during my administrative career.

In general, though, I work well with my colleagues at Crescent and form good friendships in the Canton community during the ten years I'm there. Working at Crescent is challenging, frustrating, and upsetting at times. But it's also an enlivening, enriching experience.

CAI is not like most Muslim work environments. We operate within wider parameters when it comes to male-female professional relationships. Br. Dawud is not as formal as other Muslim men I've encountered at work. His attitude and behavior sets the tone for the rest of the staff. He often tells me, "You are the weather in the school." But just as the teacher is the weather in the classroom, he himself affects the overarching atmosphere. He jokes and talks openly with us about life outside of school. He is raising three young adults as a single father. His youngest son attends middle school at Crescent.

Br. Dawud deliberately engages me and certain other teachers in deep and thoughtful conversations. He encourages us to let down our guard and speak our minds. This professional camaraderie leads to friendship. I am not alone in thinking this; over the years, many female staff members come to consider Br. Dawud a close friend and confidante. But more conservative family and community members do not understand or appreciate the value of our work relationships. The intense psychological atmosphere of our school leads to greater synchronicity in developing our curriculum, but it also causes greater emotional tension and stress than might exist in other schools. My mother succinctly summarizes the nature of Crescent's work environment by comparing it to her own teaching experience in an elementary school in the sixties. She has met Br. Dawud and finds him charming, considerate, and attractive. When I try to describe the male-female dynamic at Crescent, she smiles and says, "Oh, it's the harem complex!" She isn't making any reference to our religion, just to the idea that in schools there are often many female teachers and one male administrator in whom many women confide. This situation is changing, of course, as more women move into leadership roles in schools. However, sometimes the Muslim community is a few years behind the public sector in general societal changes. I find Mom's comment right on point.

Building the Tarbiyah curriculum is time consuming, dynamic work. Our program is gaining notoriety. Br. Dawud and I, along with one or two teachers, begin traveling to national and regional Islamic education forums to speak about the *Tarbiyah Project*. He speaks of the philosophy and vison behind it, and I speak about its implementation on the school and class-room levels, using teacher-designed learning experiences as examples of the work. Br. Dawud travels overseas to speak in the Philippines, Singapore, and the Arabian Gulf states. Educators from the US, Indonesia, Singapore, and Arabic-speaking countries are hosted at CAI to learn about the project. Once again, fascination with my job and my colleagues takes priority over my family life, much to the resentment of my husband and children.

Alhamdulillah, many of the teachers I worked with are still at Crescent Academy. The school is now an accredited learning institution with six hundred students. There is currently a director and a principal, though neither Br. Dawud nor I are at the school. Sadly, Br. Dawud died of cancer in 2010, the same year I decided to resign. The Tarbiyah Project is his legacy, as are the hundreds of students impacted by the quality of education they received at Crescent during his tenure there. He was much beloved and is missed dearly by many.

> *Don't you see how Allah sets forth a parable: a good word is like a good tree – its roots are firm, (rooted in the earth), and its branches in heaven- producing its fruit in every season by permission of its Lord. And Allah sets forth parables for the people in order that they might remember (S. Ibrahim, v. 24-25)*

CHAPTER 32

Red Alert

I was at Crescent for only one year when 9/11 turned the world upside down. Elementary schools don't normally have TVs and radios playing during the school day, and social media is still in its infancy in the early 2000s, so we don't hear the news as it's happening. We get a few phone calls from parents that alert us to the situation, and then we turn on a TV to see the image of the towers falling. All stations are replaying that scene over and over. I think of my family, my parents on Long Island, and my aunt and uncle who live in Manhattan and say a quick prayer for their safety. It hasn't really sunk in that this could actually have happened. As I enter the classrooms to inform the teachers, I think, *Is this actually happening?* It all seems so surreal. I go to the middle school first. One boy in the eighth grade mirrors my own thoughts and asks, "Is this really true, or is it a movie?" "Apparently, it's true," I say, not really sure if I believe it myself. We stayed in school that day, despite a threatening phone call left on the masjid's voicemail. But the next day we close the school for fear of further threats and reprisals against Muslims.

Not having a TV at home saves me and my children from seeing those horrific images endlessly repeat. We hear and see all we need to know on the radio and laptop in the days and weeks that follow. My parents, I found out, were fine, although very angry of course. My father had friends who worked in the court across the street from the Twin Towers. That courthouse was destroyed in the collapse, and some of his colleagues died. We also have relatives and friends in Manhattan, including my Uncle Murray and Aunt Pixie, although they live uptown on the West Side and are nowhere near Ground Zero. The whole city came to a standstill that day, and on Long Island, everyone waited anxiously for their loved ones to come home. Trains and busses weren't running, and tunnels and bridges in and out of the city were blocked.

In the weeks and months that follow, New York City and other metropolitan areas are under very strict security measures. At movie theaters, museums, and other cultural venues my parents attend, purses and bags are searched upon entry. Airports stay on high alert and staff check bags and suspicious persons with extra scrutiny. The new security methods eventually become commonplace.

Our family had lived in Jersey City, New Jersey for twenty-five years. Many of our friends there worked in Manhattan, but all were safe, thank God. Liberty State Park, situated on the Hudson River in downtown Jersey City, previously boasted of a panoramic view of the New York skyline including the Statue of Liberty, Ellis Island, and the Twin Towers. After 9/11 that view is irrevocably changed. Meanwhile, some of my friends in New York and Michigan are now afraid to leave their homes in *hijab*. Some women actually decide to stop wearing a scarf at this time, saying it makes them a moving target.

Everyone in our Michigan community and Muslim communities throughout the US are horrified and ashamed that the attackers had been so-called Muslims. Muslim spokespersons in every community are telling the media that the criminals who blew up the Towers had hijacked our religion. They do not practice the faith of Islam because there is no murder or suicide bombing or killing of that nature permitted in Islam. We declare that our faith does not condone any of those actions and to kill even one person is like killing all of humanity. But nobody is listening to us. For many Americans, the attack on the Twin Towers and the Pentagon is their first introduction to Islam. Despite President George Bush's speech urging people not to blame Islam and the Muslims, six hundred people are killed in the days following 9/11 in random acts of violence directed at Muslims and Islamic centers. Some of these victims are not even Muslims, but turbaned Sikhs that were targeted out of ignorance.

To be honest, I personally face no discrimination in Michigan directly after 9/11. Despite the fears of many parents, nobody else called to threaten our school, and classes resume after just one day. There are a few isolated incidents, however. For example, one teacher arrives at school quite shaken up because as she stopped at a red light, a man came along and spit on her window. The bus driver says she feels like a moving target with a bus full of Muslim children. One father wants us to consider the possibility of "snipers in the trees" around the school campus. For the most part, however, we continue our lives as normally as possible.

A few months after the attack, I'm walking through our neighborhood when my daughter Safiyeh, now a sixth grader, looks up at the sky and says, "I guess we really aren't safe anymore." At that moment, I realize how much our world has changed because of 9/11. Her generation and those that follow will feel its impact for many years to come. The many actions and reactions that have occurred since in the War on Terror began have only added fuel to the fire. At present, we live in dangerous times indeed as presidential candidates like Donald Trump speak of putting a ban on Muslims entering the country and closing down masjids until the government can "figure out what's going on."

I became a Muslim in 1979 after the Iranians took Americans hostage at the US embassy in Iran. Now, as then, there was a resurgence of interest in Islam. Studies show that rates of conversion actually rise after events like 9/11. People who are searching for the truth will be guided to it, especially in the wake of traumatic events. Post-9/11, Muslims in the US are forced out of their comfort and complacency and into a flurry of pro-activism.

The Muslim Community of the Western Suburbs, and other Islamic centers nationwide start inviting groups of schoolchildren and townspeople to open houses and food festivals, so that they can get to know the real Islam, away from media portrayals of terrorists and suicide bombers. Occasionally, fears and prejudices brewing under their skins might surface, like the time someone in my daughter's high school class asks her if Muslims make bombs in their masjids.

At Crescent, time marches on. As I'd done in the past, I spend inordinate amounts of time on the job. Safi and Sajdah have to stay after school almost every day. They don't like me being their principal any more than Tahera and Imran had liked me being one of their teachers at Al Ghazaly. There are a few times when I embarrass them. And there are also times when they embarrass me.

We have an annual reading contest at school. Students and classes compete to see who can read the most books in a given amount of time, usually a month. One year, the teacher in charge wants to motivate students to read a certain number of pages. She sets a total school goal of something like one million pages. If the students meet or exceed their goal, the principal will have to eat an ice cream sundae with both hands tied behind her back. I foolishly agree. They exceed their goal and I am given a gigantic ice cream sundae with whipped cream and chocolate syrup to eat for breakfast, seated on a chair at morning assembly, with my hands tied behind my back. This elicits a good laugh from the students. But on the way home in the car that evening, Safi and Sajdah tell me that I can never, ever embarrass them like that again. Not that I want to!

Both girls go through middle school at Crescent, graduate, and attend the local public high school. Everybody knows that middle school can be the worst, most awkward years of adolescence. It's made just that much worse when your mother is the school principal. I have to enforce the rules for them, as I do for all students, or I'll be accused of favoritism. The eighth-grade graduation ceremony becomes particularly embarrassing for me because my daughter decides to violate the dress code by wearing jeans under her graduation robes instead of dress pants. As she sits slouched in her chair on the stage, the jeans are quite noticeable. One parent of an eighth grader comments, "I went out and bought my son dress pants just for this occasion, and look what the principal's daughter is wearing!"

To be fair to my children, it is an exceptionally difficult time for them because their father and I are going through the final stages of divorce. In 2000, I had asked him to come to Michigan so we could be together as a family and try again. But it soon became clear to me yet again that I could not stay in the marriage. The sociocultural differences that had been there from the beginning were as glaring as ever. To compensate for our lack of common interests and communication at home, I am again spending most of my time on work-related issues. I am also traveling and giving presentations on the Tarbiyah Project and brain-compatible learning with Brother Dawud and other Crescent staff members. My husband does not approve of these trips. He also feels the school is exploiting me by having me speak in front of both men and women at the annual fundraising dinners. He sees that, as a principal, I am working even harder than as I did as a teacher. On top of that, I am in the public eye more. In his view, women should not be in the spotlight. He resents Br. Dawud and the board for putting me there.

By the time I do get home from work, I'm completely exhausted. I only want to sleep. Rather than providing me with fulfillment, my marriage further saps my psychic energy. I'm happier by myself than I am with Mohammed. He is also depressed, unemployed, and spending large parts of the day sleeping. Staying married isn't worth such a heavy emotional cost. I see a lawyer and begin formal divorce proceedings. I'll stop and start the process twice before finally going through with it in April, 2006. Before the divorce is complete, two happy occasions take place: Our oldest daughter gets married, and I go to *Hajj* once more.

And He provides for him from sources he never could imagine. And if anyone puts his trust in God, sufficient is God for him. And God will surely accomplish His purpose. Verily for all things has God appointed a due proportion. (S. Talaq, v. 3)

CHAPTER 33

Rejuvenation

Me with Bilal, my first grandchild, 2006

*There is a polish for everything that taketh away rust; and the polish
of the Heart is the invocation of Allah.*
—*Hadith of Prophet Muhammad* ﷺ

In 2004, during my term as principal at Crescent, two American wom-
en come to our *masjid* wanting to hang up flyers. The flyers advertise a
seminar to be given by a sheikh named Sidi Muhammad al Jamal, who is
visiting from Jerusalem and will give three days of lectures at a local college
campus. It was unusual for a sheikh to have his photo on a flyer, and those
in charge at the *masjid* are reluctant to hang it up. But I note the information and plan to attend.

When I enter the lecture hall that weekend, I see a whole roomful of Muslims who look as American as me. This is something new and exciting. American-born Muslim converts, whether black, white, or Latino, have always been the minority population at any large religious gathering. Who are these people, and who is their sheikh? I soon find out he preaches the basic message of mainstream Islam but with an emphasis on God's love. When prayer time comes, I don't see many people praying, so I ask *Sidi* if he teaches prayer. He smiles and says, "I teach them everything, little by little." He seems such a gentle, grandfatherly man that it's easy to believe he doesn't push people. He just showers them with his love and attention. Or you might say, God's love and attention is being channeled through him.

On the first evening of the three-day program, my husband accompanies me, patiently allowing me to explore this new group. I'm intrigued enough to attend on the second day as well, so I go alone. I find out that the Eastern Michigan chapter of this group meets weekly for *dhikr,* so I start attending these gatherings. The group calls themselves the Shadhuli Sufis. There are many different schools of Sufism, such as Shadhuli, Naqshabandi, Qadri, and Chisti. Each school has its own particular practices and follows a line of teachers reaching back to the time of Prophet Muhammad 灩.

Dhikr, also known as *tasbih,* is the act of remembrance of Allah (SWT). The objective of a Sufi—someone who practices this form of Islamic mysticism—is to keep God in remembrance all the time, until the process becomes so automatic that the heart says *dhikr* with its every beat. There are different formulas for *dhikr,* depending on what school of Sufism one adheres to. I have always found it unnecessary to adhere to one particular school of thought, so my approach to remembrance is somewhat eclectic. I consider myself very fortunate that my first lessons in Islam, back in Washington Square Park with Abdullah, were all about remembrance.

Sufism and its practices are sometimes frowned upon by traditional Muslims, including my immediate family members. Their attitude is to stick to what is known and not to delve too far into the mysteries of the unseen. But for me, Sufism brings a deeper level of meaning to my practice of Islam. Ironically, as my children developed their knowledge of Islam in school, I became so busy with my duties first as a teacher and then as an administrator that I'd neglected my own spiritual growth. The Michigan *zikr* circle rejuvenates my Islam, which has become somewhat rote and dry. I need something more, something that activates my heart and my imagination. Once I begin making *dhikr* again, I find my prayers seem to carry more meaning. I am once again focusing on their meaning, not just their ritual. I am now able to deepen my practice of the faith.

I begin reading Sidi Mohammed's books in translation. He uses some wonderful phrases about being with Allah (SWT) in His garden all the time. He says there are other ways of knowing besides the knowledge of the intellect. In fact, to know with the heart, we sometimes have to give up on our rational intellect altogether. That's a hard concept for a life-long reader like me to grasp. However, the reason I became Muslim in the first place was because Islam rang true to my heart, not my head. Thirty years ago, I began to develop my concept of faith based on my heart knowing I had a relationship with Allah (SWT). Sufism was a natural continuation of that process.

I pick up a few other books on Sufism, including one by Abdul Qadr Jilani, the founder of the Qadri school of Sufism. He was a very powerful teacher, or *murshid*. In fact, he is said to be the *murshid* of anyone who does not have a living teacher. Most Sufis pledge allegiance to a teacher. This is called taking *baaya*. The practice stems back to the time of Prophet Muhammad ﷺ. Various individuals and tribes would pledge allegiance to him and swear to follow his teachings and his ways. This is what Muslims today call the *sunnah*, or practices of the Prophet. They include much more than just how to pray. There are prescribed ways to eat, do business, have relationships with people, etc. Every aspect of daily life is covered. Those who want to be close to the Prophet, to be part of his *ummah* (community), and to have him intercede for them on the Day of Judgment, try to stay as close to his example as possible in their daily lives. This is true whether one is Shi'a, Sunni, or Sufi in orientation. I try to take what I consider best from all schools of thought and practice.

The people who introduced me to Islam thirty years ago were mostly Shi'a. My ex-husband and the people I associated with for most of my adult Muslim life were Sunni, or mainstream Muslims. In 2004, I begin delving into Sufism, trying to reach past the known world into dimensions of the unseen. In fleeting moments throughout my life, I've gotten a glimpse of other states and realities, and this has fueled my yearning for a greater closeness to Allah (SWT). For most of us, this is a lifelong quest. Teachers, like Sheikh Mohammed Al Hanooti and Sidi Muhammad al Jamal are there to provide guidance and support. Both of these great men have passed from the world into the Hereafter in recent years. I learned valuable lessons from them both regarding teaching by example. May Allah (SWT) grant them the highest places in *jennah* and reward them for all the people they brought to the faith.

A few months after I started attending the local Michigan *dhikr* group, Allah gave me a sign that I was headed in the right direction. I'm sitting on my prayer rug one evening, saying the remembrance after prayer. A light rain is falling, and my murmured *dhikr* syncs with the steady flow of raindrops. The boundary of my actual body and my actual breath seem to dissolve into the rain. I become one with the space I am in and for just a few moments, I am gone, absorbed into the Unity of All That Is. That is the place of bliss I do not want to leave, but again, it is not my time to stay. I must come back to the reality of my earthly life. The numbness slowly leaves my limbs and I realize I'm back in the temporal world once again.

Once again, Rumi says it better than I can:

Dissolver of sugar, dissolve me,
if this is the time.

Do it gently with a touch of a hand, or a look.
Every morning I wait at dawn. That's when
it has happened before. Or do it suddenly
like an execution. How else
can I get ready for death?

You breathe without a body, like a spark.
You grieve, and I begin to feel lighter.
You keep me away with your arm,
but the keeping away is pulling me in.

(translation by Coleman Barks)

CHAPTER 34

A Guest at the Kaaba

The view from my window at Dar ul Tauhid, Mecca

In the winter of 2005, I get another chance to go to Mecca, an offer I can't refuse. A Saudi media station is sponsoring American converts with all expenses except airfare covered: a free *Hajj*! The offer came via one of the teachers at Crescent, a well-known singer in the Arab world, Mohamad Abu Ratib. The plan is for me to accompany him and his wife Batoul on the trip. Once in Saudi, we will meet up with a group of Saudi nationals who are also performing *Hajj*.

We set out from Detroit and arrive in Chicago, ready to begin the international leg of our journey. When we arrive in Chicago, we find that the Air Jordanian flight to Amman Jeddah is overbooked. There is only one ticket issued for the three of us, and it's in Batoul's name! As we wait with many other patient people in the crowded airport, we keep hoping that two someones will cancel at the last minute, freeing up two more tickets for our group of three. Batoul is not prepared to leave without her husband, even though she has a ticket. At five minutes to boarding time, the reservations clerk waves Batoul's ticket teasingly in the air and tells her, "Either you take it, or I give it away." With a rush of determination, I snatch the ticket from the clerk's hand. "I'll take it," I shout over the crowd. She quickly transfers my information to Batoul's ticket and off I go, flying down the hallway to the gate. Br. Abu Ratib has to come rushing after me with my forgotten coat, and it is then that I remember, *I haven't the faintest idea what the plan is.* "Who should I contact when I get there?" I shout out over the security checkpoint.

"Go to Dar ul Tauhid!" Abu Ratib shouts back. I memorize the name as I fly toward the departure gate and make it onto the plane just before the doors close.

I'm flying solo! I'm excited, but I try to relax and settle into the long transatlantic flight, first to Amman, then on to Jeddah. *Labbayka Allahumma labbayk, labbayk Allah shareeka laka labbayk. Inna al-hamda wa'l-ni'mata laka wa'l-mulk, la shareeka lak. (Here I am, O Allah, here I am. Here I am, You have no partner, here I am. Verily all praise and blessings are Yours, and all sovereignty, You have no partner.)*

The prayer of the pilgrim going to his Lord can be heard all over the plane, sometimes in the low murmurs of individual voices, and sometimes loud and choral, led by a strong male voice and chanted in unison. It is the prayer of anticipation as we start our journey. There is an atmosphere of unity amid the diversity of ethnic faces on the flight. This diversity will be multiplied many times over once we reach the airport in Jeddah and, most of all, at the Kaaba itself. Many of the men have already shed their western workday identities in favor of the simple white garment that marks them as *Hajjis.* They will shiver beneath airline blankets until we reach our destination. Female *Hajjis* are free to wear their customary Islamic clothing for pilgrimage, but they must not cover their faces in the vicinity of the Kaaba itself.

We land in Jordan, exhausted but anxious for the last leg of the journey to Jeddah. After flying on a smaller, more crowded plane from Amman, we disembark in Jeddah and face the first of several checkpoints, this one simply for the right to retrieve our luggage. I show my passport with its *Hajj* visa stamp, issued just a day before we left the States. There is a letter attached that says I have permission to travel as a single female. I'm estranged from my husband, midway through the divorce process, so I've made my eighteen-year-old son Imran my *mahram* (male guardian). His signature, along with the letter from our imam, should pass muster with the Saudis, who do not allow unaccompanied females into their country without good reason.

The customs agent questions me anyways, "Where is your husband?" I point to the letter, unsure of whether he can actually read the English. Abu Ratib would have been very handy just about now. *Three words of his polite and polished Arabic would have sufficed for this agent,* I think to myself. The guard's next words bring me back to reality. "Where your group is?" I can't tell him I have no group, can I?

At the next checkpoint, I explain my need for a group to my seatmate from the plane, a very pleasant Sri Lankan woman from Detroit. She speaks a few words to the male leader of her group, and he agrees to let me tag along with them. So I stay at the end of their line until we pass with our luggage through the next checkpoint. The plan works. I thank them, then off I go to find my way to Mecca

I remember from last time that once you get to Jeddah, there are many buses waiting to go to Mecca so I get on a bus, only to find that the buses are reserved for certain tour groups. The drivers will not let me, an unattached woman, get on their buses. I go to what looks like a ticket window and try to explain my situation to the man working there. "Ok, wait, wait over there." So I sit down to wait, confident that the problem will soon resolve itself. I have promised to be patient, and I am repeating *labbayk* and other prayers to myself to help me stay calm and unafraid in the face of these small problems.

I wait a long time. I watch people rush back and forth, dragging luggage and family members as they go searching for their correct buses, find them and then call over the other members of their party to board the bus. Finally, the man who had shown me where to wait hurries over and points me in the direction of a small van-like bus. I show my passport to the driver and get on board, dragging my luggage with me. I notice that this bus has a very diverse group of people on it, from Africans to Asians. The bus is going to drive us all to our hotels, I think, though the driver has not asked me where I am going.

We crawl through the customary city traffic, made that much worse by the annual influx of Hajj pilgrims. When we get near Mecca itself, the driver begins making stops at various small hotels. When there are only a few of us pilgrims left, he stops at what appears to be some kind of office building. Here a group of African men get off, pulling their bundles from under the bus. Now I am the only one left. The driver gets back on and I say *"Dar ul Tauhid,* please." He says, "Last stop here," and escorts me into the building. We enter a large room filled with people. There are Arabs, Pakistanis, Africans, and Asians. Most of them, though not all, are men. The driver leads me to a counter, says a few words in Arabic to the young man behind it and then leaves. That young man takes a look at my passport and asks my full name, age, etc. He asks why I am traveling alone, and I explain the story of Abu Ratib and Batoul and the plane ticket. I end with, "I'm supposed to go to Dar ul Tauhid."

He looks at me quizzically and says, "Dar ul Tauhid, are you sure?"

"Yes, yes, my group will be coming soon." By now, I am getting a bit frustrated. Plus, I am exhausted.

The boy says, "Ok, ok, please sit down here and wait." He also shows me where the bathroom is. I'm relieved to have somewhere private to go and take off my headscarf, wash my face and comb my hair, which hasn't been released from a ponytail for almost forty-eight hours and is giving me a headache.

There is really nothing to do here but sit. I try to talk to the young Egyptian boys. They are employees at this place, which is some kind of holding center for pilgrims who have no place to stay in Mecca or somehow don't have the right credentials for their *Hajj* trip. The Egyptian boys want to practice their English and have taken to calling me "mother," perhaps out of respect for my age. They tell me I will have to wait until the supervisor comes and is able to hear my case. This is not great news, but at least there will be someone to decide what to do. I'm hopeful that when I tell him *Dar ul Tauhid* is my hotel, he will just send me there. Meanwhile, I can sit here, be patient, and do my prayers. The Egyptian boys bring me tea occasionally, and I try to nap on the hard, plastic chairs. I am so tired I do fall asleep for short periods of time. I spend most of the day in that room. I am upset, but I am trying my best to be patient and above all, not to cry.

I am finally taken to another room. This one has a big desk at one end and is set up like a private office. Again, I am offered tea. The supervisor enters. He is an Arab, but he does not appear to be Saudi. He wears a white *thobe* and sports a dark beard and glasses. He gestures for me to sit and then does the same.

"What can I do for you, madam?" I explain my story for what seems like the hundredth time. "Do you have a phone number for the people you are supposed to be with?" I do not. "Why do you want to go to Dar ul Tauhid? Are you sure that's the hotel you belong to?" I explain about Br. Abu Ratib. Finally, he says, "Ok, if you're sure, we will take you there. But it is highly unusual."

Oh please take me there, I beg silently in my head. I am anxious to start my pilgrimage. "Thank you so much. May Allah reward you. *Jazak Allahu khair.*"

So I get into a van with a driver, one of the Egyptian boys, and my suitcase. We drive to the main part of the city, as close to the Kaaba as we can get.

"Mother, this is as far as the car can go. Do you want me to help with your suitcase? You have to walk the rest of the way, but the hotel is right over there." He points to a very grand building on the side of the plaza just opposite to the main entrance to the Kaaba. I am surprised but pleased with the elegance of the hotel. He walks me to the door and I go in, straight to the reservations desk. I ask about a reservation in my own name and then in Abu Ratib's name.

I am met with a look of puzzled surprise. "No reservations in that name, Madam."

"Are you sure? I'm supposed to meet my group here."

"Yes, madam, very sure."

Ya Allah, the situation is getting more puzzling by the minute. I ask to speak to someone in charge and sit down at a desk in the grand lobby until a Malaysian gentleman joins me there. He is handsome and dignified looking. As for me, after almost three days in transit I am starting to feel rather frayed around the edges, and like I might break into tears at any moment. I explain my story.

"Madam, I do not know why your reservation does not appear in our book. Normally all our rooms are booked well in advance. If I lived nearby I would call my wife and have you stay with us because we must take care of all pilgrims, especially those who are alone like you. But my home is far from the city."

"Please, I need a room. I have plenty of money to pay for it." I begin opening my wallet to show him my cash. By now I am crying and desperate.

"Madam, please put your money away. Let me see what I can do. Please calm down, all will be well, *Inshallah*."

He walks away and I start saying a prayer in my head. *Please Allah, you sent for me to come to You. Now please give me a place to stay until Abu Ratib arrives. You do we worship and on you we depend.*

The hotel manager returns. "I have a room for you for just one night. In the morning you will have to go elsewhere, I'm afraid. Now follow me please."

"*Alhamdulillah*, I am so grateful. How much is the room please?"

"No charge Madam. This is strictly off the books." He is speaking in an undertone so nobody near us will hear.

We go up to the second floor, and he opens the door to a palatial suite of rooms. The bathroom is as big as my bedroom at home and the bedroom is so big it echoes when I speak! But the best feature of all is a huge picture window that faces the precincts of the Kaaba itself. The manager leaves quietly, informing me that I may help myself to the complimentary breakfast buffet in the morning.

I sink to the carpet in front of that window. The view is as mesmerizing as a movie. I'm enthralled. This second-floor room is at eye level with the scene outside. A never-ending flow of pilgrims dressed in white are crossing a large marble plaza. I raise my eyes higher and see the majestic Kaaba itself, framed like a glittering jewel between the doors of an open gateway. Thousands of pilgrims either stream towards or encircle it in a whirlwind of motion. My heart aches to join them in an instant.

But I am bone weary from my journey. I cannot get up off the floor. I cannot tear my eyes from the movie, yet I must. In order to go to the *haram* itself, a ritual bath is required. After my ordeal of the past two days I need a bath badly. So I run some hot water in the large porcelain tub and slowly sink myself down. Sweet relief for my aching bones and feet. My eyes close of their own accord for a short but refreshing nap. I awaken with a start for I'm anxious to be gone. I dress in brand new white clothing, the outfit I've reserved for this meeting with my Lord in His House.

I find myself crossing the plaza, drawn like an iron filing to a magnet. The Kaaba stands majestic at the center of the scene, clothed in rich robes of velvet stitched with gold. I'm pulled into the vortex of emotions swirling in a never-ending circle. A heady mix of fervent prayers arises from the crowd, spoken in a multitude of tongues. I get as close to the Kaaba as I dare for my first seven rounds of *tawwaf.* The closer I get, the more I'm overtaken by the surging waves of pilgrims. The mass of humanity propels me round and round. *Labbayk Allahumma labbayk, Labbayk Allah sharika laka Labbayk. In al hamda, wa ni'mata laka wal mulk. La sharika lak.*

After the initial *tawwaf,* I retreat to one of the balconies where I have some space to pray a few cycles of prayer. I perform them with a heart full of awe and devotion to Allah, the One who has called me here to be His guest and has provided so amply for my needs. I break down in tears as I beg forgiveness for the countless sins, both big and small, that I've committed since my first *Hajj.* Back then I was a baby in Islam. Now I have so much more for which to answer.

I stay at the Kaaba all night, emerging only in the morning for a sumptuous breakfast at Dar ul Tauhid, Mecca's five-star hotel on the plaza, where I happen to have a room. Then I go in search of a payphone to call home. Tahera is the one I call. When she asks me how everything is, I say "Fine, *Alhamdulillah*."

She says, "Mama, Abu Ratib called."

"Oh, did he?" I ask, as casually as I can muster. "What did he say?"

"He told us what happened with the tickets. Are you okay?"

I reassure my daughter and hear my son-in-law in the background. He says, "I told Abu Ratib my mother-in-law always lands on her feet." I'm silently grateful for his support.

"Mama, Br. Abu Ratib sent a number for you to call," my daughter says. It's the number for our Saudi tour guide. I call him right after I get off the phone with Tahera. He's been expecting my call and tells me to wait for him outside the gates of the Kaaba. Before I leave Dar ul Tauhid, I write a heartfelt note of thanks to the Malaysian hotel manager for his gracious hospitality to this lone pilgrim.

The tour guide picks me up in a car. He sits in front with his driver and I sit in the back. He explains that our group is to meet up at Dar ul Tauhid, Jeddah, near the airport. We did not have a reservation in Mecca. Mystery solved! I am sorry to be leaving so soon, though I know I'll be back.

When we get to the hotel in Jeddah, the tour guide pulls out a billfold and hands me some Saudi riyals. He tells me to order room service and just wait in the hotel. Abu Ratib and Batoul are scheduled to arrive in a day. I try to thank him, but he is already back in the car and ready to leave. I realize that Saudi men have as little contact with women as possible. I can't help feeling a bit snubbed, but it is only a precursor to what is to occur during the next two days. Whenever I leave my room for the lobby or to take a walk outside, I notice the absence of women. The few I do see are wearing black *abayas* and face veils. They are accompanied by men and occasionally children. There are no single women in the lobby when I sit down for a cup of coffee and no single women in the restaurant where I am placed behind a screen in the "family" dining section for women.

When I go out to explore my surroundings it is the same. The only women I see are a big group of Africans having a picnic down by the pier. Jeddah is one of the few port cities in Saudi Arabia, and there are places to picnic along the coast of the Arabian Sea, also known as the Persian Gulf. Once night falls, even those women disappear and I feel very much alone. I hear the jeers of men whizzing by in cars, and I realize I am not wearing a veil, so they must be mistaking me for a different kind of woman. On my second day, I opt to stay in my room and order my food from room service. I wait anxiously for Abu Ratib and Batoul.

They arrive on the third day with the story of how difficult it was to get on a flight out of Chicago. Now we will join our Saudi companions. I will later name this *Hajj* my "deluxe *Hajj*" because it was so much more luxurious than the first *Hajj* I made in 1989. Well-connected Saudis can make *Hajj* almost every year of their lives. They do not have to wait for a visa, like non-Saudis do. They do not travel on rickety old buses with broken air conditioning, the way I had in 1989. Nor do they stay in make-shift tents at Mina the way we did then. On this *Hajj*, there are no traffic jams, no broken air-conditioning units, and no waiting around at checkpoints. We join our group on a thoroughly modern tour bus and are whisked off to the Kaaba using separate tunnels and roadways reserved only for Saudis.

I make *tawwaf* again with Batoul, and I'm amazed to discover a totally different side to my quiet friend. Batoul and I have been working together at Crescent, where she teaches Quran and Arabic. We haven't talked much on a personal level, since she prefers Arabic and I speak English. Now she grabs my hand and insists that we move toward the interior circle so that we can touch the Black Stone. This means pushing our way against the flow of traffic through thousands of people as they surge around the Kaaba. I would never have attempted to do this on my own. But Batoul is determined, so we link arms and plow ahead until we are right in front of the stone and can reach out our hands to touch it and murmur a quick prayer before the swelling crowd pushes us on. The Black Stone is the eastern cornerstone of the Kaaba. It may be a meteorite that came to earth during the time of Adam and Eve. It's surrounded for protection by a silver frame and every pilgrim longs to kiss, or at least reach a hand toward it during *tawwaf.* Only a small number achieve this goal, but Batoul and I have done it. I grin to think of the powerful alter ego who has just emerged from my friend and led me to this honor.

I do my *Saii,* the walk between the hills of Safaa and Marwa. Hajar, the mother of Ismail, ran between those hills in search of water for her thirsty baby. She ran back and forth, crying to Allah to send water for her and the child. The baby was laying on the sand and began crying and kicking his heels. Suddenly, a spring of water welled up at his feet. This is the water of *Zam Zam* which still flows from the same spot to this day. Its holy water is taken as a cure for many ailments and always drunk with a prayer. It's chilled and pumped throughout the harem complex to refresh the pilgrims. In modern times, the *Saii* is a paved marble walkway between the two small hills. Pilgrims walk and run there to remember Hajar, ask God's forgiveness, and pray for prosperity in their lives.

I am much more conscious of the symbolic meanings behind all the acts of *Hajj* this time around. Another important rite is the stoning of the devil at the *jamarat,* three stone pillars. They represent three places where Abraham stopped to throw stones at the devil who was trying to persuade him to disobey God by refusing to sacrifice his son, Ismail. The pillars are free standing. All the Hajjis want to throw the stones as Abraham did. Imagine the chaos of hundreds or thousands of people throwing stones at once! Most people don't lightly toss them. They visualize the devil as they throw, and they put some muscle into it. It used to be that the stones would often hit other people. However, between my first pilgrimage in 1989 and this one in 2005, the Saudis have built a wall behind the pillars. Now, instead of hitting people, the stones hit a wall and fall into a trench, which is much safer.

Women are asked not to go to the *jamarat* but to have men throw stones for them instead. Most women go anyways, preferring to throw their own. Br. Abu Ratib accompanies Batoul and I to the *jamarat,* and we throw our stones. As I throw, I imagine the devil, and I ask God to forgive me for all the evil deeds I've done, both knowingly and unknowingly. I ask Him to protect me from further sins after *Hajj.*

It's 3:00 am one night when I get a call on Abu Ratib's cellphone. It's my father. He and my mom had been watching the *Hajj* proceedings on the news. It was reported that there had been a stampede and many people had died inside one of the tunnels. My mother panicked at that news and wanted to make sure I was alright. She contacted Dawud Tauhidi and got Br. Abu Ratib's number just so she could call and make sure I was alive and well. I later find out from Dawud that he had spent almost two hours on the phone trying to calm her fears, but to no avail. As I speak to my dad that early, early morning, I am standing in front of our tent, looking out toward the *jamarat*, where, at 3:00 am, everything is calm and peaceful. The pillars are illuminated and I can see dozens, not thousands, of people throwing their stones. There is a deep contrast between the mob scene my parents saw on TV and the inner tranquility I feel at this moment. I have completed the requirements of Hajj at this point. I can spend my time in extra prayer and reflection, while getting to know my fellow pilgrims. I wish I could take away my parents' worries and fears and replace them with the peace and contentment I feel.

The majority of our time at this *Hajj* is spent encamped at Mina. The Saudis do not camp like everybody else does. Their camps consist of large tent-like structures erected on platforms. The twenty or so women in our group share a tent. We are given sleeping mats, bedding, and prayer rugs to use. The tent is equipped with air conditioning for the daytime and heating for the night. There are toilets, sinks, and showers inside, as well as a refrigerator filled with cold water, juices, sodas, and snacks. There are even servants, young women from Asian countries who serve and clean up after our lavish meals and keep the tent and bathrooms tidy. The food is catered in high style, and there is so much of it, one does not know what to eat first. I can't help but think, *Hajj is not supposed to be like a luxury cruise.* However, I rationalize, *This is not something I've chosen. It's been given to me and I should benefit from all the physical comforts by focusing on the spiritual aspects of the journey.*

Ironically, an epidemic of food poisoning breaks out on our third day and most of us succumb to it. The fourth day at Mina is spent largely in bed and the bathrooms. Antibiotics are given to all of us who suffer, and thankfully the problem is short-lived. I feel very sorry for the Asian women who have to clean the bathrooms. In fact, I don't like the way the Saudis order them about.

I am the only American and the only convert among the group. The women are very interested in the story of my conversion, so I give a little talk one night. It is very well received and my companions ask many questions afterwards. I get to know one young woman particularly well. She becomes my translator during the trip. Sawsan has been to *Hajj* before. She is a university student who spent time with her parents in the States, where she learned English.

As we sit in our tent on the Day of Arafat, she remarks, "You seem so content with your life. How did you reach that stage?" I don't know how to answer such a question. If I seem calm and peaceful on the outside, it is because of *dhikr*. When I look at her, I see a little bit of myself on my first *Hajj*, always looking for what would come next and trying to understand everything that was happening. This time, I'm content to sometimes sit and watch the action swirling around me while I immerse myself in contemplation. I reflect, *She will get to that stage also, but it can't be explained, only experienced when it's time has come.*

The international character of *Hajj* is a marvel to behold. There are thousands of people in any given location at any time. When the *athan* for any particular prayer is made, all the people must find a place to stand in rows, shoulder to shoulder and heel to heel. Normally, men and women pray separately, with sufficient space between their rows so that they don't physically touch. In Mecca, that is not possible, so you just do your best not to touch a stranger. People try to gather in rows ahead of the prayer time to ensure they'll be able to have a place. More than once I look down the row I'm sitting in and see women from every corner of the earth. As we shift our places to make room for each other, ours is the universal language of smiles and caring and love.

As a spiritual journey, *Hajj* transformed me, bringing me closer in love and worship to Allah than I was before my pilgrimage. As I circled the Kaaba, stood in prayer, performed the symbolic acts and sat immersed in contemplation and remembrance, I reaffirmed my commitment to faith. I emerged from this *Hajj* determined to make my relationship with Allah (SWT) the top priority in my life and to stay away from sin. But in order to do that, I knew I had to be true to myself, to face the facts of my life situation, and take firm steps to resolve long standing internal and external conflicts.

Hence, (Oh Muhammad) proclaim thou unto all people the (duty of) pilgrimage: they will come unto thee on foot and on (every kind) of fast mount, coming from every far-away point on earth. (S. Hajj, v. 27)

Divorce

I came back from *Hajj* renewed, refreshed, and ready to divorce my husband. Mohammed hoped I'd come back with a new attitude toward our marriage and a willingness to try again. But at *Hajj*, I'd had a chance to reflect on the larger patterns of my life. I knew if I stayed married I would continue comparing Mohammed to other men. I would continue looking for intellectual stimulation and emotional satisfaction outside my marriage. I was not going to keep beating myself up over what I could not change. I'd reached middle age, the time to know who I was and what I was worth to others and to myself. I could not forsake my own chance at happiness to fulfill someone else's needs. It hadn't worked before and it wouldn't work now. Besides, the emotional cost was just. Too. High. Both Mohammed and I had tried hard enough. We'd stayed married for twenty-five years! Our oldest daughter, whose conception was Allah's reason for our elopement back on February 1, 1981, who was born exactly nine months to the day we got married, was herself now married. Now that she was settled into her new life, our divorce seemed both timely and acceptable.

I'd started divorce proceedings in the spring of 2005 but then called them off. Now I called my lawyer and asked her to reopen the case. Michigan has no-fault divorce, so I didn't need to prove any wrong-doing on Mohammed's part or my own. I just needed to state there were irreconcilable differences. I tried to get an Islamic divorce first by going to our local sheikh. He said, "Sister Sommieh, Mohammed is my close friend. A divorce will make him too unhappy, and I just can't do that to him." He sends me to another sheikh who advises me to get a legal divorce through the court system first. "Once you have a legal divorce," he says, "the Islamic divorce will be easier to obtain because, first and foremost, as Muslims we must follow the law of the land."

Lawyers' fees are expensive, and I have to ask my father for help, which he grants, no questions asked. He and Mohammed do not see eye to eye on many issues. Dad and Mom have known of our marital problems over the past ten years and can see they are getting worse. Even the children do not protest the divorce. I think they, of all people, understand how big the gulf is between Mohammed and me. They are sick and tired of the arguments and fighting they witness. Some of it has turned physical. Our son has even had to intervene on at least one occasion.

A court date is set for us to sign the divorce papers, but Mohammed opts not to show up. When his lawyer calls him, he says he's sick at home. The judge says she does not believe him and orders the lawyer to sign on his behalf. It's that simple. I have obtained a civil divorce in the State of Michigan. The terms of the document are fairly simple. Tahera is married and out of the house, and Imran is over age eighteen. He can choose to live with one of his parents or on his own. He had already moved out of the house while in university. Safi and Sajdah are minors and will live with me. Mohammed is ordered to pay some child support based on his income level. He has unlimited visitation rights. Also, the house cannot be sold until our youngest child, Sajdah, turns eighteen. Those are the main points of the agreement.

I take this document to an *imam*, or religious community leader, who has been recommended to me. There are two forms of Islamic divorce. One is called *talaq*. This is a form of divorce requested by the husband. The other form of Islamic divorce is *khulaa*, when the wife initiates the divorce. The *imam* draws up the papers for me. Mohammed is required to sign them, but again he refuses. Both the civil and Islamic divorces require Mohammed to move out of the family home, but he will not. I move out of our bedroom into a spare room, and we try to live that way for several months. It is very difficult, as you might imagine. A solution presents itself in the form of necessity, *Alhamdulillah*.

Safi is due to start high school in the fall of 2006. When we purchased the house in 2000, we didn't pay enough attention to the school district assignment. After all, we expected the girls to go to Islamic school at Crescent for many years. Well, many years have passed. The alternative to public school is the local Islamic high school. Although I don't think it's the best place for Safi, I give in to pressure from the rest of the family to send her there. After a few months, we realize this school is not a good choice for our artistic and intelligent daughter. The course options are too limited and are often taught out of sequence. It is also a cliquish environment where one has to be either Arab or Indo-Pak to fit in, and Safi is neither. Public school is the only other option and our house is not in the Canton school district. So I actually move out of the house and get an apartment in Canton for Safi, Sajdah, and myself. I am now paying a mortgage as well as rent on a nice, three-bedroom apartment. I maintain that arrangement for two years.

Mohammed and Imran live together in the house until 2008, when Mohammed goes to Bangladesh. One afternoon I'm caught off guard by a phone call from him. He speaks of our marriage and how he learned so much from me. I admit I'd learned a lot from him as well. He apologizes for whatever he contributed to our breakup, and I do the same. Mercifully, he ends the call before we both start to cry. I am unsure of why he's called like that, seemingly out of the blue. However, a few months later, the chil-

dren learn from their Bengali cousins that their father has remarried. They
are surprised he has not told them himself. They feel as if he still considers
them children and therefore does not announce his news directly to them.
But it was never his way to come out and say anything direct. He would
always hint at something instead or beat around the bush.

I am relieved of some guilt now and happy that Mohammed has found
someone to share his life with. Rumors of his wife's very young age abound
in the family. The children eventually meet her once he brings her to the
US and settles her in Canton. They say she is younger than him, but not
that young, maybe in her early thirties. Unfortunately, the marriage does
not last. Several years later, he returns to Bangladesh again and marries a
widow. He currently travels between two countries, just as I do, spending
some part of the year in the US and some part of it overseas.

In the winter of 2008, Imran is living in the house by himself and going to medical school in Detroit. We are in the middle of a very cold
winter when he leaves town for a few days. In the interest of saving on utilities, he turns the heat in the house down to about 50 degrees before he
leaves, but he doesn't tell anyone. Meanwhile, I've been having strange
dreams about the house. Some kind of low-level anxiety is at work in my
brain, but I don't heed the hunches. I keep visualizing mice tearing up paper, destroying the basement, and leaving their droppings everywhere. I
want to go over to the house and check on things, but I don't manage to
find the time.

It is a normal work day at Crescent when I get a call from Imran, who
has just returned from his short vacation. "Ma, how do you turn the water
off in the house?!" he shouts urgently into the phone. At first, I don't understand.

"I don't know, Imran."

"Maybe there's a valve to shut it off in the basement," Br. Dawud
prompts from the chair opposite my desk.

"Ok, lemme see… Yeah, it's off now, but Ma, the whole entire house is flooded. You need to come over here and see this right now."

I drop everything and drive over to the house. Sure enough, one entire side of the house is flooded, clear down to the basement. In the beginning, I think the flood has started in the basement, but as I slog my way upstairs I realize the water is flowing downward, not rising up. The master bedroom is the wettest place of all, especially the bathroom, where I find a totally ruined wall behind the shower faucet. Apparently, a pipe inside that wall had frozen then burst.

The house is truly a wreck. I run down to the basement where we keep boxes of memorabilia, old books, and files, and I start to salvage whatever looks salvageable. I throw lots of stuff out, including a box of Mohammed's very important stuff. To me, it looks like soaking wet paper, but there are old coins he has been saving at the bottom and some of those were worth money. We lose many things of sentimental value in the flood, including old photos and documents. I thank God when I realize we have homeowner's insurance and they will pay for the massive cleanup and renovation needed to make the house livable again.

And who knew there are companies, such as Coach's Catastrophe, that deal with just this kind of thing The wood frame of the house and the cement flooring has to be dried out completely. Some of the sheetrock can be dried up, but the rest has to be removed and rebuilt. There is more than $70,000 worth of damage to deal with. *Alhamdulillah,* the insurance company is prompt and they also provide money for renovation. I will get a whole new house before the project is finished. That's the good news.

The flood at the house is a big trial. To me it signals my negligence and neglect of important things. After all, I do own the house and it is a responsibility. Mohammed had left Imran to deal with it and to pay the heating bill while he was away. That wasn't fair. But ultimately, I have to clean up the damage. The catastrophe company takes care of the interior, but I must deal with the driveway myself. All the flood water had seeped out of the house and collected on the driveway. It's January and the temperatures are frigid. All that water has frozen, making the driveway into an ice slick that's at least four-inches thick. I buy salt, salt, and more salt. On the weekend, I hack at that ice for two days, trying to clear it from my driveway. It's backbreaking, exhausting work. I don't know why, but I have to do it myself. It's some kind of penance.

It takes about a month to complete the clean-up and for the house to dry out enough to plan the next steps. I have the insurance money in hand for renovations. This will be my brand new, post-apocalypse, post-divorce house. I'm going to plan and design it to my heart's content. I need new floors, some new walls, and a fresh coat of paint over everything. After that I'll need new furniture. Luckily, the leather sofas in the family room are undamaged. But the living room was directly under the bathroom with the burst pipe, so it has to be gutted entirely.

One of our school employees is married to a building contractor. He comes over, surveys the damage, and then gives me an estimate of what needs to be done and the approximate costs for the work. He helps me every step of the way, from choosing flooring to painting walls and installing electric fixtures. My favorite part of the restoration is choosing the color scheme. I have always loved color—bright, simple color. Up until the flood, our walls had been white and beige, the same dull colors one sees in many homes. My new home will be different. Sunshine yellow and apple green colors will grace the walls. Upstairs, my bedroom will be painted turquoise, with a beach colored carpet—a sea and sand effect. The girls pick the color schemes for their bedrooms, too.

I leaf through magazines and books on design. I buy pints of paint color to slosh on the walls and see what I can live with. I choose carpeting, hardwood flooring, an abstract rug, a white leather couch, an eggplant-colored chair, and a Danish modern kitchen table. I have window shades custom made for every room in the house. Tall, black shelving from IKEA forms symmetrical columns on each side of the family room fireplace. When everything is in place, I stand back and admire the effect. My friends love the paint box colors, the way the lemon-yellow hallway blends into the lime-green kitchen with its electric blue tile backsplash. My house is a showpiece.

Mohammed returns from Bangladesh a few months after the flood. In order to collect the homeowner's insurance to do the repairs and renovations, I've had the house remortgaged in my name alone. I've reclaimed it and made it mine. This time, he gets an apartment and makes sure it's in the right school district for Safi and Sajdah to finish high school. They'll continue to live with me but will be able to use his Canton address.

Material wealth comes and goes. I thoroughly enjoy the refurbished house for two years. By 2010, I have other plans, and the house will become a burden once again.

Oh you who have attained to faith, let not your worldly goods or your children make you oblivious of the remembrance of God: for if any behave thus, it is they, they who are the losers. (S. Munafiqun, v. 9-11)

CHAPTER 36

Another Step Forward

School Picture, 2008

"Sister Sommieh, if you would just let me take your picture and put it on one of those internet matchmaking sites, I'm sure you'd find someone you like. You're still young, after all."

A well-meaning friend and Crescent parent was trying to convince me that online dating was the way to find a new husband. It was 2010, four years after the divorce. I had been busy with my career and my grandchildren. Tahera now had a boy and a girl. Safi was studying in Chicago, and

Sajdah was in her last year of high school. Imran was in medical school and living in Detroit.

I also have been teaching water aerobics at the local Fitness USA since 2009, a part-time job I love. I've always been fairly active, either going to a gym, using a treadmill at home, or even just walking to the park with the kids. I've had brief encounters with kickboxing and a long acquaintance with yoga, which I find to be a great way to relieve anxiety. Exercise always lifts my mood. After discovering water aerobics at the gym, I started attending a class three days a week. When the teacher had to leave, my classmates encouraged me to take over, and the gym hired me to teach the class. This is not your old lady water aerobics, but an action-packed, quick-paced workout. It's great fun and guaranteed to elevate your mood. Water aerobics is truly a no-sweat workout. The gym is women-only three days a week and men-only the other three days. I revel in the fact that I can wear a simple one-piece bathing suit and not worry about being seen by any men. I save my *burkinis* for the beach.

My post-divorce life has been fulfilling in many ways. But perhaps it's time to get married again. My nights are long and lonely. Sajdah and I live together in the house, but we each have our own lives and schedules and spend much of our time apart. I reconsider my friend's advice about online dating. I feel connected to my Sufi group, but have no romantic interests there. Although he is also divorced, Br. Dawud and I are just good friends. We've both been around long enough to know that an office romance is a dangerous idea. I make *du'a* and ask Allah to help me find a suitable partner. I even ask Him to find me a Sufi man. My views on Islam have expanded to include the more mystical dimensions of God's Oneness, and the role of Prophet Muhammad ﷺ. I'm looking for someone who might have similar views and common interests.

There is no fooling around in Islam. You get to know someone strictly for the purpose of marriage. Islamic dating websites are set up with that goal in mind. I weigh the pros and cons, thinking, *At fifty-two, I'm not getting any younger, so why not give it a try?* I use one of my school portraits as the introductory photo. I am wearing *hijab* and clearly state in my profile that I wear it all the time and that I am a practicing Muslim. The website I choose has a free option where you don't contact someone you are interested in directly, but the website itself sends them a note saying you have expressed interest in their profile. They can contact you if the interest is mutual. I view the profile of a man who lives in Massachusetts and works as an accountant. His profile says he likes a natural, simple life, and that he's intelligent, educated, and enjoys reading and Sufi music. I express my interest in wanting to learn more about Mr. Tariq Ashraf Khan, and he writes me back. We begin corresponding through email. I learn that he is a Pakistani national and has been educated in British boarding schools. We exchange numbers and I call first, just to hear his accent, which is beautiful. We begin having long conversations about everything under the sun, from politics to calligraphy to string theory. We are also both writers and exchange poetry with each other. We exchange photos as well. I am thrilled with how handsome and charming Tareq looks in his pictures. He asks me to call him Asad, a favorite nickname. He calls me Stef. I find this very endearing because it brings me back to my younger days. He buys me a cellphone exclusively reserved for our conversations, so we'll be in touch all the time. I often neglect my work and home responsibilities to engage in long conversations with him. I learn that Asad has been in the U.S. off and on for twelve years, working in various capacities from driving a taxi to working as an accountant. He is well-traveled, having also lived in Saudi Arabia where he was a personnel manager for Peugeot. In his early adulthood, he was in the military, where he wanted to be a pilot before deciding to drop out entirely. I'm impressed with his ability to talk about literature, poetry, and art. I'm thrilled to know we share these interests in common. Additionally, he knows much about Islam and the history of Sufism. All this and that wonderful British accent besides, I've fallen in love with Asad long before we meet in person. It's like a poem by Rumi:

Lovers don't finally meet somewhere. They're in each other all along.

As if someone has sprinkled fairy dust in my eyes, everything is new and beautiful and right with the world because I've found my soul mate.

After a few months of increasingly intimate talk, we arrange to meet in New York, where I am going with Safi, Sajdah, and Safaa, a Moroccan exchange student who is living with us for winter break. Poor Asad has to meet me, my children, my parents, and some relatives, all in one weekend.

The girls and I drive from Michigan to New Jersey to visit old friends at their eighteenth-century farmhouse. I stay overnight in the oldest part of the house, a cozy little room with whitewashed walls and a fireplace. The night before meeting Asad, I'm on my knees praying for all to go well. I don't want everything to turn out to be too good to be true. That same night, Asad calls to tell me he had actually driven by the house where I'm staying, just to see where I am. The sweetness behind that gesture further softens my already melting heart. On the day we're to meet face to face, my whole being is buzzing with anticipation. Days before, I had carefully chosen a skirt and sweater in my favorite color combination, turquoise and brown. The girls are going to spend the day with friends at the Museum of Modern Art (MOMA). Asad and I will meet there and go someplace where we can talk.

At the museum with the kids, I have one eye on my phone. Asad texts to say he'll be a bit late due to traffic. When he gets to the museum, he texts again from his car. I fly out the museum doors and see a slightly smashed up rental car. Apparently, he's had a small collision on the way. I climb in. We say our *salaam*s and eye each other up and down for the first time. He is even more handsome than in his picture. We both smile and then briefly clasp each other's hands. I nervously rub my thumb back and forth over his hand till I realize what I'm doing. I stop immediately. We know each other so well already.

It's warm for December, and we decide to go to Central Park for a stroll. Eventually, we find a large boulder to sit on. The conversation flows almost as easily as it has on the phone, and the afternoon passes in a lovely haze. We take a pedicab ride through the park and have coffee while basking in the sunshine and joy of finally meeting face to face.

The plan is to use his car to pick the kids up at the museum and take them somewhere for dinner, but we end up going back to my friend's house in New Jersey instead. She wants to kill us when we arrive unannounced and unfed. But, gracious hostess that she is, she quickly throws a meal together. Meanwhile, Asad and her husband get to talking. My friend's husband tries to find out more about Asad at the dinner table, such as what he does for work, his education, and his past history. He's acting in the role of an unofficial *mahram*, trying to help me determine if Asad has good husband potential. After he leaves for the evening, the three of us talk. While Asad had been warm, friendly, and charming, my friends have some reservations about him. "Maybe his answers were too good to be true. Maybe he's too old for you. He says he's just looking for a housewife to settle down with. You've always been a working woman. How will you stand being at home?" These are some of their concerns, but I am hardly listening. My heart is humming a little tune of joy. The feeling of being in love overrides all the red flags my friends try to wave.

The next day, Asad again meets us in the city. The girls and I are going to stay there for two nights to see a Broadway show, take in the sights, and have dinner with my parents, Uncle Murray and Aunt Pixie. Asad has arranged to stay at the same hotel, and I've cajoled my father into getting him an extra ticket for the show. Honestly, the only thing that matters to me in all of this is the opportunity to spend time with Asad.

He proves to be a knowledgeable tour guide when we visit the Museum of Natural History, where the exhibit is all about the famous Silk Route from the Middle East to China. It passed through his country, Pakistan, and the country of his ancestors, the Pathan tribes of Afghanistan. He is quite familiar with that history, and I am easily impressed as he guides me by the elbow through the crowd and whispers interesting snippets of information as we tour the exhibit.

He does not enjoy *West Side Story*. The opulence of Broadway theatre, compared to the poverty of millions in his homeland makes him think of it as a mere extravagance and waste of time. I do not find this out until later, of course, when I visit Pakistan and see the poverty there for myself. One of my own ongoing internal conflicts has been reconciling the relative opulence of my life in the West with the knowledge that billions of people worldwide, and even in my own country, do not have clean water to drink or adequate food, clothing, and shelter, let alone entertainment.

We have dinner in a French restaurant frequented by my parents. It is all pleasant conversation and small talk until Asad notes, "The woman at the next table seems very interested in us." She and her husband are my parents' age. Her interest, encouraged by her drunkenness, leads her to stand up and say, "We do not want people like you here. This is our restaurant. Why don't you go back where you belong?" We are all silent for a moment and then my father gets up, and turns angrily to her husband growling, "And why don't you put a muzzle on your bitch and leave this restaurant?" They had obviously finished their dinner already. As the embarrassed husband takes his flabbergasted wife by the elbow, he utters some conciliatory words about being peaceful to my dad. Dad retorts with something about the man's cowardice as they leave. The proprietress of the restaurant comes over and apologizes to us for her customers' behavior. My dad is still trying to be my hero, God bless him!

There is a light snowfall on the day we leave, creating a pretty picture of Manhattan covered in snow. Our visiting exchange student has seen Manhattan; Safi and Sajdah have seen West Side Story; and Asad and I have seen that we're truly meant for each other.

Back in Michigan, the two of us continue our daily conversations. He comes to Michigan in January, and we marry in the office of the imam in Ann Arbor with Imran and Sajdah as our witnesses. We honeymoon in town, but then have to separate again, as he is working in Massachusetts and I still work at Crescent Academy. We spend the next few months flying to meet each other in Boston, Philadelphia, and Canton. Asad does sweet little things to surprise me. One day, I get to our hotel room and he says, "You must have forgotten your shoes." I turn around to find three pairs of beautiful designer shoes he has purchased, and they all fit! Another time, it is a beautiful cape, and another, some bright red lipstick, perhaps a hint that I should wear a bit of make-up.

Soon after we'd met online, Asad told me he might have to leave the United States for good. At the time, I thought very little about what seemed like a remote possibility. He hired a lawyer to try and help him achieve a more permanent status in the US, but after 9/11, many of the immigration laws had changed. I would not be able to sponsor him the way I had done for my first husband when we married back in 1980. Just a few months into our marriage, he tells me he must leave the US by April. I begin making plans to resign from Crescent and join him in Pakistan.

When my children were growing up, I'd always told myself I would travel once they were on their own. In 2009, I took an online course to get a TEFL (Teaching English as a Foreign Language) certificate. That document, along with my master's and bachelor's degrees in education, plus thirty-years of experience in teaching and administration, could get me teaching jobs overseas. My plan was to work in various countries and thereby afford the expense of travelling. Asad's impending departure catalyzed my plans. I thought of Pakistan as the first leg of my teaching and traveling career.

Prior to April, Asad left his job in Boston and moved in with Sajdah and me. We make the most of our time together, taking long walks in the nature preserve behind my home. I try to cook food spicy enough for him to eat, but a bottle of hot sauce becomes a permanent fixture on our table! I'm still sensitive about the food issue, wanting my husband to like what I cook. But this is not as big a deal as it was in my first marriage. As Asad kindly explains, "We all have different tongues and prefer the foods we're brought up on." On the sad day of his departure, we drive to Chicago together and say our goodbyes at the airport, promising tearfully to stay in touch. Once he has a home, I will come and live with him for a few months as a kind of orientation visit.

From April until August, I'm in daily contact with Asad via phone and email. He tells me of his progress in looking for a job and a suitable home for us. He's been out of the country for seven years, so it takes some serious effort to get re-established. Well-connected family and friends help to get him a job in Islamabad, the capital city.

He tries to describe the trials and tribulations of daily life in Pakistan, I do sense a change in his attitude toward life now that he's back home. He seems more serious, not as carefree as he was when I first met him. But for the most part, I'm living in anticipation of seeing him again and wearing rose-colored glasses as I contemplate life in a developing "third world" country.

My anticipation is also fueled by my desire to continue my spiritual quest in Pakistan. Asad has helped me along that path with unparalleled love and devotion. Through him, I've glimpsed the more mystical, philosophical, and gentler side of Islam. I hope to continue down the Sufi path by experiencing life in Pakistan. And I will, just maybe not in the way I thought I would. "Allah is the best of planners."

My last year at Crescent ends on a very sad note. On May 23, 2010, Dawud Tauhidi, my friend and colleague, founder and director of Crescent Academy, passes away after a relatively short battle with cancer. The day of his funeral is a day of mourning for the entire school. We hold a eulogy a few weeks later that is well attended by Br. Dawud's family, friends, colleagues, and former students. After his passing, the school limps toward the end of the school year. After ten years as principal, I will miss my colleagues, students, and their families, but I'm ready for my next big adventure with Asad in Pakistan.

Forget safety.
Live where you fear to live.
Destroy your reputation.
Be notorious.
—Jalaluddin Rumi (translated by Coleman Barks)

Tariq Ashraf Khan, a/k/a Asad

CHAPTER 37

First Impressions

Masjid and Graveyard, Hazara, Pakistan, 2011

Blog Post: August 27, 2010
West Ridge Cantonment, Rawalpindi, Pakistan

Asalamu alaykum and Ramadan Kareem to all. I hope things are well with you and your families. I am having a wonderful experience here in Pakistan. Every day brings something new. Since I arrived last week, my husband and I have been distributing the zakat monies all of you donated for flood relief. Alhamdulillah, I am happy to inform you that the bulk of the money was distributed today directly to eight needy families, seven in Rawalpindi and one in Haripur.

I've learned that many areas of the country were affected by the flood and the usual August monsoons as well. For example, in a very poor section of Rawalpindi called Lai, the water and sewer system is basically an open drain.

Every seven years or so, it overflows, completely polluting the city water supply. This year, the water came up as high as the first-floor shops and homes. People were ordered to evacuate but were given no assistance in finding shelter.

We found several families living in tents on top of the mud and rubble of the city. One group of three sisters and their mom have about 20 children between them, most of them girls. Their husbands work as porters in the local market which was also flooded. The youngest sister had been set to get married, but most of her dowry was washed away by the flood. We gave Pak Rs 75,000 to this group.

Among their neighbors are four widows, one with school age children and none with livable homes. They were given Rs. 55,000, 45,000 and 35,000, depending on their immediate needs. The balance of the donation monies is being given to two other destitute families in Haripur and Gharibabad district in Rawalpindi who will get Rs. 35,000 and 45,000 respectively. One of the men is a widower with three children and the other supports an extended family and is the only wage earner for them. He is going to open business as a denter (someone who removes dents from car fenders, etc.) with the money he received. If the amounts given seem large to you, please keep the exchange rate in mind. It fluctuates daily but seems to stay between Rs. 85.20 and 84.05 per dollar. The total amount distributed was Rs. 374,000, or $4,400.

I arrive in Pakistan in August, 2010 at 2:00 am on a humid summer night. Asad waves from the crowd in the arrivals terminal, thinner than I remembered him but still my handsome husband. An army car is waiting to escort us to Rawalpindi Cantonment Our rented home is as yet unavailable, so we spend a few weeks in the cantonment, in a sort of guesthouse hotel run by the military. In Pakistan, former military personnel like my husband have many privileges, including the use of accommodations when they travel. Cantonments are cheaper than hotels for long-term stays. They are clean, air-conditioned, and comfortable. Meals are provided as part of the cost. The cantonment will be our convenient home for a few weeks. It's a good place for me to ease into Pakistani life.

My first assignment is to distribute monies my friends in the States had collected for flood relief. They were very happy to hand it over to me personally. An agency might pocket a substantial amount of money meant for poor Pakistanis who have been displaced from their homes by the floods. My blog post of August 27 gave an account of how the money had been distributed.

I arrived in the middle of Ramadan. After one or two days of rest from my trip, it's time to get back to fasting. At the cantonment, a designated waiter serves us *suhoor* (morning meal) and *iftar* (evening meal to break fast) in our own private dining room. We have a small yard in the front and back of our bungalow, and we can also walk around the landscaped grounds. There aren't many other guests in the cantonment. The only people I see are those who work here, and they make themselves scarce. The palm trees, foliage and flowers, and even the insects are new species to me, and I enjoy the novelty of my new surroundings.

It is exceedingly hot here, however. People had warned me, but you don't know what 112 degrees really feels like until you experience it for yourself. I am learning a new dimension to fasting by experiencing the heat and other limitations, such as a lack of electricity and cooking gas. One can count on at least two power outages for load shedding during the day or night. When the fans and A/C go off, you feel the heat almost boiling your blood. I expect I'm losing several pounds due to sweat. I put salt in my water at *suhoor* time to help prevent dehydration and I'm much more interested in cold water than in food when I break my fast. We have fruit *chaat* (salad) and *pakoras* (fried chick pea dumplings) most of the time. We may or may not eat dinner later. Sometimes, we just save that for *suhoor*, which comes at about 3:15 am. Prayer is at 4:15, so we are fasting from 4:15 am to about 6:45 pm, fourteen hours a day.

Our rental is ready in time for *Eid ul Fitr*, the holiday that marks the end of Ramadan. It's a one-story home located in Chatha Bakhtawar, a village near Islamabad. It has three bedrooms, a living room, and a kitchen. There's an abundance of marble in Pakistan, so all the floors, the verandah, and even the kitchen countertop are made of marble. There are ceiling fans in every room. With the doors open for circulation, the fans do a decent job, especially if you don't move much.

Homes do not generally have large windows because that would make them unbearably hot in the long summer months. They do, however, have flat-topped roofs. Rooftops count as living space in Pakistan. It's a good place to sit in the evening, admiring the view and catching a cool breeze before sunset. It's also nice to watch the sunrise there in the morning when the birds raise a chorus. It's a place to dry the laundry but also the hair. Many times, one can see women combing their wet hair and letting it dry in the sunshine. I've even seen women threading their eyebrows or applying *mehndi* (henna) and makeup on the roof where the light is better than in the dark recesses of their homes.

Pakistani homes differ from American ones in purpose and function. Most middle- and upper-class homes have a large front gate and a walled courtyard that includes the driveway or car park. Brick, stone, or plaster walls shield the family from the street noise and traffic offering privacy. Women, who may spend most of their time at home, can be relatively free from male eyes behind the walls of their courtyards. Once on the street, many women wear *niqab* for protection from curious observers. At home, they will just have a *dupatta*, a long, thin scarf, handy in case someone rings the bell. The gates are usually adorned with floral or geometric designs, simple on modest homes and elaborate for the wealthier ones. All homes have *Masha 'Allah* engraved above the doorway, meaning, "It is the will of Allah." This is considered protection for the home and its occupants. Wealthy estates and public buildings like banks, schools, and stores have *chowkidars*, or security guards, who are armed and in uniform.

In the cities, there are apartment buildings where many families live crowded together, but in villages, most homes, whether rich or poor, contain just one extended family, which usually includes grandparents, grown-up sons, their wives, and children.

The poorest people live in hovels made from mud brick, bamboo, or reeds with thatched roofs made of dried straw and perhaps a few pieces of plastic or sheet metal. These huts are clustered in ghettoes called *katchi abadi*, which literally means "uncooked abodes" because the mud bricks are unbaked and held together by a combination of rags and straw mixed with more mud. They seem flimsy and unstable, but they can actually last up to thirty years. They have no clean water, indoor cooking, or sewage facilities. One can see these huts clustered together in ghettoes on the outskirts or in the corners of cities and villages. Their inhabitants are often refugees from Kashmir, Sindh, Punjab, or Afghanistan who have come to find work in the cities. Minority groups like Christians and Shi'ite Muslims may also live in such conditions. The slum dwellers are often squatting on unoccupied land and must move when and if the city reclaims it. Those with a bit of money can rent small concrete bunkers that also have no utilities or plumbing.

In the early mornings, you can see the men sitting with their tools by the side of the road, hoping to be chosen to break stones or work on a construction site for a daily wage of about Rs. 600. The price of one *roti*, a flat bread similar to a pita, is currently Rs. 10. If there are ten people in the family, that's 200 rupees just for bread, not to mention some lentils or vegetables to go with it.

Asad and I have a cook, a cleaner, and someone to do our laundry. They are all neighborhood women who came to us asking for work. I am definitely not accustomed to such luxury, but servants are cheap labor in Pakistan where everyone needs a job. At home in the States, I'd been doing most of my cooking and cleaning on the weekends. After thirty years of full-time work on the job and at home, I suddenly have no real work to do.

We are living near the capital city of Islamabad, where Asad works on project development fora private company.. The city is quite modern compared to Karachi and Lahore. It was planned and developed in the 1960s, largely with money from Saudi Arabia. They built the Faisal Mosque and the International Islamic University, both showpieces of modern architecture. In the first month after Ramadan, I visit Islamabad's cultural highlights. The Heritage Museum at Lok Virsa has been funded by UNESCO. It displays and preserves the cultural richness of Pakistan's traditional arts and music. The National Art Museum features mostly contemporary works, including some beautiful calligraphy and sculpture installations by female artists. In the evenings after work, Asad takes me for walks in some lovely parks. The Rose and Jasmine Garden is resplendent with every variety and color of roses under the sun, arranged in flowerbeds and tended by a large staff of gardeners who spend as much time on tea breaks as they do in the dirt. Daman-e-koh Park, in Margalla Hills, features a panoramic view of Islamabad that's especially pretty at night when all the lights are twinkling. The city fans out below us to the east and west from a central sector called the Blue Area. I hike Margalla Hills with friends in the daytime and enjoy the monkeys who swing down from the trees, looking for food scraps from picnic lunches. Near the parking lot we see a trained monkey. As his owner tells a story of visiting the in-laws, the monkey acts it out, complete with gestures and facial expressions. At one point, the monkey sits on a small chair, crosses his legs, and clasps his hands on his knees, swinging one foot back and forth, just like a proper son-in-law!

An older man plays the *rabaab,* a classical Indian string instrument. We stop to listen and give him a few coins. The most interesting display is the *paan waala.* He has set up a stand consisting of a large chest, or *paan* box, with all its accoutrements. Many South Asian men and women like to chew *paan,* the leaves of the betel nut tree, which are wrapped around a variety of fillings such as lime, slivers of areca nut, chewing tobacco, candy-coated fennel seeds, and spices. This *paan waala* is making *paan* to order with great ceremonial flair. He's dressed in green, like his leaves, and is wearing a special hat. He has dolls on exhibit dressed in native costume, doing common cultural activities, like spinning wool, riding horses, and reading Quran. The funny thing is that these are American Barbie dolls dressed as classic Pakistani characters. Asad buys a custom-made *paan* for tradition's sake. I, however, am not interested in trying this particular delicacy.

Frustrated by a sudden lack of regular exercise, I go swimming once in the pool at the Serena, Islamabad's only five-star hotel. The price of swimming there for one afternoon can feed a Pakistani family of six for a week! When my husband points this out, I feel guilty about going back. The Serena with its luxurious rooms, elegant restaurants, and two swimming pools represents the clear divide between the haves and have nots in Pakistan.

My husband has a good job and is financially stable. He comes from a landowning family of means. But he abhors what he considers extravagance of any kind and is very generous to those in need. According to Allah, all wealth is given by Him, and he tests us to see how we use this resource. The poor and needy have a share in what we've been given and we should want for them what we want for ourselves. Asad tries his best to live by these Islamic principles. I admire and emulate these qualities to the extent that I'm able. By now, I've realized the conflicts between the American outlook on life and Islamic values. I strive to come closer to the latter, though I still enjoy the former, with its emphasis on fun and entertainment. One difference between my first and second marriage is that now I have   the maturity and wisdom to step back and distinguish these opposing characteristics in my personality. I can accept and respect my husband's views without totally disregarding my own. My priorities have begun to change.

During my first visit to Pakistan, Asad and I visit the ruins of a Buddhist monastery in Taxila, more than an hour's drive north of the city. There is a small museum and several archeological sites dating from the sixth century BC to the sixth century AD. They have been designated National Heritage sites by UNESCO, the United Nations branch that funds their restoration and development. The ruins are quite fantastic. They include monks' cells, a kitchen, and a bathing pool. There are large *stupas*, or shrines, dedicated to the Buddha. There are several archeological sites in the region, all related to the same time period. I also visit Lahore, the ancient cultural capital of the country where I see Minar-e-Pakistan, a tall, needle-like monument; Badshahi Masjid and Lahore Fort, constructed by the Mughals; and the tomb of Mohammad Iqbal, the Poet of the East. We also travel to Sialkot to see Iqbal's home and attend a wedding party.

Every city and village in Pakistan has its own flavor, culture, and spoken dialect. Travel on bumpy, dusty roads is often difficult but the variety of sights and people makes it a rewarding experience. Asad and I travel the country in a small gray Suzuki with a manual transmission. Travel in Pakistan is far from easy, yet it's through travel that I get an overview of the two colliding worlds that comprise this country. There are the rich and the poor and the divide between them is getting bigger all the time. On the road, we see all manner of vehicles, from the horse and donkey wagons of the farmers, to the large Pajero land cruisers and Toyotas of the upper class. There are huge trucks carrying everything from livestock to gasoline. Many have top-heavy loads of straw or recyclable materials. The trucks themselves are amazing to western eyes, because they're decorated in colorful folk art paintings and designs. Truck art is a cottage industry in South Asia. Lines of poetry, cozy mountain dwellings, eagles, tigers, famous people, and the ever-present seductive eyes of a woman are all to be found on the trucks that crisscross the landscape. Trucks in the western world are very boring and non-descript by comparison. Small Suzuki vans are crammed with passengers sitting on hard wooden benches. Buses colorfully decorated and equipped with jingling bells sway down the road with young men hanging from their sides and sitting on the roof for lack of space inside the vehicles.

But the most ubiquitous form of transport is the motorbike. Most people cannot afford a car in Pakistan, so one sees whole families traveling together by motorbike. A father or son is driving. If he has a helmet, he is the only person wearing one. There may be a small child sitting in front of him and a child or two behind, clutching at his waist. Behind that child is the wife. Perhaps she is holding another child or an infant on her lap. Her *dupatta* is blowing in the wind, often reaching dangerously close to the wheels of the bike. Death by strangulation as the *dupatta* gets wrapped around the spinning wheels of the bike is a common accident here. A proper woman sits sideways, a more ladylike position than straddling the bike, but her sandaled foot dangles quite close to the ground seated like this. She must be careful to hold it high enough so as not to scrape the road. The only women I ever see straddling a bike are the very elderly ones who cling tight to the male body in front of them for fear of falling off. I fantasize about riding a bicycle or a horse, just for the shock value!

Everyone is on the road in Pakistan, all rushing to who knows where. Traffic jams are frequent when entering the small cities along the highways. Checkpoints also cause pile-ups. The general idea seems to be to drive as fast as possible, passing the cars and trucks on your right and left, slowing down only for speed bumps, checkpoints, and toll plazas. It's a reckless ride, and I often close my eyes to try and stave off my panic. My husband makes fun of me using my imaginary brake on the passenger side of the car, which is on the right, by the way, in the British style.

And then there's the shopping. In a village such as ours, there are small corner shops selling basic necessities such as packaged goods, boxed milk, bottled water, chips, cigarettes, biscuits, and laundry detergent. Large cities like Islamabad, Lahore, and Karachi have supermarkets, some of them quite extensive and modern. We go to the supermarket once a month to buy hard-to-find items such as breakfast cereal, deodorant, canned tuna, and instant coffee. Fresh fruits and vegetables are purchased from stands in town or from wooden carts called *rehris.* These are basically pushcarts with one to three wheels handled by the *waalas,* who circulate the neighborhoods. Housewives and servants come out of their homes to buy what they need for the day. Not everybody has a refrigerator, and if they do, the lack of electricity doesn't always keep food fresh. I quickly learn that the customer is not to handle the merchandise, but can protest if the salesman throws in some unripe or rotten produce as part of the sale. Things are weighed in grams and kilos, not ounces, pounds, or number of pieces. Old-fashioned scales with weights help determine the proper amounts.

Chickens are chosen alive, then killed before your eyes if you care to watch. The nauseating sight of the butcher's bloody apron is enough to make me walk away once I've chosen my birds. The meat is certainly fresh, though I can't vouch for the health of the chickens! Fresh fish from Rawal Lake is available at the side of the road where the *waala* will clean it for a small tip, but once the weather gets hot enough to melt the ice, the stands close up or switch to selling something less perishable. Food is local and seasonal, unless it comes in a box or bag. Nestle has monopolized the packaged juice, bottled water, and yogurt markets. Pakistanis can buy fresh yogurt in shops, but I need to be careful, since the tap water used to make it is dangerous for me. Fresh juice made from sugarcane with no water added is a delicious treat.

Other *waalas* sell household goods like sheets, tablecloths, and pots and pans from their carts. Still others go through town advertising their services for knife and scissor sharpening or sewing machine repair. Some of these men still call out their wares and services with rhythmic chants. Others have small speakers that repeat their sing-song ditties. Initially, it's pleasant to listen to, but it quickly becomes annoying. Between the *waalas'* cries and the blaring *athans* emanating from every street corner masjid, Pakistan has a serious noise pollution problem.

There is other pollution as well. Unfortunately, only the wealthy areas of the big cities have adequate trash pick-up and disposal systems. In the villages, everything ends up on the ground and in the open sewers that run along the streets. Shoppers are not people here, but the word used for the ubiquitous plastic bags that litter the ground everywhere you turn. Trash collects wherever the wind blows it. Animals like chickens and goats graze right on top of the trash. Water buffalo, cattle, and occasionally horses are left to graze on any trashy, grassy plot available, watched over by shepherd boys who should probably be in school.

Both small and large cities have bazaars. These are large outdoor markets that convene on certain days of the week. For example, the Itwaar Bazaar is only open on Sunday. Everyone goes in search of bargains, for the stalls in the bazaar are cheaper than the shops in town. Some old men make a business out of carrying the many parcels customers accumulate. And, like everywhere else in Pakistan, there are the beggars. Give money to one and you will have ten to twenty more come and swarm you. They are mostly children, though there are the occasional mothers and old women too. The beggars, the heat, and the bargaining make the bazaar a difficult place for me to shop. But it can't be beat as an interesting place to stroll and purchase anything you can imagine, from ladies' lingerie to spices and household goods. It's like a giant flea market.

Pakistan is a rough-and-tumble place. People are desperate to earn a few rupees to buy their family's next meal. This is reflected in the attitude of the shopkeepers. Bargaining is essential and requires language skills that are certainly beyond what I have as a beginner. One needs to know the numbers and especially the abbreviations for those numbers. If a shopkeeper realizes you do not know, he will automatically raise the price as high as he can. There are many times when my husband asks me to just point at an item I want. If I open my mouth, anyone will know I am a foreigner and deliberately cheat me out of my money. It's not good Islamic behavior. It's desperation but also greed that motivates them to act this way. When they see a foreigner, they automatically think he or she is rich and can well afford to be cheated a bit. Maybe they are right, but it does make shopping a stressful experience. Conversely, if you stay in Pakistan for more than just a short time, you must start thinking in terms of their currency, not yours. My husband is earning a good salary but it's in rupees, not dollars, so I have to start thinking accordingly. The Pakistani rupee is decreasing in value at an alarming rate. When I first went to Pakistan, the exchange rate was eighty-five rupees to a US dollar. Now (in 2016) it takes one hundred and five rupees to equal a dollar. Rents are high and so is the cost of food and all utilities. It is a serious mistake to keep saying, "Oh, this purse is only five dollars." Five dollars is almost five hundred twenty-five rupees, just seventy-five rupees short of the money a man might make to break stones, by hand, in the hot sun, for an entire day

Woe unto those who give short measure: Those who, when they are to receive their due from other people demand that it be given in full- but when they are to measure or weigh whatever they owe to others, give less than what is due! (S. Mutaffifeen, v. 1–2)

Badshahi Masjid, Lahore

239

CHAPTER 38

Bloom Where You're Planted

Child Labor in Pakistan

I came to Pakistan in mid-August, 2010 with a plan to return home by Thanksgiving. This would give me enough time to decide whether or not I could make a life for myself with my husband in Pakistan. Once the novelty of the place wore off, what, besides Asad, would sustain me enough to be so far away from my parents, children, and grandchildren for months at a time? Pakistan is certainly a difficult place to live. If Asad had had the choice to stay in the United States, he would have. Life is so much more comfortable there. In Pakistan, one has to cope with shortages of all kinds on a daily basis. We never know when the power will go out, nor for how long. Eating by candlelight may seem romantic, but I can tell you, cooking by candlelight is not!

And once I had seen the sights, I did indeed become bored. After all, I worked my entire adult life. What could I do here, and who would I do it with? Asad worked all week and wanted to rest on the weekends. His family did not live near us. I was starting to meet other women but did not consider anyone a close friend yet. And then there was the language barrier. While everyone in Pakistan speaks a little English, it was not enough for a real conversation, and my Urdu was slow to develop.

As a former British colony, Pakistanis have bought into the idea that English is more important than Urdu. Of course, it is true that English is a global language; yet media marketing, power, and politics have made it so to the extent that languages like Urdu are actually being forgotten. My husband is vehemently opposed to the eradication of Urdu. Along with the loss of native language comes the loss of cultural identity. He himself is the product of a British education, and while he is fluent in both languages, he prefers to write poetry and literary essays in Urdu. But for me, speaking English is a job skill in Pakistan. I thought, *If everyone in Pakistan wants to speak English, why not start teaching again?* I had taught English for twelve years in New Jersey before starting my administrative career in Michigan. I'd recently earned a certificate in teaching English as a second language, so why not take on some students for tutoring?

I mention this to Asad, and he suggests that I visit the private schools on the main road of our village to volunteer my services. Out of the four schools I visit, one principal is seriously interested in having a native English speaker on staff. At least one of the others seem to think I could be some kind of spy or that they would get into trouble with the government for having a foreigner on staff. Madam Huda says, "I'm embarrassed to tell you the salary we can offer," and I tell her not to worry about it. Volunteers are a rarity in Pakistan, and she jumps at the opportunity. We set up a schedule and I begin teaching conversational English for two hours, three times a week to third, fourth, and fifth graders. It is more difficult than I think it will be. When you do not speak the local language, it is easy for the students to not pay attention to you. Even in a private school such as this one, English is a textbook subject to be memorized. Neither the students nor the teachers have any experience with actual conversation. I achieve some moderate success by trying to teach a few songs to the younger children. Madam Huda capitalizes on my presence by having me attend parent-teacher conferences. In a highly competitive private school market, she makes her school stand out. The parents are duly impressed.

It's during the five-minute walk from home to school and back that I start to notice gangs of dusty, ragged children working by the roadside, cutting dry grass or picking up recyclable trash. The recyclables go into the empty rice sacks they've slung over their shoulders. One little boy is carrying a sickle that's almost as big as he is. He cuts some dry grass and then tries to pile it on the seat of an old rusty bicycle that another boy is wheeling by the handlebars. These children are either barefoot or wearing broken plastic sandals. They themselves are as grubby and tatty as the grass they cut. They are not in school, though they are certainly of school age. The oldest looks to be no more than ten years old. In the evening, I ask my husband about them.

"Who are all these children I see picking up trash by the side of the road? Why aren't they in school?"

"They have no money for school," he tells me.

"What about the government school? Isn't it free?"

He gives me a sad smile, "Even the government schools aren't free. They charge money for books, uniforms, and other fees. Besides, those children are Pathan, mainly from Afghanistan. Their families are refugees here. They are not registered with the government and have no proper documentation so they can't attend school," he concludes.

I'm quite perplexed by this because in the US even homeless children can go to public schools, which are free of charge.

Once I'm aware of these children, I see them everywhere. One day, I see a bunch of them gathered near the creek where the water buffalo like to wallow. They are gesturing excitedly at something lying near the bottom of a tree. "*Sayb, Sayb,*" one of the younger girls shouts. I wonder at her excitement, so I look down toward the creek and see a windfall of old rotten apples decaying at the bottom of a tree.

They notice me too, since I do not wear *niqab* and have a foreign sounding voice when I greet them with *salaams*. They usually smile back, and after a few more encounters, I know them by name. If I have a couple of coins or some biscuits in my pocket, I give them out, but there are always more hands reaching than I have money or biscuits for. The boldest ones follow me to the grocery store, and I buy bags of chips or biscuits to distribute. This makes them very joyful.

One day, the doorbell rings. *"Bhaaji, Bhaaji,"* some young voices call out. This means older sister and is a term of respect. My husband and I go to the door and find a small group of street children there, asking us for bottles. As a foreigner in Pakistan, I drink only bottled water, so we happen to have many bottles. We lead the kids to our stockpile and indicate that they can take all the bottles. They think they've discovered a gold mine! Each boy and girl scrambles to get as many bottles as they can. They frenziedly stuff their sacks full of plastic and their mouths full of biscuits. Of course, they come back the next day, and the next, hoping for just as many bottles, which we don't have, but there is always something to give them; a cardboard container, a packing box, plastics, broken glass. They want to take everything and anything they can trade for a few rupees.

Recycling is a cottage industry for refugee and migrant families in Pakistan. It's how they earn their bread. One large sack of recyclables is worth about Rs. 30, enough for three *rotis* to contribute to the family's evening meal. When the kids bring home full sacks, their female relatives sort the trash, and the men take it to the recycling centers to exchange it for cash. It's weighed by the kilo. So glass or metal, even if it's sharp and rusty and cuts your toes and fingers, is a prized possession.

After getting the trash and having a bite to eat, the children are ready to play. The girls begin asking if they can play in the courtyard. I enjoy watching their games. They like to play a kind of hopscotch where they draw a court in the dust and throw a stone to determine how they should move. I buy some jump ropes and balls for their visits. They are tough kids who fight over who gets to hold the ball or whose turn it is to jump. But they fill my quiet home with the sounds of childhood, something I've missed since leaving my school and family life in the States. I begin writing about the children on my blog.

Blog Post: November 11, 2010

Pakistan is a tough place to live, but you can easily fall in love here. Laal-meenahis about seven, but she is tall, like a nine-year-old. She's thin and lanky, but strong, and she has beautiful, brown, understanding eyes. Anaargul is a little older, about 12 maybe, with the deepest, most glittering eyes of all. There is a whole group of them, including Heer Bibi, who wants to wash every chance she gets, especially her hair. There is no clean running water in the ramshackle huts they call home. They sleep three, four or more to a bed, a simple charpay meant for one. They dream of having a double bed when they get married. After the bed comes the swaddled baby lying on the bed that Anaargul fashions from clay this morning. Not to be outdone, little Shazia makes a whole man and they all chuckle at her creation.

These are my Afghan girls. There are also three boys. Ali is the oldest, tall and lanky. A younger boy is short and chubby. He likes chasing the girls and climbing the columns that flank the sides of our home. The third boy is quiet and dignified. He usually likes to stay out of trouble. Ali recently found a broken MP3 player somewhere in his ramblings and was trying to get it to work. But when he saw my camera batteries had died, he took the batteries out of that MP3 and put them in my camera. It still didn't work, so he tried some other batteries he had in his pocket. No luck. He collects all kinds of scrap metal, which fetches more money than plastic bottles and discarded cardboard boxes. So does the broken glass I've seen them stuff into their bags.

They eat lunch, and then play their games. They love the space of the courtyard for tag, climbing the columns, and high jump games. They are highly imaginative and spontaneous. They've never been to school. One can't even imagine their boundless energy being contained in a classroom. That doesn't mean they shouldn't have the opportunity of going to school. For now, the world is their classroom, with all the harsh and complex reality that is Pakistan today. They are all our children.

One night I dream of a courtyard full of children, laughing, singing, playing... and reading. I tell my husband of this dream and he raises his hands and says, "*Ameen* (May it be so)." A friend from Michigan who reads my blog writes back, "You seem to love these children a lot. Why don't you start a school for them? I'll help you." That is all I need to hear.

I'll never forget the day Saima, Anaargul, and Marina, the older crowd of girls, save my life on the highway. I've hailed a taxi to go to the Daewoo bus station for a four-hour trip to Lahore. After I enter the taxi, the driver asks me how to get there! As is our usual plan, if a driver doesn't seem to know where to go, I call my husband and he instructs the driver in Urdu. This usually works just fine. But this time, after yelling at the driver, Asad tells me, "Get out of that taxi and get another one. This guy doesn't know where he is going."

Okay...

I gesture for the driver to stop. We are less than a quarter mile from where we started out. I hop out and he has the nerve to ask me for money. Asad, still on the phone, tells me to just walk away, as I have already started doing. Suddenly, who should materialize by the roadside, as if out of thin air? There are my girls, walking back to Chatha from Chaak Shazaad, a bigger town where they have gone to collect recyclable trash. There they are, walking in a graceful line, carrying bundles of dry grass on their heads and trash bags on their hips the way mothers carry babies. Looking for all the world like the beautiful young women they are soon to be.

We are delighted to see each other. They take one look at the taxi driver, and then glance quizzically at me. In my very poor Urdu, I explain the situation and they start yelling at the driver, all of them together until he drives away! I've never been so happy to see anyone in my life! They stay and chat with me and then wave goodbye as I get settled in a new taxi. When I get back from Lahore, they are already in the courtyard, making me more tea sets.

My three months in Pakistan are almost up. I'm due to go home for Thanksgiving with my family, but I have found my purpose and a reason, besides Asad, to return. I will start a school for these children. Once I'm home, I begin telling friends and family of my intentions. Most of the Canton community know me and trust me as the former principal of CAI. Many of them are of Indo-Pak descent. They understand the problems of their homeland and are happy to contribute to this project. Saima, who had written that first supportive email, sets up a meeting in her home for people who would be interested in funding the project. Backed by this group of donors, we form a non-profit corporation, register it with the State of Michigan, and open a bank account. I get busy with visualizing the dream and Sitara School is born.

Sitara means star in Urdu. It is one of the first words I've learned. My husband's legal name, Tariq, signifies a particular morning star in Arabic. Asad, which means lion, is a nickname he chose for himself in adolescence. I see the children who will soon attend our school as little stars. Each one can shine brightly with the light of faith and knowledge, if only given the opportunity. Maybe this project is just the sort of thing my Sufi sheikh, Sidi Muhammad, had in mind when he told me I needed to "give more to people."

In preparation for my return to Pakistan and to raise some money for the school, I sell off most of the furniture in the house on Amber Court. I also decide to get rid of all thirty of my journals. I spend a few days selecting significant excerpts from each one. Then I ceremoniously feed the remaining pages, piece by piece, to a roaring fire. As the books burn, I reflect on the contents of their pages: the good, the bad, and the ugly. Since I can't take these books with me on my travels, destroying them is the safest thing to do. If something should happen to me, I wouldn't want my children to be burdened with the contents of those pages.

Back in Pakistan, Asad is getting ready for my return and the start of Sitara School in February, 2011. We plan to use an extra room of our home as our first classroom. He equips the room with tables, chairs, and a whiteboard. Everything is in place when I get back. We advertise for a teacher, someone who is knowledgeable about the national curriculum and the books we'll need to get started. Madam Noreen comes to see us. She has experience teaching prep class, which is like kindergarten in the US. Soon she is taking me to bookstores and purchasing school supplies.

My street children know I am back, and they know something exciting is going to happen. I began by giving them crayons and coloring books when they come to visit. I want to see if they are able to sit still, at least for a few moments at a time. They like the crayons, although they sometimes fight over the colors. To my surprise, a few of the older girls can already write their names and some numbers in Urdu and English. They are eager to show me their skills. My husband says they may have attended one of the temporary schools set up by the UN when they were living in Afghanistan. It is heartening to me that they may have had some type of school experience already.

We soon show them the classroom. The whiteboard has just been hung on the wall. The desks are in place. When they see that room, their eyes become as round as saucers. They run around, touching everything in their giddy excitement. Madam Noreen explains that we are starting a school for them and that they should return the next day with their families and friends. Sitara School is taking on a life of its own. I am humming with anticipation and excitement but also apprehension. Can I really handle this? Thank God for Madam Noreen!

My small group of Afghan children get the word out. The next day there are twenty curious kids of all ages at my door. One of the first things we teach them is how to wash their hands and faces with soap. They don't have running water at home, so this is a novelty, as is our indoor toilet. They know how to squat, but need instructions on how to wash and how to flush. We are really starting with the basics, but Madam Noreen is a practical woman. She did not sign up for toilet training, but realizes it's what the children need, so she obliges!

I have to quickly learn some survival Urdu in order to communicate with my students. I try to memorize the names of the colors, and some schoolroom phrases like *write your name, form a circle, share, don't hit.* These feisty kids need a lot of basic training before they can sit down to learn.

We feed the children a hearty lunch every school day that first year. We hire a wonderful cook named Samina. She is one of a kind. She comes from a Christian background but is married to a Muslim. She has an older daughter from a previous marriage and a cute little toddler nicknamed Nimmi. Samina is just one of the people Allah (SWT) sends to Sitara. On her second day with us, she brings a large clock for the school room and tells me, "Time is very important and should not be wasted." Her excellent work ethic comes from her father, who had been the cook on an American military base when Samina was a child.

Most Pakistanis do not live by the clock. It isn't until a year later, when we begin teaching the students to tell time, that I realize it is a new concept for them. They aren't used to counting hours and minutes. Things just happen when they happen in their lives. Learning how to tell time actually means learning the concept of the passage of time and how we can measure it. For the first time, it dawns on me that many people are not late because they are inconsiderate, they are late because they do not have a clear concept of hours and minutes. Perhaps this is not surprising in a country that is 60 percent illiterate.

The first year, many children come to school just because of the lunch. We serve lentils or vegetables with rice most of the time. Once in a very long while, we have chicken. Red meat is reserved for holidays and special occasions. In our second year, when we have many more children, we begin serving only a snack, such as fruit or biscuits. We realize that lack of food is not as much of a problem for these children as education is, and we prioritize our spending in favor of books, computers, and teachers' salaries. We do need to teach manners regarding food however. Most of the children come from big families. They are used to eating quickly, shoving as much food into their mouths as possible, and grabbing more before someone else does. This is especially true of the boys, in whom these behaviors are condoned. They think nothing of grabbing a piece of roti or meat out of the hands of a younger or slower child. Girls are taught to hang back and prefer their brothers over themselves. They are often charged with feeding younger siblings and putting the needs of others before their own. We have to make both boys and girls understand that we have enough for everyone to get their fair share.

Many of the eight to twelve-year-old girls come to school with a baby on their hip. This is because their mothers work outside the home or have too many other children to deal with and want a break. Most of the babies don't wear diapers, even cloth ones. The girls take them outside when they think the baby might need to relieve itself. Imagine trying to focus on learning when you have to worry about whether the baby needs to go!

When we say "no babies," some of the girls don't return to school. So we compromise by starting a play group for the young children who are at least three years old. I buy toys at the bazaar and set the little ones up in our living room area so they don't distract their older siblings. Samina, who brings her own young daughter, watches the babies while I take over when she needs to be in the kitchen.

Regular attendance is an ongoing problem. Many students drop in and out of school as it suits them and their parents. Other students come for a little while, then disappear. I am told they go back to their villages, which are usually in northern Pakistan or Afghanistan, for a wedding or another occasion. They may be gone a month or more before returning. We try offering toys or other prizes to students who attend regularly and come to school on time, but this strategy has limited success.

We hire Madam Rizwana, our second teacher, once we have more than twenty children. Madam Noreen and Madam Rizwana both live in the village and walk to school, along with some of the students, who come from their side of town. The walk is about twenty minutes, through whatever weather we have. Sometimes the teachers get a ride, but the students often arrive, wet, muddy or shivering. They have to wash their feet before coming into the classroom. In the winter, they all huddle around one of several kerosene or gas cylinders we use to heat the space. It's more warmth than most of them have at home.

With two teachers, we can divide the students into two groups, roughly determined by age and ability. As far as curriculum and learning, most of our children have to start with the basics of ABCs and 123s in both Urdu and English. Even the ten-year-olds have not been to school consistently and therefore have gaps in their understanding of basic concepts. For many, Urdu is a second language. At home, they speak Pashto, Dari, or Hindko, dialects of the northern regions of Pakistan and Afghanistan. Migrants from the south might speak Punjabi or Sindhi. Every school in Pakistan, even public schools in the poorest villages, will claim to have *English Medium Instruction.* Unfortunately, English is seen as a superior language to Urdu. It is a global, international language. It is the language of the conquerors. Every Pakistani is convinced that learning English will help their child succeed in life. While this may be true, the society, from the top down, has thrown out the baby with the bathwater. They have devalued the national language of Urdu to such an extent that even three-year-olds in play group are taught words like "red" and "circle" in English instead of their native tongue.

From a pedagogical standpoint, this is just plain wrong. Study after study has shown the importance of the mother tongue in understanding basic concepts such as number, shape, color, letter, and letter sounds. Our brain is programmed from birth to think in the language of our home culture. Asking three-year-olds to start their formal education in a foreign language places a huge roadblock in their way. Based on my own educational training, I have gone against all conventional practice in Pakistan and encouraged my teachers to use the children's mother tongues in the classroom. This is a challenge to the teachers, because it goes against their own training in turn. I've had to constantly interrupt lessons to remind them to use the mother tongue, or at least the national language, Urdu.

At first, only Madam Rizwana agrees with the importance of this practice. She has a master's degree in Social Studies and appreciates the value of culture and language. She often talks about the traditional arts and practices of "our Pakistan." On holidays and special occasions, she wears beautifully embellished *shalwar kameez* styled in the manner of her ancestral village in southern Punjab.

Madam Rizwana is currently the principal of the Sitara, though I held that role myself from 2011 to 2013. My job in the early years is to teach English and computer skills to students and teachers. When we establish the Teachers' Institute in 2012, I begin teaching formal pedagogy and hire a young man to teach computers. As the founder of the program, I 'm also the school director. Asad takes care of the school finances including bills and major purchases. He writes quarterly and yearly financial reports for our Board of Trustees in the United States.

The school year in Pakistan begins in April and ends in March of the following year right after final exams. After Result Day, when students get their report cards and awards, school is dismissed until the first week of April when the new term begins. Summer vacation in the capital region of

Islamabad is at least two months, depending on how hot the weather becomes in June. I am leaving the country at the end of May in 2011, before the real heat of summer sets in and will return in August to help reopen the school. Before going home, however, I suffer a nasty bout of food poisoning.

The week I'm scheduled to leave, many people want me to visit their homes. I also want to treat my staff to a nice lunch at an Islamabad hotel. The Pakistani version of an all-you-can-eat buffet is usually held in hotels at tea time, which is at 4:00 pm. A regular tea consists of biscuits and tea with milk and sugar, boiled till it is thick and rich. A high tea will also include food. The hotels have made a practice of offering these buffets for a set price, and they are very popular. One sweltering afternoon in May, I take Madam Noreen, Madam Rizwana, and Madam Samina to tea. It is too hot to eat much, but of course I want to try all the delicacies on offer. There are finger sandwiches as well as bread, rice, and a variety of curries, including chicken, beef, and fish.

It is hard to know if I initially get sick there or if it's the fresh mango *lassi*, or smoothie, I drink a few hours later at a student's home. Or is it a combination of all my gluttony? The next day I have a major case of diarrhea. I try the local remedies to no avail. I get sicker and sicker, till finally I have no control over myself and can't even make it to the bathroom. That's when Samina steps in. She sizes up the situation, exclaims, "Madam, this is not good," and calls a cab to take us to the only decent hospital in Islamabad. She uses the address of her former employer to have us admitted since we don't actually live in the city itself. Samina helps me through the admission process, which consists of a bunch of people talking all at once to a man behind a window. I am taken to a bed in what appears to be a waiting room for women. I am very weak at this point, and I'm happy just to lie down. I am given an IV. Samina waits faithfully by my side throughout the ordeal until Asad arrives from work. She explains to the curious bystanders that I am an American madam, and she is my housekeeper.

I'm not sure how much time passes while I lay there in that sort of twilight state, but at least I do not have to use a chamber pot. I am curled in a fetal position and become gradually aware that if I extend my legs, I can touch something that moves at the end of the bed! *Is there an animal of some kind down there, like maybe a big rat?* I scrunch myself up in fear. When I hear the lumpy bundle groan in pain, I realize there's another woman at the other end of the bed! I am wondering if maybe I'm hallucinating this woman when Asad rushes into the room. I whisper "Asad, is there someone else at the other end of the bed?" He affirms that yes, there is. "They don't have enough beds in here for each person to have their own. Welcome to Pakistan. Would you like to get out of here now?" With that, he helps me to the car, Samina follows, and we all go home.

I am due to leave the country in three days. Asad worries that I'll be too sick to leave. I just stay in bed and let life happen around me. Samina has to pack my bags. On the third day, before going to the airport, Asad makes me some eggs. It is the first and only time I've eaten scrambled eggs with chunks of garlic, but it's the thought that counts.

Chatha Bakhtawar Bazaar with students, 2012

CHAPTER 39

Sitara's Success

Welcome to Sitara, 2013

From 2010 to 2016, I crossed the globe five times, traveling from North America to Pakistan and back again. Along the way, I enjoyed visits to Istanbul and Konya, two vacations in the Emirates, and one in Lebanon with my daughter's family. I also spent one year in Saudi Arabia. My dream of teaching and traveling had become a reality.

I enjoyed my summers in the States and Canada visiting family and friends. During those six years, Imran, Sajdah, and Safiyeh got married. Tahera and Imran now have children of their own—my grandchildren. My parents are great-grandparents many times over. Family is precious and irreplaceable, and mine has been very accommodating as I've crisscrossed the globe. I've lived with my parents and oldest child for months at a time since I no longer have a stateside home of my own. In Pakistan, I'm at home with just Asad now, after he and I shared our first two homes with the school.

By the time I return to Pakistan in August of 2011, Asad and Sitara have both moved out of our one-story home and into a bigger facility where we'll live on the second floor and the school will use the lower level. But as the school expands they need the upper floor too, so we move out for the sake of our privacy, quiet, and sanity.

Our new place is just a few streets away, and I can walk around the corner and down the dirt lane to my school. The children always wait for me at various lookout points. The first ones to spot me shout, *"Madam aa rahi hae!* (Madam is coming). "*They push and shove to be the first to shake my hand and fight for the privilege of opening our gate. I feel like a movie star every morning!

Asad's nephew Noori comes to live with us and join the school. He is five years old and a wonderful child to have around. Both Asad and I enjoy the experience of having a "grandchild" in the house. I introduce Noori to the joys of bedtime stories, pancake breakfasts, and biscuits with milk. I make him wash his hands, brush his teeth, and use a handkerchief. He stays with us a year, and I miss him when he goes back to his village, where he is able to skip a class level in school because he's learned so much English at Sitara. In 2016, Noori is ten years old, living with his family in the village and studying at a government school. He still remembers pancakes, Choco-Prince biscuits, and one or two friends from Sitara.

Sitara is improving in many ways. We have formal registration documents and requirements that include national identification cards for the parents and immunization records for the children. Refugees fleeing war or natural disaster often have no paper work and must go through the process of registering with the local authorities. These documents are required for us to exist as a registered school in the district, and we need this status in order to get our textbooks from the Ministry of Education.

In Sitara's first years, it was rare that we got a student who had actually been to school somewhere before and already had a grade report. Whether students were five or ten years old, they were all starting school for the first time. Some older boys even came to enroll themselves without their parents. That is how eager they were to learn.

Going to school is an accomplishment for these children. We want them to feel proud of themselves and their school, so we have uniforms made. The first uniforms are a lavender and white *shalwar kameez* for the girls and a grey one for the boys. These tunic tops and loose fitting trousers are the standard traditional dress for all Pakistanis, whether children or adults. In 2013, we switch to a ready-made uniform with a blue and white-checkered *shalwar kameez* for the girls. The boys wear a checkered shirt and gray pants, in the Western style, as is more popular in schools and among the parents. We order uniforms, shoes, socks, and sweaters and distribute them free of cost to the students. Uniform Day is a special occasion, and shoe fittings may take a whole week as Asad and the teachers go back and forth to the stores to get the right sizes for everyone. Some students want to save the nice clothes and shoes for weddings and other occasions, but we explain that the clothes and shoes are for school and that they should wear them every day. We continue to emphasize cleanliness and see most students making an effort to wash their faces, comb their hair, and trim their nails, especially on Fridays.

Once we have more than fifty children enrolled, we divide them into more or less age-appropriate groups. Our very first students have progressed beyond the basics. We have a play group, nursery, prep class, and first and second classes. Students in third class and up are mainly from our original group of students. They continue to progress at their own levels. The goal is to get them ready to take their fifth-class exams, which they begin doing in 2013.

Our school has eight desktop computers and a data projector, making us the envy of the neighborhood. There is no other school in our village where students as young as seven years old can learn word processing. Technology is a shortcut to learning for these children, and they love it. I research websites that teach phonics and math skills, and show the teachers how to use them. Technology in the classroom is new for the teachers too, so I hire a young guy from COMSATS, the local technological university, to run a computer skills course for the staff. Of course, power outages are a fact of life in Pakistan, so there must always be a no-tech plan B waiting in the wings, just in case.

My favorite time of the day is the early morning, before assembly begins. Students come to school early to sit in the library and read. Sometimes they bring a book to my office for some one-on-one reading—the absolute best use of my time.

The thing that hurts me the most is when kids just disappear. They go to their village and don't return, or they move out of the area without letting us know. Sometimes it's more dramatic than that. Once, when one of the older girls leaves, we're told she's needed to watch her younger siblings at home. A few months later, however, we learn she'd been taken to the village to be married. Although we don't know her exact age, she couldn't have been more than fourteen or fifteen.

One Saturday morning, Asad and I are at school when a Pathan mother comes in dragging her four-year-old daughter by the hand. This girl, named Mina, is tiny and ragged; she never smiles. But she is extremely smart and one of our best young students. I smile in welcome and ask Mina to run and get her notebook to show her mama. Mom starts speaking to me in a loud, agitated tone of voice. I can't understand much, but I hear the word *roti*. Assuming she's asking for bread, I run to the kitchen to see if we have any. When I return, I find Asad engaged in a shouting match with the mother. She grabs her daughter by the hand and storms out. I ask him what has happened, since I am clueless. He says, "She doesn't want her daughter in school anymore."

"Why?" I ask uncomprehendingly. Mina was doing so well with Madam Noreen and could write all her letters in both English and Urdu. "She asked me for *roti*. I went to the kitchen to get it and came back to hear the two of you arguing. What did you say to her?" I'm interrogating him now, thinking he's picked a fight with her for some reason.

"I told her that she needed to think about the girl's future, but she's thinking only about the next meal. You thought she wanted *roti*, but what she said to you is, 'Who will earn her bread?'" I am shocked into silence by the thought that this four-year-old child is expected to earn a daily wage. A few days later, I see Mina with the rest of her family, dressed in a ragged frock a few sizes too big for her. She is standing barefoot in the swamp, picking through the trash. I go home, suddenly very tired. I get into bed, pull the covers over my head, and cry myself to sleep. *Am I making any difference at all in the lives of these children?*

Alhamdulillah, there are also successes. We take the students on field trips to national heritage and history sites. These experiences open their eyes to the world around them. As our principal, Madam Rizwana says, "They only know this village and the one they come from. None of the rest of the world exists for them unless we show it to them." Fauzia, an older girl, has been struggling to read English until the day we go to Lok Virsa, the national heritage museum in Islamabad. We stand there looking at the cultural exhibits highlighting different regions of the country and their handicrafts. All of a sudden, I feel Fauzia tugging my sleeve. She pulls me over to a large sign in English and begins reading it aloud! I praise her and her face breaks into a delighted smile. She continues for the rest of the trip reading the signs out loud, as she realizes she has indeed learned to read English. In 2015 Fauzia passes her fifth-class exam. She is still at Sitara. I am told her father comes to Result Day (Report Card Day) and parent meetings crying tears of gratitude because his three children are at Sitara. He himself is an illiterate man who cuts stone for a living, but he wants better for his children, both the girl and the boys.

Sitara keeps me very busy. I try to visit the classes and model best teaching practices. Teachers in Pakistan receive little classroom training. Schools and universities, alike, require only memorization and regurgitation, the lowest form of learning. Cheating is a way of life here, and it's no different in the field of education. But that's not what I want for our students and our school. Along with teaching them academics, we are teaching them how to be Muslims and what being Muslim means in terms of their daily behavior and interactions with others.

A Sitara student is:

> Regular and Punctual
> Hardworking
> Clean (Inside and Out)
> Truthful and Honest
> Respectful

These qualities are painted on the courtyard wall and reviewed on a regular basis in morning assemblies, when we sing the national anthem, and recite *Lab Pai Aate hai Dua*, a poem written for children by Sir Allama Muhammad Iqbal.

The Sitara Teachers' Institute (S.T.I.) I started in 2012 works to more effectively educate my staff and other aspiring teachers. I begin preparing and teaching lectures in the evening hours and after school. I'm impressed with the caliber of student teachers who attend from other schools, as well as our own.

The philosophy of STI focuses on *Teaching for Understanding*. This also becomes the motto of our school. All the reading and study I've done in the area of brain-compatible learning has made me a firm believer in this tenet of pedagogy. Both children and adults learn best when they can connect new knowledge to what they are already familiar with, or what is relevant to them. I am inspired to impart what I know to the current and next generation of teachers in Pakistan.

Before I leave for the summer in 2013, one of my young teachers has a dream. She tells me she sees herself helping me across a field of flowers. I tell her, "You are the future of Sitara, and you will carry on this work when I am gone." *Alhamdulillah*, it is so. She is Asma, now our school's vice principal and the STI's main teacher. Sitara has a core group of dedicated teachers who live in the neighborhood and are committed to the school's success. The future is in good and trustworthy hands.

My longing comes to my lips as a prayer
O Lord, may my life be like a candle
May the world's darkness disappear because of me
May it light up with my sparkling light

May I add to the elegance of my homeland
As a flower makes the garden elegant

May my life be like that of a moth, O Lord
May I love the lamp of knowledge, O Lord

May my life be supportive of the poor
May loving the old, the suffering, be my way

O Lord, Protect me from the evil ways
Show me the path leading to the good

(Lab Pai Aate hai Dua, by Sir Muhammad Iqbal, translated by T.A.
Khan)

CHAPTER 40

Balancing Act

Hunza Valley farmland, 2016

In addition to the people I meet through Sitara, I begin to establish strong friendships in Pakistan. I join the New Muslim Club, an international group of women in Islamabad who are married to Pakistanis. Only a handful of these women are new Muslims who have recently embraced the faith. The ones in my age bracket (fifty and above), however, had mostly come to Pakistan as young women and embraced the faith before or soon after marrying Pakistani men. They have raised children in Pakistan and studied the religion here, through courses at the International Islamic University and Al Huda International, or online through less formal classes and one-on-one tutoring. At least one of them has memorized the entire Quran, a very praiseworthy accomplishment considering Arabic is not her first language.

The purpose of our monthly meetings is both social and academic. We meet in a member's home or apartment and open the meeting with a reading from the Quran. We then have a guest speaker talk about some important aspect of the faith. We always share a delicious international lunch and reserve time to enjoy each other's company. The women are from all around the globe, including China, Japan, the Philippines, Belgium, France, England, Canada, and the U.S., not to mention a few Pakistani members as well. The global nature of this group's membership reminds me of the days I spent with the Muslim Students' Association in New York during my college days. Here, I encounter a similar feeling of love, and the feeling of sisterhood that unites us women from around the globe.

I'm also able to pursue my interest in Sufism in Pakistan, where many different Sufi groups co-exist. My husband belongs to the Chisti-Qadri order, which means he follows the teachings of Moinuddin Chisti and Abdul Qadir Jilani, two famous Sufi scholars of the twelfth and thirteenth centuries AD. My husband's *murshid,* or teacher, passed away many years ago (may Allah be pleased with him). Asad was one of the calligraphers who worked on his tomb, a simple but beautiful structure. One of Asad's fellow students and spiritual companions, Baba Mohamad Jaan, becomes my *murshid.* There is a language barrier between us, but my husband translates any matter of importance. Baba Jaani is known and loved by legions of people in our part of the country. He is kind, loving, and wise. Baba does not offer advice unless asked and then it is usually offered in the kindest and gentlest manner. I am happy to join their affiliation. However, just as I have done throughout my life, I never give my allegiance totally to any one teacher. My complete allegiance and obedience is only to Allah and His messenger, Muhammad ﷺ . I consider any other form of submission to be something that might lead me into the dangers of *shirk.*

Shirk is a very serious offense in Islam. Allah (SWT) states in the Quran that it is the only sin He will not forgive. *Shirk* means setting up partners with Allah and imbuing them with powers that should be reserved only for Him. I am always thankful that I came into Islam from Judaism and not Christianity because Judaism is inherently monotheistic, whereas many branches of Christianity worship Jesus (peace be upon him) as the son of God. To Muslims, Jesus is a prophet, just like the other prophets, Adam, Moses, Abraham, and Muhammad 🕌, peace be upon them all. The prophets may intercede for us on the Day of Judgment. Ordinary people, including our teachers, are not prophets. We may perceive them as holy men and women who are spiritually more advanced than us, though only Allah knows the truth about someone's spiritual level. In Islam, it is incumbent on each individual to study and learn the faith so he or she does not lapse into *shirk* by attributing God-like powers to another human being. The problem in Pakistan is that more than 50 percent of the population is illiterate. They cannot learn the basics of the religion themselves and they often rely on holy men, whom they call saints, to intervene with Allah on their behalf. Pakistan is a land of shrines dedicated to these holy men. Every village has at least one shrine and some villages have one on every corner. The most famous deceased holy men have entire complexes built in their honor. Most people also rely on the holy ones that live amongst them for advice, spiritual counsel, intercession, and *taweez.*

Taweez are Quranic incantations that some people use as others might use magic spells to attain something they desire. These rituals become complicated, and people who pose as holy men sometimes exploit others, extracting high fees for their "spiritual services." My husband and I stay away from these doubtful matters. On the other side of the coin, many of the *mullahs,* or religious leaders of the various Islamic movements of Pakistan have been unduly influenced by Wahhabism, an overly strict and sometimes extreme version of Islam in which even Prophet Muhammad🕌 is divested of spiritual power. The reason given by Wahhabis to view him and all prophets as just ordinary men is to ensure that Muslims do not begin worshipping him as the Christians worship Jesus. The Wahhabis are also more restrictive than the Sufis when it comes to women's role in Islam. In Pakistan, the *masjids* do not provide adequate places for women to pray. If there is a women's area, it is usually some dirty corner room in an obscure part of the building. However, shrines are open to everyone. I have found them to be very peaceful and tranquil places where I can at least say my prayers in comfort when I am out and about. I just need to make my intention very clear that I am not praying to the deceased, nor am I praying to Allah through the deceased person. No such intervention is needed in Islam. I can pray *for* that deceased person, that Allah may be kind to him and give him the best of rewards in the afterlife, especially considering what he or she has done for others, but I do not ask for intercession at the shrines.

As always, I try my best to keep to what I consider the middle road: a balanced interpretation of Islam that ensures active practice of the five pillars of the faith, while leaving room for some of the mystical aspects of Islam that enliven my soul. I have learned, too, that intangibles, such as the unseen world, are not accessed through logic and intellect but through faith and God's grace.

Allah (SWT) holds my heart in His hand and lets me experience whatever He wants me to know. My understanding of the religion is based on my direct and personal relationship with Allah. When I feel close to Him, all is right in the world. When I allow anything or anyone else to take priority over my relationship with Him, be it for a moment or some longer period of time, I feel somehow dissatisfied and unfulfilled.

Life in Pakistan is much simpler and less materialistic than in the US, at least for Asad and I. With fewer distractions, I have more opportunities for worship and reflection. That said, we still need to deal with the more mundane aspects of daily life. In 2012, my husband loses his job. It's a case of last one hired, first one fired. The rate of unemployment is very high in Pakistan. There is also the age factor. Asad is in his late fifties. It's more likely that I can find paid employment teaching English as a second language in a country other than Pakistan. I begin a diligent online search for a position teaching English somewhere in the Muslim world. I'm pretty sure I don't want to be an administrator again, although those positions are available too. I hope to get a university teaching position, but I explore all my options. Once I'm settled somewhere, I can apply for a visa for my husband. We are confident that Sitara will carry on without us, under the mature direction of our new principal, Madam Rizwana. We appoint a local board to help the staff as needed. We, and our overseas donors, will remain financially responsible for the school.

I get a call back on a position I'd applied for in Fujairah, one of the small states of the United Arab Emirates. Most people think of Dubai and Abu Dhabi as the UAE, but it is actually a coalition of seven states that also includes Fujairah, Ras ul Khaimah, Sharjah, Ajman, and Um ul Quwain. The latter five are not as wealthy nor as commercial as the former two. They have beautiful natural landscapes including mountains, deserts, and the sea and sand of the Arabian Gulf. I go for an all-expense paid interview to Fujairah and enjoy touring the region while I'm there, even visiting a friend who is teaching English in Abu Dhabi. I don't end up accepting the job in the end, but I certainly enjoy the vacation in the comparative luxury of the Emirates. Swimming in the Arabian Gulf is absolutely delightful.

After continuing my search and sending my CV all over Middle and South Asia, I ultimately accept a university teaching position in Saudi Arabia. I leave Pakistan in the summer of 2013 with the expectation of reuniting with Asad in Saudi Arabia that fall. But I won't even set foot in Saudi until April 2014, and I don't see my husband again until October of that year when his Saudi visa finally comes through.

I know Allah by the destruction of my plans.
—Ali ibn abi Talib, 4ᵗʰ caliph of Islam (r.a.)

CHAPTER 41

Gypsy Grandma

Tahera's children: Bilal, Bayan, and Layal, 2014

"Good afternoon," I smile and hand the customs agent my identification. It's a blustery, snow-blown December afternoon with single-digit temperatures. I've just crossed the Ambassador Bridge from Michigan headed to my daughter Tahera's home in Windsor, Canada. She lives about ten minutes from the border on a good day. Let's see how this day shapes up.

"Is this your address in Michigan, ma'am?" the blonde woman in uniform asks me. In my experience, the women in customs positions always speak just a bit more brusquely than the men.

"It was," I answer truthfully, perhaps my first mistake. She's referring to the Michigan address on my enhanced license. *Enhanced*, meaning my driver's license contains a microchip with all my pertinent bio-data and can be used instead of a passport at this border crossing. "The house in question has been sold."

"Where is your residence now, ma'am?" While asking these questions, she's pulling up my data on her computer screen.

"Well, I've been in New York the past three months," I answer honestly again.

"And before that, where were you?"

"I was here in Windsor with my daughter."

"Are you employed, ma'am?"

"No, not currently." Uh oh… I can tell where this is leading. The next question could be, "And how do you support yourself, ma'am?" Basically, "Are you trying to freeload off of the Canadian government?" But she doesn't ask that.

"And what are you carrying with you today?"

"Personal items, clothing, a laptop."

"Any alcohol, tobacco, firearms?"

"No, officer."

"Ok, ma'am, thank you. Take this yellow paper I'm giving you and drive over there. Park your car and go into the customs and immigration center. Show them the yellow slip, and they'll take care of you."

Damn. I've been down this route before. The Canadian Customs and Immigration officials are polite and courteous but painstakingly thorough. Good thing I have lots of documents with me, including the one that lists the balance in my US bank account! Although they are very kind to refugees, Canada is not too fond of wanderers. If you can't prove that you have binding ties outside of their country, you might just decide to stay awhile and benefit from their government's largesse. That's not my intention. I just like staying with my daughter and her family. But customs doesn't know that. To them, I'm a Muslim woman with no apparent residence driving a borrowed car. They can also tell from their files that I've travelled a lot in the Middle East. And that I go back and forth to Pakistan. Hmmmmmm. Sounds suspicious, even to me.

As a Muslim woman who wears a headscarf, I try to navigate airports and border checkpoints carefully and calmly, with all necessary documents in hand. I've learned not to wear a black headscarf and not to pair it with an *abaya*. A tunic top and jeans with a colorful scarf works best on North American or European soil.

"Traveling while Muslim" has become a liability. In 2016, it reached the height of ridiculousness when a bearded Italian man was pulled off a plane because he was spotted making "suspicious notations" on paper. A fellow passenger thought he was writing in Arabic and felt somehow threatened. It turns out he was a mathematics professor coming to the US to give a lecture. The suspicious notations were mathematics symbols and formulas. In 2015, an American Muslim family was asked to leave an airplane, and countless single Muslim men with beards have this experience because fellow passengers or airline personnel feel somehow threatened by their presence.

Nothing as drastic as being taken off a plane has happened to me yet. In most U.S. airports, my headscarf merits an extra pat-down after I walk through the scanner. Once, in Chicago, the extra pat-down was preceded by the agent calling out, "We've got a non-threatening headscarf over here," which is meant to get the attention of his female co-worker. I wonder what they would have shouted if I was deemed a "threatening headscarf?" Another time, when I was traveling to Boston to see my husband, I had a present for him in my carry-on bag. It was a metal cylinder packed in a cardboard box. I watched as the customs agent scanned my bag twice before calling his supervisor over for a conference. I noticed the looks of concern that passed between them. It finally dawned on me to say, "It's a kaleidoscope."

"Oh, a *kaleidoscope*," they echoed with audible relief. At least there was no gun-toting terrorist on *their* watch.

As the current political climate in the US grows more Islamophobic, traveling while Muslim is getting more and more difficult. On my last flight from New York to Islamabad in March, 2016, I was pulled aside at customs for a hand-wiping. I was then told I had traces of explosives on my hands. That was a really crazy accusation, and I was naturally incredulous. My entire carry-on bag was unpacked, and I was not allowed to touch any of my possessions. Then I was taken into a separate, curtained room and given a very thorough pat-down that included my private parts. Nothing was found, so I was allowed to continue on to my plane.

Not one to leave you hanging, Canada does finally let me in to stay with my daughter in Windsor. I spend 2013–14 living mostly with Tahera, but also with my aging parents in New York. My mother has non-Alzheimer's dementia. Life in their household revolves around her needs and the "changing of the guard," meaning the schedule of the home health aides who care for her round the clock. My father, thank God, is still in excellent health and is working almost full-time at his law firm, in addition to going to the gym, and continuing to acquire artwork for his collection. My brother Andrew comes to visit them in New York, and we have a family reunion with Sajdah, her husband Kareem, and Safi.

Compared to Pakistan, life in North America is easy, but it takes me months to readjust. I'm in limbo, waiting for the Saudi job to materialize. I also miss my husband. Windsor, Ontario has a vibrant and active Muslim community with two excellent Islamic schools. I meet Tahera's friends and fellow colleagues at the masjid and in the community. In Pakistan, women's lives are centered around the family. They rarely get involved in community or masjid affairs. I have always appreciated the Islamic centers in North America as places to connect with others of my faith for social as well as religious activities.

I enjoy my grandchildren, who are growing up quickly before my eyes. Bilal is eight, Bayan, six, and Layal, four. Imran's son Qays is almost a year-old. I reconnect with old friends and former students, take some online courses, and teach one myself. Asad and I speak daily on Skype, and I keep waiting for news on my job in Saudi Arabia. After much red tape and phone time with the Saudi Cultural Center in Washington, DC, the first job offer falls through. I am disappointed, but then I almost immediately receive another offer from Skyline Global Recruitment. They send me a ticket to Riyadh, and I'm finally on my way. When one door closes, another one opens.

Amazing is the affair of the believer, verily all of his affair is good and this is not for no one except the believer. If something of

good/happiness befalls him he is grateful and that is good for him. If something of harm befalls him he is patient and that is good for him.
—Hadith of Prophet Muhammad ﷺ

CHAPTER 42

Arar, K.S.A.

I arrived to teach in Saudi Arabia in April 2014, a full year after starting the application process to work there. The universities were right in the middle of spring break, a detail was overlooked by whoever booked my ticket. I was hired by Al Khaleej Education and Training to teach English at a location, a location undisclosed up to this point. I was hoping to be placed at a university near Mecca or Madinah, perhaps in Jeddah but preferably not in Riyadh. I'd been warned off Riyadh by a family friend. He called it "a heartless and uncaring place." The general attitude of Americans working in Saudi Arabia seemed to be, "The money is good, but life there is not much fun." I was there because I'd finally gotten a job where my husband could join me on a family visa. We hoped to go to *Umrah* or *Hajj* while in the country. I knew that by Western standards Saudi Arabia is a very restrictive country, but since I was Muslim, I thought the benefits might outweigh the disadvantages.

When I arrive, a company driver picks me up at the airport and tells me we need to get my medical checkup and identification cards processed right away because his orders are to take me to Rafa the following morning. When I ask him where Rafa is, he waves his hand vaguely in the air and says "It is in the north, a very green place that most people like." *Green,* as a geographic descriptor, is a relative term in Saudi Arabia. The country is basically a desert. The princes of the ibn Saud family, who rule the various provinces, have spent money to plant and irrigate. Most towns have a nice park or two but I don't think any Westerner would describe Saudi Arabia as *green*! My driver is Sudanese and Sudan is also a desert country, so he isn't looking at Rafa from a Western point of view.

My main concern is where the town lies in relation to Mecca and Madinah, the country's major spiritual centers. According to Google Maps, north of Riyadh, there are only small towns perched on the edges of the desert until you reach the borders of Jordan to the east and Iraq to the west. Rafa is clearly in the middle of nowhere.

After the medical tests (apparently the two rounds I'd paid for in the States were not quite enough) and after exchanging some currency, I am driven to the hotel. I call my husband, who advises me to refuse the placement in Rafa. I have an Al Khaleej handbook on my laptop, so I begin calling any staff person who I think might speak English. One sympathetic soul calls back, despite the late hour, and advises me to cancel the driver for the morning. He tells me to walk to the head office, which is near the hotel, and explain why I don't want to work in the middle of nowhere.

The Al Khaleej company office is staffed by young male clerks from Jordan and Egypt; well-educated men who speak, read, and write English. Employment is largely determined by nationality and level of education in Saudi Arabia. Sudanese and Indo-Pak men are usually drivers. If they have some money when they arrive, they may run a small business for a Saudi overseer. Egyptians work as hotel clerks and restaurant managers. Men with masters' degrees and doctorates are employed as doctors, teachers, and engineers, the highest of those positions going to white males from western countries or South Africa. Educated females from western or Asian countries are invariably teachers, doctors, or nurses. Uneducated women from the Philippines, African countries, and South Asia are domestic workers in homes, universities, or hospitals. Some are nannies in the homes of wealthy Saudis. Less educated men from those same countries work in the construction industry. Both men and women in the non-professional job sectors are poorly paid, housed, and fed. They have to withstand inhumane treatment by Saudi employers, including substandard living conditions and even sexual harassment.

However, most foreign workers in Saudi Arabia feel they are better off than they would be in their own countries, where drought, famine, war, and other problems wreak havoc with people's lives. Their families back home desperately need the money they earn. On payday, the Western Union office is an international scene with lines of patient dark-skinned men, interspersed with the occasional Europeans or women, all there to wire money to villages, towns, and cities from Addis Ababa to Auckland.

At Al Khaleej headquarters, I'm eventually ushered into the office of Mr. Walid, a tall, older Sudanese man. I explain my situation and he nods his head as if listening, but he doesn't give me any response except to ask if I want a cup of tea. Apparently, I need to see a bigger boss. After tea, I am taken to the office of Mr. Saif, a small-framed Jordanian. He looks at me over the tops of his glasses and says, "Yes, Madam? What can I help you with?" I explain my situation once more. I point out that when I was hired in the US, I was assured that Al Khaleej had jobs all over the country, not just in the remote areas. I'd hoped to be closer to the holy sites, perhaps in Madinah. He asks sarcastically, "Why? Do you think the people who live in Madinah are angels?"

Mr. Saif tersely explains that the company only has positions in the Northern Borders Universities (N.B.U.), a group of campuses dotting the northern province of the country. Rafa is the northernmost outpost. If I don't want to go there, I can wait in Riyadh until spring vacation is over and hope for placement elsewhere, but he makes no promises. Al Khaleej will pay for the hotel until a suitable position is found, but they will not pay for meals. Instead, they'll give me an advance on my salary, which will not actually be paid until I'm working at one of their universities. Mr. Saif is curt and businesslike. He's clearly displeased with my refusal to go to Rafa, but he cannot force the issue.

A few days later, I meet with Bill, a company liaison between teachers and management. Bill advises me to go to Arar, an hour's flight from Riyadh. Arar is small but has a new English program and greater opportunities for advancement in curriculum development and teacher training, my two main professional interests.

"Al Khaleej is the best of the worst," Bill says. "You're here in Saudi to make your money and get out." Well, that's a practical attitude. With more than thirty years' work in Islamic education, I've never worked solely for the money, so this will be a new experience. *Take it or leave it*, I tell myself. I don't want to go home after spending so much time and effort to get here! Besides, I haven't seen Asad in a year. Saudi Arabia is one of the few countries he can enter with a visa. I accept the position in Arar. I will teach English at the Northern Borders' female campus.

I wait out spring vacation in Riyadh where I have a tiny hotel room just big enough for a bed and dresser. The bathroom is a small alcove with a sink, shower, and toilet. The only window in the room faces an alleyway. That dingy room is a catalyst to go out and explore my surroundings. I don't meet any other women in this hotel until the last few days I'm there, so I spend almost two weeks alone. I walk extensively in the dry, desert heat and find stores, homes, hospitals, masjids, and many, many cars, often parked haphazardly and clogging the already congested streets.

Riyadh is the official capital of Saudi Arabia. It's a cosmopolitan city of business and commerce, and it isn't as conservative as the provinces. While most Saudi women wear a black *abaya* and face veil, in the large cities the veil is not mandatory. I feel comfortable in a long over garment that is not black and a floral *hijab*. The same is not true away from the cities, as I will soon find out.

Riyadh is a great city if you like shopping malls. I usually don't, though it's a novelty to find so many long skirts and tops in shops catering exclusively to women. The drawback is no fitting rooms. Ladies try on clothing at home and return items as needed. I also visit the city museum, quite a cab ride away, though otherwise unremarkable. I also walked to several masjids near the hotel and am happy to find nice prayer areas for women.

Saudi Arabia has its own version of Jim Crow laws to curtail the activities of women. For one thing, women cannot drive. It's more common to see a twelve-year-old boy behind the wheel than a woman. A few brave souls are trying to change this law. They go out on the streets and drive, often getting arrested or paying fines for their misdemeanors.

One evening, I'm craving meat, so I walk into a fairly nice restaurant, intending to order takeout to eat at the hotel. I notice a few tables where men are seated. One man is clearly a Westerner from the looks of him. I send a small smile of recognition his way, but he takes no apparent notice. It's a hot day and I'm tired, so I sit down at an empty table with the takeout menu. No sooner have I sat than a waiter comes rushing over exclaiming,

"No, no Madam. What are you doing? You cannot sit there. Get up, please."

"But I just want to place my order. I am not going to eat here."

"You want to order? Please go and stand over there and someone will come and take your order." He gestures toward a dirty, unswept corner near the kitchen that has one lone table and chair. "You may wait here."

I am angered, insulted, and hungry. Not a good combination. After waiting a few moments, I decide not to spend my money in such a place, and I leave.

Apparently, a woman cannot eat or even sit in a restaurant unless it has a "family section." This rule is to prevent mixing of the sexes. "Family sections" are for all-female groups or families. They are usually behind curtains or other partitions so that non-family men will not see the women, and perhaps so that women can eat without *niqab*. This is just one aspect of Saudi society where the separation of the sexes is taken to unpleasant, unfriendly extremes. For a Westerner, these rules make life in Saudi unnecessarily restrictive for both women and men. They stunt the personality development of Saudi boys and girls because they never learn how to relate to each other in a professional and courteous manner. An animosity and sense of distrust exists between them that is sometimes palpable.

In my last days at the hotel, I meet a contingent of young American and British teachers just returning from Thailand. After two weeks on my own, I'm very happy to meet them. They fill me in a bit on what to expect in Arar and at the university. "We've learned to make our own fun," one of them says when I ask what there is to do on the compound. She says it with a giggle. Months later, I learn that for them, "fun" means distilling their own alcohol, a substance strictly forbidden in Saudi, but not unheard of on expatriate and US military compounds.

The flight to Arar is just an hour from takeoff to landing. Besides us teachers there are Filipino nurses and families with children on the flight. The children are especially active on the plane, standing up on their seats and jumping around in the aisles. The stewardesses who try to make them sit down for their own safety are ignored by children and parents alike. I'd heard about how spoiled Saudi children are; now I'm getting my first glimpse of their bad behavior.

It's evening when we land in Arar and are met by the Al Khaleej driver, Suhayl. In twenty minutes, we reach the teachers' compound, an ugly rectangular building complete with its own guardhouse and armed guard! A high boundary wall topped with barbed wire completes the prison-like edifice. It sits perched at the edge of the desert looking like the last outpost in town. If I had not lived in Pakistan and Palestine, where barbed wire is the order of the day, I would be alarmed. Apparently, the other teachers have grown used to this place, because no one comments upon it.

The apartments inside the walls are quite nice, at least. After the cramped hotel room, each apartment's good-sized bedrooms, large kitchens, and living rooms feel luxurious. Many public buildings in Saudi Arabia have barbed wire and armed security as well. One just gets used to it. No attacks on foreigners occur in Arar during my stay there, although incidents do happen in other parts of the country.

I elect to share an apartment with Barbara, the South African woman who I met in the van ride from the airport. Our bedrooms are at opposite ends of a first-floor apartment. We share a kitchen, living room, and laundry room, but each of us have our own bathroom. The apartment is completely furnished with everything from pots, pans, and cutlery to sheets and bedding. I am happy and thankful to Allah (SWT) to be settled down in my own place. I make my prayers and am pleasantly surprised by Barbara's offer to share dinner. God bless her. Our personalities work well together as we are both quiet and keep mainly to ourselves. Sometimes we connect in the kitchen and share our meals.

Work resumes at the university the day after our arrival. Suhayl, a soft spoken Indian man and a very hard worker, will drive us to and from the university each school day. He will also take us shopping twice a week. There is a grocery on either corner of our street if we need something in between our shopping days. Men and women are totally segregated in the compound and on two different campuses in different parts of town. Suhayl has one schedule to keep with the men and another one with the women. In addition to driving, he takes care of minor repairs in the apartments and gas, water, and cable services. I once hear him remark, "Work is worship" and that is indeed how he conducts his life. As an Indian man in Saudi Arabia, he is not paid very well, though he does have room and board with Al Khaleej. He tells us the people he feels sorry for are the Bengali domestics and construction workers. The pecking order is very severe in Saudi Arabia, and Bengalis and other unskilled laborers are on the very bottom.

My colleagues and I work in the English prep year program at NBU. All incoming freshmen women and men at Saudi universities must pass a mandatory year of English, which is called prep year. It is supposed to prepare them for the rigors of the university curriculum to follow. Most of their subject area textbooks will be in English, so it's important they master the language. Prep year programs have been instituted in most universities where English is a second language. The success or failure of these programs and their role in the globalization of English could be the subject of a book in itself!

Al Khaleej has not notified the university and English prep year office of my arrival. I am graciously welcomed, but at first, they do not know what work to assign me. NBU is in the last two months of the spring semester. All teachers have returned after spring vacation, so there is little for a newcomer to do. I find no available desks in the staff rooms so I sit wherever I find an empty chair and move when its owner returns from class. For the remainder of the Spring term, I'm a floating substitute, filling in whenever and wherever I'm needed. I review the books and curriculum to familiarize myself with their contents. I get to know my colleagues over coffee, tea, and snacks. After chatting with Dr. Mona, the university president, I agree to collaborate with another staff member to prepare and present a workshop for teachers on *Making English Relevant*. The main point of this assigned topic is how to make English enjoyable and relevant to our particular students. The teachers applaud the workshop. They all agree that the workshop ideas are wonderful. However, they don't think they will be able to fit these ideas into the rigorous syllabus they must follow. I don't quite understand what they mean until I try implementing my own ideas during the summer school program.

I'm thrilled to have achieved one of my life goals: to be teaching at a university. But NBU is like no university I've experienced before! The students arrive between 7:00 am and 8:00 am when classes begin. They exit their cars and vans or buses clad head to toe in black *abayas* and *niqabs*. Sometimes a bit of leg with a sneaker or a fancy shoe peeks out from under an *abaya*. Their handbags are huge totes, big enough to carry their books, makeup, mobiles, and other paraphernalia. The students enter the reception hall, bypass the expensive, nonfunctioning scanners and head toward the robust female security guards who check their bags and the length and tightness of their skirts at random. The black skirt is the students' uniform. It has to be ankle length, and not too tight and without slits. The security guards note any violations of the dress code and may send students home if they show up in a skirt that's too tight, too short, or too risqué.

As they step over the threshold leading to the interior campus of their all-girl university, they begin to disrobe. First the *niqabs*, then the *abayas* come off. Out come the cheap body sprays that make the entryway reek of synthetic fruit flavors or ocean breezes right in the midst of the desert. Then they swarm, chatting and giggling, to any convenient restroom to apply their makeup and brush their long, silky hair over the sinks where we teachers will later find the remains of this grooming and bonding ritual. I can hardly blame them. This all-female enclave is the only place in their family-centered lives where these Saudi girls can express themselves among their peers. The administration tends to pamper the girls as well. Dr. Mona is very lenient up to a point. When that point is reached, she resorts to yelling at students or staff members. She can be heard all over the building. But so can the students, who often, shockingly, yell right back at her.

Above the waist, any top of any color or style is acceptable, as long as it's not transparent. And these girls know how to make that freedom count. Low cut tops abound. We teachers often have to ask girls to cover up their well-endowed figures in class. What's actually under those black *abayas* never fails to amaze. They can also sport any footwear they like and carry any type of bag, whether designer or faux designer. Mobile phones must not have cameras because they are all out of *hijab* on campus, so no pictures are allowed.

Given the strictures of Saudi society, the university campus is the only place the girls are free to socialize with their friends, so that is their number one priority and the reason most of them come to school in the first place. I had thought university teaching would be a step up from working in elementary schools back home. I purposely did not take an administrative position in an elementary or secondary school overseas because I thought I would relish working in a university. But teaching at Northern Borders is like teaching in an American middle school. All hormones, all the time! I have even seen girls slap each other across the face in the midst of a fight. Conversely, I've seen them kiss and hug with just as much passion.

These young women are eighteen, nineteen, and twenty years old. Many are already married and some have children. But psychologically, they seem like young adolescents in so many ways. Also, they are rude to their teachers. They come to class very late and disrupt the flow of instruction to greet their friends, who are clearly more important to them than the teacher is. They don't turn off their mobiles, even though it's the rule. And when their driver calls, they beg to leave, even if class is not over I have personally taken girls' mobiles and spoken to the people on the other end, telling them that these girls would come out when class was over. According to male teachers at the compound, the problem is much worse on the boys' campus. Male students don't wait for drivers. They have their own cars.

I once confiscated some mobiles that rang in class and handed them over to the administration. Dr. Mona, who had put this rule in place, was not particularly pleased when she had to meet with the mothers who came to retrieve the mobiles and get their daughters readmitted to class. She asked me, "Miss Sommieh, was this reaction really necessary?"

The attitude of many Saudis toward foreign workers of any kind, from servants to doctors, is that we're in their country to serve them. We are performing jobs that they cannot or do not want to perform themselves, and they are paying us good money to do those jobs. There are exceptions to this attitude, most notably among the non-Saudi students, girls who live in Arar with their parents or husbands, but are originally from Sudan, Turkey, Egypt or Syria. They view their educations as a privilege, not a right, and they act accordingly, excelling in studies far beyond their Saudi peers.

One of the reasons for the non-productive attitude of Saudi students is the fact that they are actually paid by their government to go to school. All Saudi university students receive a stipend of about 800 riyals a month just for attending school. There is no minimum grade requirement for receiving this money, just an attendance quota. The girls will argue more over unexcused absences than they will over failing grades. If they fail English, they can take it again, and continue getting paid. Eight hundred riyals is about $210 a month. And it's for them, not their parents. As Saudi citizens, the parents have stipends of their own.

My colleagues and I are teaching English as a foreign language. It's not a subject most students enjoy. They enter university with widely diverse levels of competency in English, yet they are all thrown into the same freshman-level classes. A placement test is issued at the beginning of the term, but the results are never used to place students at their proper level. Instructors are given a pacing chart and textbooks and then told to follow them to the letter, as if they are a script. The teachers from non-Western countries do not see a problem with the scripted approach. They have taught English in a similar fashion back home in Sudan or Pakistan. But for the Westerners, and especially for me, a specialist in curriculum development, this approach is unrealistic, inefficient, and unproductive. I view teaching as the art of developing lesson plans that will help students truly understand a concept or an idea. The Saudi objective in teaching English has much more to do with helping students to memorize the correct answer so they can spit it back out on test day.

The Oxford books we use are well written and attractively illustrated but far above the students' instructional levels. Arabic and English are very different languages. Most of the girls don't yet know how to spell their own names with vowel letters, whereas the totally unrealistic pacing chart expects us to move quickly from *What is Your Name?* and *Where are You From?* to *How to Read a Train or Plane Schedule* and *Who was Sherlock Holmes?* The textbook does try to view English from a practical standpoint as a global language of communication. But these girls are far from ready to make a hotel reservation for their winter holiday in Colorado or to navigate a table comparing that vacation to one in sunny Italy. Most of them cannot yet read a simple paragraph!

I can't help comparing my NBU students to the young women I worked with in Pakistan. They were young teachers who wanted to improve their English. They had already mastered basic grammar and wanted to understand more advanced concepts such as the subjunctive tense. They also wanted to be able to speak conversational English, something they could only learn from a native speaker. How motivated they were and how respectful! I really miss them as I now find myself having to focus as much attention on confiscating nail polish and mobiles that ring in the classroom as I do on teaching. "Teacher, no English!" is the common refrain of students who don't even bring their books to class. They voice the phrase disdainfully, with a sweep of their manicured hand, as if pushing the missing books off their desk.

Teaching English at Northern Borders quickly becomes an exercise in futility. Even if I try to reach the students on their own level, I am told by the students themselves to just stick to the book and give them the answers. It's so sad for me to see that most of them are so jaded, they just keep doing things the same way even though it hasn't worked for them before. Many girls have to take English two or three times before they pass. It is a requirement for their university degree in any subject. If they don't pass during the school year, they are advised to take it during the summer, when it is supposed to be easier.

Since I arrived in April and didn't have any classes of my own, the university requests that I take charge of the summer program. Eight hours of English a day for six weeks—including Ramadan. Doing the same thing that didn't work all year, except more intensively. While I'm glad to be in charge of something, the program is more of a joke. Neither instructors nor students can pay attention to one subject for eight hours. I am glad when it's over and I can finally go home to enjoy my summer with family and friends. I come back in the fall to fulfill the terms of my contract and bring my husband to Arar.

The new semester at the university is a bit better. Since I am there at the beginning of the term, I'm given a regular course load and my own desk. I'm able to start with my students from the beginning and can therefore modify the course material at least a little bit to make it more accessible. The main problem is that the university assumes the students have been learning English since at least fifth grade and therefore have some competency and fluency. But this is true for only a handful of incoming freshmen. The vast majority have retained next to no English from their elementary and secondary schools. I wish I could have had some influence over how English is taught in the Saudi public school system. But I'm enough of a realist to know that change in such a bureaucracy comes slowly, if at all. I would have needed a doctorate and to have been employed in the upper echelons of the system before anyone would care to listen to my ideas. I'm much better off at Sitara, where I can see the results of my efforts.

NBU has great online resources to go with our textbooks, and all classrooms can access the internet, so that makes for more interactive lessons. We also have the Rosetta Stone program in the language lab. Students enjoy its self-paced nature, although the soft easy chairs and dim lighting in the language lab sometimes lull them to sleep. Many students do not actually do the Rosetta Stone work themselves, but pay someone outside the school to complete the work for them. We try to crack down on this scam, but it is nearly impossible. It's only when they fail the final that we know for sure they haven't done the work. A great bonus for us teachers is being able to use the costly Rosetta Stone program for free to learn any language we want. I am using it for Arabic, while another teacher is using it to study Japanese.

The most wonderful aspect of my job at Northern Borders is working with my colleagues. We are an international group of women from all over the globe. In our small English department of about twenty-five teachers, we have Indians, Sudanese, Egyptians, Americans, Brits, South Africans, Pakistanis, and Jordanians. It is both enlightening and inspiring to live and work with women from such a variety of cultures; to eat our ethnic foods together; and to discuss our families, friends, and lifestyles. With smartphone applications and Facebook, it's easy to stay in touch even when we are no longer on the same continent.

The oldest woman among us is almost sixty. She's a chain-smoking South African who's been working in Saudi forever. The youngest is an Egyptian girl in her early twenties who lives with her parents in Arar. For some of the elder teachers, teaching in Saudi is a retirement job to pay the bills back home. For others, it's a step up in their teaching careers and a much needed income for their families. Whole families from developing countries like India, Pakistan, and Sudan are working in Saudi, where life may be difficult but is better than it is at home. That's not necessarily true for the Americans. They end up staying just one or two years before going back home or moving on to a more exotic, less-restrictive locale.

Muslim or not, we all wear the black *abaya* and *niqab* when we're in public. Arar is a small town and if we don't wear it, people stare at us. One morning, the police actually come to the university to check on one new teacher who had refused to wear the *niqab*. She is told she must put it on if she wants to keep her job, so she complies. At least we are free to show our hair and dress as we like within the walls of our campus, just like the students are. After years of wearing *hijab* at work, I enjoy the opportunity to dress up and wear earrings. No Western-style slacks or jeans are allowed on campus, however. Except for the Pakistani *shalwar kameez*, all teachers must wear dresses or long skirts.

Another advantage of living in Saudi Arabia is hearing the *athan* five times a day. When it sounds from the masjids on every corner, work comes to a stop. Stores and businesses actually shut their doors while everyone stops to pray. It's the law of the land that businesses will shut down during prayer time. This five-times daily reminder encourages me to make my prayers in the early part of each prayer cycle.

Bill, the human resources manager from Al Khaleej had advised, "The best way to use your time in Saudi is to study something or write something." It's good advice. I live without my husband for half of my twelve month stay in Saudi, and I'm definitely lonely sometimes, but I'm able to use most of my free time to study Arabic, Islam, and Quran through an online program called Ribaat. Sponsored by an all-women's organization called Rabata, Ribaat promotes female scholarship through online courses taught by qualified Muslim women from all over the world. My teachers are inspiring. Through Ribaat I've been able to improve my Arabic recitation of the Holy Quran and deepen my understanding of Islamic history.

Alhamdulillah, in the fall of 2014, I am finally able to get Asad a three month, renewable visa. Al Khaleej is very accommodating and gives us our own large apartment on the compound. Vicky and Dave, a couple from South Africa are the only other married couple on the premises. I move into it just one day before Asad is due to arrive and clean my heart out until the place is sparkling. I am running on the extra adrenaline of anticipation. It has been a year and a half since I've seen my husband.

I go with Suhayl to the airport to wait for Asad's plane, but I wait in the wrong place. I don't realize he's coming out of the arrivals area and I am sitting in the departure lounge thinking, *Why is the plane late?* He's already out of the terminal with his luggage heading toward the parking lot where Suhayl spots him before I do. Asad looks so thin and so frail that he scares me. Never a big eater, he hasn't taken care of himself at all while we we've been apart. I'll need to fatten him up.

We have another one of our joyous reunions and happily settle into married life in Saudi. I love coming home to him and complaining about my day, then having a cup of tea in our large, roomy kitchen. We try go-ing out for walks, the way we had in Pakistan, but find out that Saudis don't walk. In fact, people keep stopping their cars and SUVs to pick us up. It's embarrassing! Asad tries to find a job or start a small business in Saudi, but finds it's not possible without a Saudi sponsor and a permanent visa. He doesn't need to work, but he would benefit from something to do while I am at work all day. He finally ends up tutoring a young Egyptian man who is trying to diminish his accent and get a job in Europe.

And among His wonders is the creation of the heavens and the earth and the diversity of your tongues and colors: for in this, behold, there are messages indeed for all who are possessed of (innate) knowledge. (S. Rum, v. 21-22)

CHAPTER 43

Mecca and Madinah

Prophet's Mosque interior, Madinah, K.S.A.

The most beautiful part of my Saudi experience is making *umrah* with Asad. *Umrah* is a voluntary pilgrimage to the holy sites of Mecca and Madinah to be made any time one wishes, unlike *Hajj* which must be performed during the Islamic month of Zhul Hijjah. Making *umrah* while living in Saudi is very easy. Since we're already in the country, no separate visa is required. There is no long and exhausting plane ride either, just an hour-long flight to Riyadh, then another hour to Mecca. The four-hour bus ride from Mecca to Madinah was the longest part of our trip.

There is a huge expansion project going on in Mecca. The area surrounding the *Kaaba is* being enlarged to accommodate more pilgrims, who already swarm the city in the millions every year. Mecca has become very commercialized, full of shopping malls, fast food, and luxury hotels. In 1989, there were still small hills surrounding the city where people who could not afford hotels would camp. Many of the pilgrims from poor countries would bring merchandise from home to sell on the street in order to fund their trip. In 2014, no trace of those earlier days remains. But regardless of the difficulties encountered by construction detours, we can still give ourselves up wholly to the sacred rites and reap the benefits, *Inshallah.*

We join the *tawwaf,* circumambulating the Kaaba seven times with the crowd, holding onto each other at all times for fear of getting separated by the mob of humanity. I have a list of people to pray for and make sure over the next four days to include them all. The beautiful black and gold-robed Kaaba is a magnet, both literally and figuratively. I cannot tear my eyes away. If I lose sight of it for a moment, when I turn around, no matter where I am, I can see it. At each glance, it takes my breath away.

Madinah is also undergoing expansion. The simple, thatched-roof structure that was the masjid in the Prophet's time no longer exists. A grand cluster of interlinked buildings with movable skylights and an expansive plaza currently replace earlier renovations. The original tombs of the Prophet ﷺ and his two companions have been beautifully adorned with gold grillwork, marble, and calligraphy. The masjid itself is a long, expansive structure with adjoining wings to accommodate millions of visitors. Men and women worship in separate sections. Every wing is fully decorated with beautiful archways, carved pillars, calligraphic designs, luxurious carpeting, and chandeliers. A large staff of artisans and workers keep everything spotlessly clean and in pristine condition. It's a tremendous privilege to work in Madinah or Mecca and these positions are often handed down from father to son for generations.

Men and women are segregated inside the masjid and the tomb areas, but families meet outside the buildings on a plaza that stretches from one end of the complex to the other. By day, huge open parasols completely shade the plaza from the hot sun. They close up automatically at night. The rooftops of each adjoining wing are also movable, shifting in place from day to night. The ingenious design of these beautiful structures provides maximum comfort for the pilgrims. As in Mecca, pilgrims come from all over the world. Families buy food in the shops opposite the plaza and picnic there. People in colorful clothing, speaking hundreds of languages, are united through smiles, small courtesies, and acts of devotion. People feel blessed and happy to be in al Madinah al Munawwarah, the radiant city.

Asad and I go our separate ways, planning to meet in the late evening. The Prophet's masjid is very spacious and can comfortably hold the throngs of pilgrims who enter there. I'm reacquainted with *Zam Zam,* the miraculous spring water piped in from Mecca and kept cold in every building. I thoroughly enjoy my time in prayer and reciting Quran for the three days we spend there. It's very peaceful. There are no explicit rites to perform, though everyone's goal is to visit the tomb of the Prophet 🕌 himself.

The wives and companions of the Prophet 🕌 were directly and profoundly affected by his charisma and love for them. But he loved us too, and even cried for us, his *ummah* of the future. In one *hadith,* he speaks of the Muslims of our time, telling his companions, "Surely, I wish to reunite with my brothers." His companions reply, "Are we not your brothers?" He answers, "You are my companions and brothers. After me, there will also come a community who believes in me though they have not seen me."

We can't be with him in the flesh, though we may see him in dreams and visions, or experience his love in some other way. He himself has said that if you see him in a dream, you have truly seen him because the devil cannot take his form. I have been blessed to have had three such encounters with the Prophet 🕌 in my life.

On my very first *Hajj* in 1989, I was in Arafat, the place where one stays for an afternoon between prayers. It is a time of making *du'a* and asking forgiveness. In the past, Arafat was just a burning desert plain, but now it's been made comfortable with air-conditioned tents and buildings. The women in my group stayed in a building where fans blew noisily, but they could not dissipate the hot, dusty air that circulated in that warehouse. I was doing my remembrance and *du'a* and became drowsy. I closed my eyes and saw the Prophet 🕌. He was sitting in a room talking to people who were seated in a circle with him. I wanted to enter the room, but I could do no more than stand in the half-open doorway. He looked up and smiled at me, a very radiant smile. He was very handsome, dressed in white, and had long, black, curly hair.

The second time I saw him was even more wonderful. It was 2013, and I was in Windsor, Ontario. I had already stayed at my daughter's house more than six months, waiting for my visa to go to Saudi Arabia. I hadn't seen my husband in over a year. I was trying to be patient but it was hard, and I was lonely. I prayed, fasted, made *du'a*, and read Quran as much as possible. One day after prayer, I was resting on my prayer mat when the Prophet ﷺ appeared again, sitting in a circle of companions. This time he beckoned for me to enter the room. I came to him and sat down. I actually put my head in his lap, and he stroked it and told me, "*All will be well.*" I was so overwhelmed by the loveliness of this experience that I began to cry and did so for quite some time. He had said, "*All will be well.*" And so it was. My visa finally came. I got the job in Saudi. My husband was able to join me there, and we both were able to make *umrah* to Mecca and Madinah.

A visit to the Prophet's tomb is the highlight of a trip to Madinah. When I'd been there in 1989, the tomb was accessible to women as well as men. But in 2015 this is no longer the case. It seems unfair and unjust that only men can enter the room where the Prophet ﷺ and his two companions, Abu Bakr (r.a.) and Umar (r.a.), are buried. Women can only get to an area behind a tarp and cannot actually see the tombs. I am certainly frustrated and upset by this and have to make do with my husband's description of the gold grillwork and the *rowdah*, a very special area in front of the tomb. The Prophet ﷺ himself called this area a piece of heaven.

I pray for a chance to get closer. On the women's side, one can pray two prayer cycles in front of a tarp that faces the tomb, but it is very difficult to get to this area. It is cordoned off and only small groups are let through. There's lots of pushing and shoving as people strain to take cellphone pictures of whatever they can glimpse over the high dividers that separate the women from the area they yearn to see.

I wait for a chance, and finally, one comes. Suddenly a door opens to let some women exit the area nearest to the tomb. The guard does not close the door right away so a small group of women climb over the cordons and run down the corridor. I run too, until I find myself at the back side of the tomb, facing the tarp. The tomb can just barely be detected as a shadowy object on the other side. I lean my head against the tarp and touch it with my hands so I will be as close to the tomb as possible. The guard motions with her stick to forbid us from touching the tarp. I pray my utmost prayers for peace and blessings upon our Prophet ﷺ and his companions who lay behind him. I pray for his family and then for mine, I pray fervently, remaining in my prostration for as long as possible. I'm completely overcome with emotion by the time the guards shoo me out of the area. Tears stream down my face. I move to the right side, adjacent to the tomb but still blocked from view by a solid wall. I place my head and hands on that wall and begin another cycle of prayer and supplication. I remember my parents, my husband, my children, my grandchildren, my friends, and the *ummah*. I pray for health, safety, and peace. I feel a response to my prayers and I cry even more, calling out to the Prophet ﷺ and to Allah (SWT). I stay as long as the guard allows, before leaving reluctantly. Blessings wash over me, filling me with happiness. I have gotten what I came to Madinah for. I've been touched by my Prophet ﷺ and answered by his Lord and mine once again. I'm humbled and grateful. My yearnings have been satisfied.

In 2014, I was sitting in Windsor, awaiting my Saudi visa and wishing for my husband in Pakistan. I made a prayer asking Allah (SWT) to let me see the Kaaba and the Prophet's grave at Madinah once more. The answer came back, *Whether you go there or not does not matter. See the Kaaba in front of you when you pray. The Kaaba resides in your heart.* I knew this to be true then. Still, it was a blessing and a gift to have made the journey once more.

In the Name of Allah,
Most Gracious, Most Merciful

Did We not expand for thee thy breast?
And lift from thee thy burden that weighed heavily upon thy back?
And did we not elevate thy reknown?

For truly with hardship comes ease!
Truly with hardship comes ease!
So when thou art free, exert thyself
And let thy desire be for thy Lord.
(S. Ash-Sharh, v. 1-8)

CHAPTER 44

Home is Where the Heart is

Shigar Fort in the Hunza Valley, 2016

One year in Saudi Arabia was enough for me. Asad's visa expired after six months, and he went back to Pakistan in April, 2015. I finished the terms of my contract in May. I'd had plenty of time to think while in Arar. One of the things I realized is that I didn't want to work just for a paycheck. I'd never done so before, and I didn't need to start doing so at age fifty-seven. Teaching had always been a passion for me, a way to express my creativity and a way to serve others. If I can't teach creatively, then I don't want to teach at all.

I also thought a lot about my family. I missed them being so far away, and I knew they missed me, too. My father was talking about having hip surgery, and my mom's health was deteriorating due to her dementia. Both Tahera and Imran's wife Karen had babies on the way. *Inshallah,* Safiyeh would soon marry. Maybe it was more important to be available for them right now than to teach and travel. After making *istikhara,* the prayer of seeking guidance, I knew I needed to give some time to my family.

Alhamdulillah, it's a good decision. I am able to help my father with his surgery and recuperation and also enjoy the births of two new grandsons and a granddaughter. Tahera has Salman, and Karen has twins named Adam and Aminah, who are born prematurely. Safiyeh meets Ryan, a wonderful man who has been Muslim for two years, and we hold their wedding in March, 2016. My father, his two sisters, and my brother's family are all able to attend the ceremony and reception, along with more than 250 friends and family members. It is a wonderful, liberating feeling to have all my children married and settling into their adult lives.

After the wedding, I return to Pakistan to spend time with Asad and check on Sitara. Upon returning from Saudi, Asad had rented a two-bedroom home in the small city of Haripur, Hazara, the first district in Khyber Pakhtunwa, or the K.P.K. The week before my arrival, he runs around town, getting kitchen crockery, sheets, and towels. When Asad is alone, he lives truly as a traveler in this world, keeping nothing with him from one day to the next. This is one of the ideals of Sufism. It's only when I'm with him that he feels the need to make a home. We reunite in March, 2016. Good morning and good night hugs in real time top virtual reality any day. I like the simple rhythm of our days together in Pakistan. I enjoy our mealtimes, even though our palates do not match. What tastes just right to me is bland as dishwater to him. He's been known to call my cooking "hospital food!" But as time passes, my tongue gradually adjusts to more spice. It's a matter of survival, especially when eating with friends and relatives. I'm also more relaxed about cooking than I used to be. I invite neighbors and nieces into my kitchen to teach me how to prepare traditional dishes.

This part of the country is full of green, agricultural land. It's a coolness to the eyes, even on a hot, hot day. The wheat crop is golden and ready for harvest in springtime and once again in the Fall. Loquat trees in orchards are weighed down heavily with a small orange fruit that grows only in this region of the country. Loquat tastes like a cross between apricots and lychees, tartly sweet and full of surprisingly large seeds. Peeling the skin and spitting out the seeds leaves just a small juicy morsel to eat. After loquat season come melons in several varieties, followed by mangos, my favorite fruit of all. We always start our breakfast with fruit in Pakistan.

Our home is just ten minutes from Asad's paternal village of Kot Naji-bullah, where Asad's mother, Ammi ji, still lives on a small estate built by her youngest son. Her home is right off the main road, but once you enter its gate, you're in a calm and peaceful oasis. A small garden is her pride and joy, so we've brought a new plant for the gardener to install. Ammi ji takes out her store of old photos to show me my husband as a boy, as a teenager, and as an army officer. It's a treat for me to see his progression from toddler to man.

Though she's well into her eighties and uses a walker, my mother-in-law is a very active woman. She reads the news and keeps up with current events. She reads the Quran, does endless *dhikr,* prays for everyone, and keeps busy by sewing small frocks for babies. They are creative and beautifully designed from leftover pieces of fabric. She still sews her own clothing as well, and has done so all her life. Nothing is wasted in her household. She's happy with the needle threaders I've brought, as her eyesight is not what it used to be.

She gives the frocks as baby gifts whenever a girl is born. She loves baby girls and always has. "As a child, I would run to any home where I heard there was a new baby girl. And I would stay there. I did not want to leave." She says all this in Urdu, and my husband kindly translates. He's told me the back story of this fierce love for baby girls. His paternal grandmother was very cruel to his mother when she bore a girl as her first child. She even denied them food and milk. When her second child was born a son, his mother was resentful of all the love and attention her in-laws showered on the baby, just because he was a boy. That child was my husband, the oldest boy in a family with one sister and two younger brothers. His older sister died of cancer in 2014, and his mother still cries when she thinks of her. Asad is gentle and deferential with his mother, showing her the utmost respect. She often asks him to bring her little things, like two lemons or a half kilo of nuts, no more, no less, and of course he does so.

As this is my fourth trip to Pakistan, I adjust to its rhythms more quickly than before. I awake to the *athan*, and my morning's work is punctuated with chatter from children off to school and the rhythmic chants of the *rehri waalas* calling their wares out in the street. They sell everything on their wooden handcarts from fruits, vegetables, and housewares to services like machine repair and knife sharpening.

Electricity is once more an on-again, off-again proposition. Some days, it may stay on all day, but on other days it cuts off in the morning and doesn't return until evening. It comes and goes without a schedule, so one learns to use it immediately when it's available. We have a small home generator to power our fan and a few lights, but it cannot accommodate the refrigerator or computers, so we just work when we can. It is easy to become lethargic about getting things done when the power just fades in and out, but I try to deal with it like a Pakistani; that is, with good humor and praise to God when it works. As we move toward the summer, the afternoons are sunny and hot. I give in to my body's desire to nap.

It is 5:30 in the afternoon when I hear a familiar knock at the door. Our neighbor Rehanna doesn't have the best sense of timing. I'm not dressed for company, having stayed in my summer nightgown all day. Its blowsy cotton helps to beat the heat. I've been drowsy and have dozed a bit too long this afternoon.

My husband goes out to let her in. It's him she's come to speak with anyways. *I'll just go and say salaams on my way to the kitchen. I've got work to do. Why did I sleep so long?* These are the thoughts that make me rise reluctantly from my rumpled bed, slip on my *chappals* (sandals) and shuffle into the living room. Rehanna rises from the chair to greet me with a smile, a hug, and a kiss. I return her affections, and walk into my tiny kitchen, tie on my apron, and get to the business of preparing dinner.

"Kya aap pakane, Auntie?" What are you cooking? That much Urdu I can understand. I reply in turn, knowing my husband will translate my mangled grammar and vocabulary as needed. He is my faithful interpreter, although he wonders aloud if I will ever learn to speak with proper grammar. Their conversation continues. He nods his head and contributes companionably to her running monologue about the neighbors, the shop-

ping, the children, and the problems of being poor in Pakistan. He is all sympathy, which is why she is here. He brings some much needed solace to her day.

Would I do the same if I could? I don't think so. I resent the constant interruptions as she comes knocking at my door in the morning, afternoon, and evening. Sometimes "uncle" is not home, and she wants to know where he is. She will even come in just to wait for him. When they converse, she is lightning quick in her speech, but with me she slows down, simplifies her words, and adds a few hand motions, as if she is talking to a simple child. *Kya hal he?* How are you? I ask. And how are the children? *Sab tiq?* All well? I grasp for words to cobble together some kind of conversation. Otherwise, we sit in silence, or I let her help me cook. She has a family, seven children and a husband, yet she seems to spend little time at home, preferring to be out and about in the neighborhood or the shops. She trades in gossip and has come today to tell us the neighbor's daughter is engaged. I have a feeling the whole neighborhood knows exactly what we have in our home, what we eat, and what I wear. "Telephone, Television, Tell Rehanna," as the saying goes. I hate gossip, but I try to be kind and give her a little of my time. My husband has told me, "Her mother died when she was two and her father soon after. She's an orphan. She's had a hard life. Give her what you can." Some extra fruit, some money, the noisy fan we don't really need. I can give of those things so much more willingly than I can give of my time. I want to explain that I have work to do, that I am writing, reading, studying—none of these things have meaning in her world. Why wouldn't I want to just sit companionably and peel garlic and cut vegetables? Well, my dinner prep will go much faster if I let her help me, so I do, just for today.

Rehanna considers herself the neighborhood welcoming committee. She has taken me for a walk, gotten my clothing tailored, introduced me to the neighbors, purchased vegetables for me, lent me her iron, and visited me with her children many times. She also washes our clothes, mops my floors, and does light housekeeping once a week. Housework is difficult in Pakistan, especially in the heat, and it's good to have the help. Her husband, a taxi driver, is currently unemployed, and my husband has given her some money for the children's school fees. Most people in Pakistan do not like the government schools, so they will send their children to private schools even if it means doing without clothing or food.

In every city, town, and village, there are many Rehannas: ordinary working class people who struggle to make a living. Husbands and fathers die young in Pakistan. The average life expectancy for a man here is only sixty-six years of age and many die before that for lack of proper medical care and nutrition, or from drug abuse which is prevalent throughout the country. Latest figures find that up to 40 percent of the population may have contracted hepatitis A, B, or C from drinking unclean water.

My seamstress is a woman with four daughters and one young son. Her husband had a sudden heart attack almost ten years ago. Her oldest daughter makes a little money as a teacher, and she sews. But there is no respect for widows, and her relatives don't help her. Sometimes people don't even want to pay her for the clothing she so expertly makes. The going rate in the villages for a suit of women's clothing is about Rs. 300 or three dollars so they barely scrape by. The children are so thin they look like scarecrows. Her only son is the youngest child in the family. His dream is to have a bicycle, though he looks too thin and weak to be able to pedal one. He says, "We don't need to eat too much food this month. If they save their money, they could buy my bike." We are thinking about buying him one for Eid but have told him he must start eating first.

The families of the children in my school have similar profiles to the people in Haripur. If they are lucky and their fathers are alive, they work for daily wages on construction sites or cutting stones. As of 2016, thirteen orphans are studying at Sitara School. Their mothers work as maids or they receive support from elder brothers who work instead of getting an education. According to Pakistani estimates, nearly 60 million people, or one-third of the country, live below the poverty line. Adult wage earners in those homes make less than sixty dollars a month. Furthermore, 12.7 percent of the country lives in extreme poverty on less than $1.20 per day.

CHAPTER 45

Power, Poverty, and Pride

Celebrating Independence Day at Sitara, 2014

Arguably the most dangerous nation on Earth, Pakistan is a bubbling cauldron of corruption and crime, where grasping politicians, greedy generals, drug smugglers, and terrorists intermix in a volatile web, made more threatening by a nuclear bazaar operated as a national sideline. Corruption and criminality run from the top down, with the political class constantly looting the national treasury and distorting economic policy for personal gain.

These are not my words, but the words of Raymond W. Baker in his book, *Capitalism's Achilles Heel: Dirty Money and How to Renew the Free Market System*, published in 2012. I cite Baker here in order to give some idea of the level of corruption at work in this poor country. He spends ten pages on Pakistan, describing the money laundering schemes of past and current prime ministers and presidents, as well as the role of the military in looting the country's wealth. I am not a political or financial analyst, but I do know what I've seen of life here over the past six years. The common citizens of Pakistan do not stand a chance of improving their lives under the current political and military regimes that rule the country. In fact, when the rulers are corrupt, most of the people follow in their footsteps as a matter of survival.

A few examples from the news will suffice to make my point. Nawaz Sharif, the current prime minister, is a convicted felon with offshore tax holdings amounting to billions of dollars according to the 2016 Panama Leak documents. The previous prime minister, Yusuf Gilani is also a thief. During his time in office, the wife of Turkish President Recep Tayyip Erdogan donated a valuable necklace as charity for the 2011 flood victims. The necklace was recently found in Gilani's possession in 2015. The donation had never been made. In a similar case, the former President Asif Zardari was found to have kept seven ambulances also donated for flood relief. He had them refitted as passenger vans for business purposes. Given these sad facts, it is no wonder that my friends in the US preferred to give their flood relief donations directly to me to distribute in 2011. I was glad to provide them with an account of where each dollar went. One of the reasons I do not expand Sitara's scope beyond one school is because I have to be accountable to Allah (SWT) and the donors for where the money goes. *Alhamdulillah,* we have people we can trust at Sitara, but if we had more than one school, it would be more difficult to keep track.

Baker's book also mentions the military. Since my husband is a retired army captain, I've had personal experience with the world of military privilege in Pakistan. Those who enlist in the armed forces make up less than half a percent of the population but they hold up to 10 percent of the nation's real estate and up to 4 percent of the nation's GDP, according to online sources. This is a conservative estimate; much of the armed forces' wealth is concealed in private enterprises. These private enterprises are run by individuals associated with the various branches of the armed forces.

Military service is coveted for all the benefits it brings to one's family. Enlistment is voluntary, requiring at least a twelfth-grade education (meaning high school plus two years in college or a military academy) for officers, and a high school graduation level for regular soldiers and junior commissioned officers. The army, navy, and air force each have their own system of public schools available to all military families, regardless of rank. Enlisted men and women and their families also have access to free medical care, subsidized real estate, and special housing in colonies that are clean, organized, and well maintained. After service, they receive pensions according to the rank at which they retired, allowing high-ranking officers to build beautiful modern homes on lands reserved especially for their purchase and use. One only has to drive through any major city in Pakistan to identify the difference between military and civilian housing schemes. In brief, the best of everything is enjoyed by the chosen few and the rest of the country makes do with shortages of all kinds.

As the wife of a man who straddles the worlds of the haves and the have nots, I've experienced both spheres of life without belonging completely to either one. I'm a foreigner here, a *farenji,* and I'm married to an atypical Pakistani. He tries to disregard the class system by being kind and loving to everyone. He spends more time with the poor than with people of the class he was born into. He helps people by listening to them, giving empathy to all, and financial help to those who need it most. They, in turn, help him with many services he and I cannot perform on our own, such as getting the car fixed, installing a generator, or shopping for household goods without getting swindled. On the other hand, our friends in the military have helped us in our travels by providing excellent accommodations and transportation at reduced rates. My husband also receives a small pension for his eleven years of military service, though he retired at the low rank of captain more than thirty years ago. A military identification card is very useful in daily life.

2016 is the year of reunions for Asad. We drive six hours each way to Sialkot, in the middle of the country, to attend the 50th Golden Jubilee of the 32nd Punjab, my husband's army unit. A few weeks later, we go to

Rawalpindi for the 40th anniversary of his class at Kakul Military Academy, which he attended directly after college. Asad keeps in touch with his army buddies through WhatsApp. These reunions are the rare occasions when he actually sees them. Many of these men have made a career out of the military, whereas Asad has not. They fondly remember him as one of the wildest in the battalion, the artist, and the rebel of the regiment. He retired from the service as a captain while many of them have reached the vaunted status of generals.

When we arrive in Sialkot after a grueling six-hour drive, we find out that there is no room for us in the cantonment because we registered at the last minute. However, the army owns a hotel in town and will be glad to host us there, free of charge. We've got about one hour to change into formal dinner attire and return to the cantonment. That's enough time for a quick shower and nap for my husband. Meanwhile, I need time to wrestle with my *dupatta.*

I have a love-hate relationship with *dupattas,* the long rectangular head covering that traditionally graces the head of every proper Pakistani woman. It used to be considered an essential part of the *shalwar kameez* suit, the traditional Pakistani dress of a long tunic top over loose-fitting trousers. Nowadays, I see many women going without this body-wrapping fabric. Trousers have gotten tighter and tunics have gotten shorter. They almost never have full sleeves unless they are custom made.

The *dupatta* fabric is often very beautiful. It coordinates with the rest of the outfit and can be placed strategically to cover any transparent material on the upper body. It's also supposed to function as a head cover. For a *hijab*-wearing Muslim woman, the *dupatta* should cover all her hair. Most people do not use them for this purpose anymore. If worn at all, they are a purely decorative shawl draped artfully over the shoulders or just touching the top of the head without concealing the hair.

For me, a *dupatta* is just too much material. If I use it to actually cover my hair, it forms a heavy, awkward-looking wrap because it is too long and too wide. I much prefer a simple triangular scarf. If I'm just using it as a shawl, then why bother? One hardly gets cold enough to need a shawl in

Pakistan, except in the midst of winter. Besides, I like to wear my clothes loose fitting enough so as not to need extra coverage on my curves.

As logical an explanation as all the above may be, on the night of the Golden Jubilee Dinner, I am wearing a *dupatta*. It goes with the princess pink and silver *shalwar kameez* I've chosen for the evening. The material was a gift from my mother-in-law. So I pin it under my chin, wrap, and then re-wrap it around my head and shoulders and hope for the best. I will need to adjust it all night long. In that way, I find it no better than the time I tried to wear a saree. I felt like the whole thing would unravel at any minute!

The Golden Jubilee Dinner is held in the evening on the lawn. When we enter the cantonment, I see the men and women congregated separately. The grounds have been decorated with twinkling lights and torches. The women's side has been arranged with comfortable couches aligned in a U-shaped curve around a carpeted area of grass. The buffet and dining tables are in front. I seat myself on one of the sofas and observe the women around me, elegantly attired in a variety of styles from glittery, to embroidered, to plain lawn of the best quality, perfectly tailored. I smile at the younger woman closest to me who smiles back, though neither of us says a word. Eventually another young woman comes over and starts a conversation in English. "*Assalamu alaykum.* I am Mrs. Lieutenant Azhar Hussayn Haq." This form of introduction seems like a throwback to 1950s America, though the Pak army etiquette is based more on the British system than the American one. When Pakistanis use the old British customs like this, my husband usually calls them *Kala Angreze* (Black Britishers), though not usually to their faces.

"*Walaykum as salam.* I'm Mrs. Captain retired Tareq Ashraf Khan." I stumble over that mouthful the first few times I utter it. It is not until much deeper into a conversation that I can ask any woman her own name or give her mine.

"Are you English?" she asks, with interest.

"No, American," I reply. "From the US."

"Ah, I love to speak English, may I talk with you?"

She has a small baby in her lap, so I make some conversation about how cute he is, asking his age, etc. She asks about my family and this is a cue to take out my phone and show some pictures, using my childish Urdu to explain relationships as I go. She eventually wanders away, but I have several similar conversations before dinner is served.

At dinner, I'm seated with the wife of one of my husband's friends, someone nearer to my own age. Her daughters and daughter-in-law are with her, as all of them have husbands in the army. Zarinah is gracious and warm, doing her best to make me feel at home. She is considered the "mother" of this regiment, the one who has kept them all connected, first by email and now on WhatsApp. She pats my hand and smiles. Her daughter translates for us both and dinner passes pleasantly.

The next day after breakfast, a very long ceremony begins at 11:30 am and continues until 2:00 pm. There is fifty years of history to cover, and the 32nd Punjab officers seem ready to recount it all. I listen as long as I can, trying to follow the gist of it until my attention wanders. I recall a conversation from the night before when I asked one woman how long she'd been living in cantonments. She answered me in practically flawless English: "The military is like one big happy family and life in our cantonments is a little bit better, a little bit cleaner, and a little bit nicer than the rest of Pakistan." She smiled brightly. I looked around me and saw that it was true. These people live a comfortable life. A full fleet of servants pour the tea, clean the house, wash the clothes, and chauffeur them to their favorite shops. Meanwhile, their teenage nannies look after the children. One or two times, I've mistaken these young girls dressed in hand-me downs as the children of their employers. When I commit this faux pas, I get a surprised or disdainful look from both servant and master. "No, she is not my daughter." No further explanation needed. I pray that no girl at Sitara will suffer this fate of servitude to the ruling class.

The Golden Jubilee Celebration ends with presentations to the families of martyrs. It is only then that I remind myself, *The military is ultimately about serving one's country and giving one's life if necessary to defend it.* As each family steps forward to be honored for their slain member, I note that most of these families are from the lower class. It is not usually the officers who die in the line of duty, but the common infantrymen. Their wives, mothers, and children come forward, empty-eyed with grief or seething with anger and frustration. They receive a stipend for the loss of their loved one and will continue to receive this money as long as they live. But money cannot compensate for their loss. As we officers' wives stand to honor each martyr in turn, I see many eyes filled with earnest tears. As one of the foot soldiers' mothers passes my front-row seat, I impulsively reach out a hand and pat her shoulder in a gesture of empathy. She turns slightly in my direction, enough for me to see the question in her eyes. "*What more do you want of me?*" they seem to ask. Then she keeps on walking to her place at the back of the hall.

Oh, Sitara, I wonder, *how can one little community school hope to bridge the divide between rich and poor through education?* This question remains unanswered. All I know is we must each do what we can. Education is what I know how to do, so I must start there. I'm returning to Sitara after a two-year absence. During that time, I've worked for a paycheck in Saudi, and taken care of my family in America. I've missed my little school in Chatha and the satisfaction that comes from seeing my students' and teachers' progress.

The school year in Pakistan runs from April to March, and the new term is about to start. Madam Rizwana and the teachers have kept me updated on Sitara's progress, supplying me with pictures and newsletter articles over the past two years. I'd been thrilled to learn we would have a new building and watched the progress of its construction in 2015 via WhatsApp. We featured the move to the new campus in our annual online fundraiser that year.

My eyes tear up as I walk through the gate and see the new campus for the first time. It is small by most schools' standards. There's a courtyard, ten classrooms, two bathrooms, office space, and storage areas. The second floor has space to build new rooms, which we will soon need because our lower classes are already full. In the courtyard are two flagpoles, one with the national flag and one with our very own school flag, both flying high and proud. I hug our principal and each of the teachers in turn, giving the longest hugs to those I've known and missed. I unpack the goodies: children's books, instructional CDs, colored dry erase markers, and plenty of stickers, easy to pack and much desired. I've brought two new Leap Pad readers and some leather wallets for the teachers. It's another happy reunion as we sit and talk about the latest developments at the school. I notice a new level of confidence and professionalism among the staff.

Alhamdulillah, the school is thriving under the good leadership of these trustworthy people. Our new *chowkidar* is also a gardener. He's beautified the campus with many flowering plants. They lend a cheerful atmosphere despite the government regulation barbed wire and security cameras we were required to install after the tragic 2014 massacre at an Army Public School in Peshawar. Schools were required to install this equipment and pay for it as well, with no help from the government.

Everyone stops by the office for a chat. After a delicious biryani lunch prepared by Ambreen, the school *mai* (housekeeper), we go to visit Madam Rizwana's family at home. Her father has returned from his job at the Pakistani embassy in Kabul. He's a gracious host and his family has prepared even more food for us. Everywhere we go in Pakistan we are fed and overfed. It is very difficult to be careful about eating in the face of this deliciousness!

We return to school on Monday for the students' first day of classes. I am joyful as I search out familiar faces that have grown and matured since 2014. We greet each other with hugs and kisses though some hang back shyly. Those who know me whisper to those who don't: *Bari Madam aa rahi hae!* (Big Madam is here!) They are eager to show off their work, their classrooms, and their little brothers and sisters. They crowd around for pictures, smiling broadly. They are happy to be at school. I leave that day with welcome back cards of all types, handmade by the students. We return for more visits in the weeks that follow.

In 2016, Sitara is celebrating its fifth year. Obviously, my role there has changed from that of a hands-on founder and principal to one who directs from a distance. My main responsibility is to raise the funds needed to run the school and teachers' institute. That includes money to pay the staff salaries, building rent, and utilities. We also provide students with textbooks, computers, internet access, and uniforms. My friends and I collect private donations, mostly in the United States, to fund all these resources. We host a yearly online fundraiser through Launchgood.com, a crowd-funding website. My husband is the accountant for the school, publishing quarterly financial reports to be shared with our Michigan Board of Trustees.

As I put together some pictures for the school website, I realize that our school now has a presence and a history. Only a handful of our original students are still with us. The Afghan and Kashmiri refugee populations are highly transient. But a few families have come to Chatha Bakhtawar and stayed, becoming long-term residents as day laborers or small-business owners. It's for these families that we will open a girls' high school in 2017, *Inshallah*. The mothers have told us they can't send their daughters anywhere else. There is no government high school for girls in Chatha Bakhtawar. Traveling to the next town for school is usually not an option for them. There is no room for these girls on the family motorbike, and public transportation is considered too dangerous. What usually happens is that girls drop out after eighth class. My Sitara girls know, however, that quitting is not an option for them. We will support them for as long as we can. A few of them have already decided they want to teach. They'll be the ones to carry Sitara forward in years to come, *Inshallah*.

Fear Allah and treat your children equally.
The best gift from a father to his child is education and upbringing.
—Hadith of Prophet Muhammad ﷺ

CHAPTER 46

Coming Full Circle

View from the Eagle's Nest in Hunza Valley, Pakistan, 2016

Anas (r.a.) reported that the Prophet ﷺ said: Be in this world like a stranger or traveler passing on his way.

The Quran urges us to travel and see the condition of people in the world, both present and past. Since 2010, I've traveled quite a bit, logging plenty of frequent flyer miles. Sometimes I forget exactly where I am, as well as the day or even the season! But the one thing that helps me remember *who* I am is my relationship with Allah (SWT). I am his servant. He is my Lord and my Constant.

Allah first drew me back to Him in 1979, and I embraced Islam by pronouncing the *shahadah,* the first of five pillars of faith in Sunni Islam I bore witness that Allah is the one true God worthy of worship, and that Muhammad ﷺ is His last prophet and messenger. The next four pillars are the activation of belief.

The day starts with *salat*, or prayer, and revolves around its proper times. I love the way the prayers help me organize my days. *Fajr* is first, performed between dawn and sunrise. It's the perfect time for a morning person like me, but more of a challenge for those who stay up late. There is great reward in it, and the promise of a productive and beautiful day. A well-known hadith says, *"He who performs the dawn prayer will be under the protection of Allah."*

The noon and afternoon *(zuhr and asr)* prayers provide a good break from work of any kind. They're a time to recap and change direction, as needed. If the day includes social events, they often take place after or between the prayers. Another hadith states, *"Whoever misses the asr prayer, it is as if he has lost his family and his wealth."*

The *maghrib* prayer is right after sunset, signaling the end of the day and the onset of evening. If it's Ramadan, or any other fasting day, *maghrib* also ends the fast and brings a feeling of success for its completion, no matter how difficult it may have been. There's time to eat a few dates and drink some water before making the prayer itself.

Isha, the evening prayer, is the most challenging for me because I'm not a night person. By 10:00 or 11:00 pm. I'm drowsy and not in the mood to think. I'd prefer to just check my Facebook page or read a novel and go to bed. So it is best for me to pray as early as possible if I hope to pray with *khushoo*, or full conscientiousness.

Prayer timings vary throughout the year and from place to place, as they follow the natural rhythms of the sun and moon, helping to keep us in harmony with the rest of creation in spite of our system of artificial light. I love to hear the *athan*, or call to prayer in Muslim countries, but I can use a prayer calendar or phone app to know the prayer times anywhere in the world.

Of course, one can pray anywhere and at any time. In addition to the five daily prayer cycles, there are voluntary ones at certain times of the day and night. *Du'a*, or supplication, can be made at any time and for any reason. Saying *Bismillah* (in the name of God) before any action is also a way to invoke Allah's blessing over anything we do. It also reminds me to look at the intention for my actions. *Is what I am about to do some-*

thing that will please Allah? Or, will He dislike it? The very first hadith recorded in most collections is about intention. Umar bin Al-Khattab narrated:

> *I heard Allah's Apostle saying, "The reward of deeds depends upon the intentions and every person will get the reward according to what he has intended. So whoever emigrated for worldly benefits or for a woman to marry, his emigration was for what he emigrated for.*

The third pillar is *saum*, or fasting, another means of spiritual purification as well as physical health. The main fast for Muslims is during Ramadan. In this month, we fast from food, drink, and sexual relations from dawn till dusk, or *fajr* till *maghrib*. Ramadan was a real challenge for me in my first few years as a Muslim, but the spiritual rewards far outweighed the difficulties. Allah is so merciful!

Besides Ramadan, there are voluntary fasts. The Prophet ﷺ himself used to fast every Monday and Thursday as well as three days in the middle of the month when the moon was full. I try to fast one day a week if I can.

Zakat, or giving charity to those in need, is the fourth pillar of Islam. A Muslim must give a minimum of 2.5 percent of her surplus wealth to the poor. In our contemporary world, there are countless opportunities to give charity, although according to Islamic law and practice, it should first be given to those nearest to us in relationship and proximity and then to those at a distance. Those who live in more affluent countries may need to look a little further from home to distribute their charity to those most in need. Giving globally is easier than ever before with the one-click donation systems online.

Hajj, the pilgrimage to Mecca, is the last pillar of Islam. This spiritual journey should be made at least once in a lifetime but is only required of those who can afford it. If you do have the money to travel, *Hajj* should take precedence over a trip to any other place for fun, recreation, or family visitation. *Alhamdulillah*, I've been blessed with two *Hajj*s and one *umrah*. May Allah accept them all. *Ameen*.

Next come the six Articles of Faith according to the Quran: Belief in Allah, His Angels, His Books, His Messengers, Heaven and Hell, and Destiny. I ask Him to help me see the reality behind professing my belief, and by that, I mean a deeper understanding and experience of each Article.

The best thing about being a Muslim is knowing that I have a direct relationship with Allah, my Creator, my Nurturer, my Lord. No intercessor is needed in this relationship. As Allah (SWT) tells us in the Quran, He is closer to us than our jugular artery! It is a huge comfort to know that my Creator knows me better than I know my own self and that He always has my best interest at heart, even if I can't see what that might mean at any given moment. *He* is Omniscient, while *we* can only experience the present and reflect upon the past.

When I first embraced Islam, I did so because it felt right in my heart. My head, or rational intellectual self, did not understand everything I was told to believe. But logic and rationality is not the only faculty we have for understanding. Ali, the son-in-law of the Prophet ﷺ and a leader of the Muslims said, "The heart is the seat of intellect." I now know this statement to be true. It took me some time to grasp the idea of believing in the unseen, such as angels, but I do understand in my heart that they exist, and I always hope to see one. The realm of the Unseen is real, even if it is not part of our common perceptual plane. Our deeds are recorded by angels who sit on our shoulders. I cannot know what that literally means. In the twenty-first century, I might conceive of them storing data in some computerized form, though seventh-century man could only visualize a written record of ink and parchment. There have been times when I think certainly an angel has come to help me in the guise of a human being, as Gabriel came to Muhammad ﷺ and his companions and also to Mary in the form of a beautiful man to announce the coming of Jesus, her son and God's prophet.

The Quran is God's final revelation to man, as revealed to His final messenger, Prophet Muhammad ﷺ. It is very similar to the other books of revelation, in their purest form, such as the Torah and the Gospels. However, those revelations have not remained in their God-given form, while the Quran has. God Himself has promised to protect it, and there is not a single Arabic Quran today that differs in any way from any other, even though translations may differ due to interpretations or limitations of language. In the Quran, readers will find biblical stories, but with important differences because the Quran was sent to correct the man-made errors of earlier revelations, as well as to provide more up-to-date guidance to humankind.

It has taken me a long time to love the Quran and develop a personal relationship with it. Mohammad Allama Iqbal, the great philosopher-poet relates the story of how his father taught him to read Quran. He told him, "Read as if the book is being revealed directly to you." It is the goal of every seeker to apply the Quran to his or her life in the way that the Prophet ﷺ and his companions did. That requires a deep understanding of the text.

My ability to understand God's word is evolving over time. The first time I experienced the entire Quran was through audiotape in Arabic and English. Tahera was in utero at the time, so she experienced it simultaneously! Later, I learned that it was commendable to read the whole Quran each Ramadan, from start to finish, so I started doing so in English. The first year I was able to complete it in one month I felt very accomplished! I read the English for the meaning, but I also memorized short portions in Arabic, so I could say them in my daily prayers. The first chapter in the Quran is only seven verses long. It is called *Al Fatiha*, or The Opening, because it is the opening of the book and also the opening of the believer's heart as he or she stands in worship. Prophet Muhammad ﷺ explained *Surah Fatiha* as a dialogue between us and Allah (SWT). Thinking of it that way enhanced my relationship with God.

I've been struggling with the Arabic for years. I learned to read the Arabic script of the Quran in my twenties, but had no idea of the right way to pronounce the letters and vowels. In my ignorance, I thought I was reading well, but after spending time in Saudi Arabia and taking classes in Quranic recitation, I've realized how much more there is to reciting correctly, and I'm finally making progress. In Arabic, the verses have a beautiful rhythm and flow to them. I still refer to the English translations to enhance my understanding, but since words and themes are repeated from chapter to chapter, I can now get the gist of their meaning in Arabic too.

I respect all the Messengers, from Adam, the first, to Muhammad ﷺ the last, and everyone in between, including Abraham, Moses, and Jesus, but also the lesser known messengers such as Ezekiel and Jonah. Moses and the Children of Israel are mentioned the most in the Quran. The story of Jesus is also told in beautiful detail. In fact, Chapter 18 of the book is named after his mother, Mary, called *Maryam* in Arabic. Muslims believe in all of God's messengers but strive to follow the example of Muhammad ﷺ, the last and final prophet. He was sent as a mercy to mankind and a role model for how to behave in each and every situation. We can follow his example through the *hadith*, collections of his words and actions compiled from the eyewitness accounts of his wives and companions, and the *sira*, biographical accounts of his life.

Heaven and Hell become easier to visualize as I reflect on the verses of Quran that describe them. And yet, there are *hadith* that say we cannot really imagine them. The Quran can only provide similes to things we have known, such as beautiful gardens with shaded pavilions or scorching fire that burns the skin off and scalding, putrid water. In reality, Heaven and Hell will be like nothing we've experienced in our earthly existence. When I'm tempted to engage in something wrongful for temporary satisfaction, I try to remember that I can have that same satisfaction and infinitely more than that in paradise if I can only delay my gratification now!

None of us knows our final destiny. We can only try to read the signs along the way. How is our life turning out so far? Are my actions pleasing or displeasing to Him? There is always more to be done. We will have to wait until we stand before Allah (SWT) on the Day of Judgment to see the overview of our life to grasp what it all meant and how it all adds up in the end. May He be merciful to me and to all of you.

As I write these final words, I'm sitting on the terrace of the Eagle's Nest, a guest house in Northern Pakistan. The place is aptly named. At my feet lies the Hunza Valley, its fertile fields and fruit orchards watered by the mighty Indus River. The river is fed by innumerable creeks, streams, and waterfalls cascading down the Karakoram mountain range. Near Hunza, the Karakorams join the Himalayas and the Hindu-Kush, forming a powerful geographic triumvirate. The scenery is so dramatic as to seem surreal. In the valley below, life flourishes in mud-brick homes and verdant fields, little towns and schools, places of worship, and places of work. The snow-covered peaks of Rakaposhi and Nanga Parbat rise nearly 8,000 meters above sea level, towering and majestic in the sunlight one moment and covered by clouds the next.

I revel in the richness of the scene. In relation to these mountain peaks, I'm just a tiny speck, yet I'm neatly woven into this tapestry of life, an inextricable part of the Whole. I will cease to exist on this earth long before these mountains crumble into dust, but for the blink of an eye of time that I am here, I have a role to play and work to do.

When I searched for Allah long ago, He revealed Himself through the sky, the planets, and the green, green earth. I had always known He was there, but my heart had grown distant as I grew older. *Alhamdulillah*, He brought me back to Himself and here I stay, enthralled by the open book of the universe and His power to command it at every moment.

Of Him seeks (its need) every creature in the heavens and on earth: every day in (new) splendour doth He (shine)!
(S. Ar Rahman, v. 29)

For those of us with insight, the dawn would have sufficed as proof of the truth even if there were no Prophets.
—Josh Malihabadi (Pakistani poet, 1894-1982)

Truly in the heart there is a void that cannot be removed except with the company of Allah. And in it there is a sadness that cannot

be removed except with the happiness of knowing Allah and being true to Him. And in it there is an emptiness that cannot be filled except with love for Him and by turning to Him and always remembering Him And if a person were given all of the world and what is in it, it would not fill this emptiness.
— *Ibn Qayyim al Jawziyya*

Acknowledgements

When I told my family I planned to write this memoir, they expressed a variety of emotions ranging from guarded curiosity to outright fear. My son even asked me to tell the story as if he did not exist—an impossibility. Everyone seemed concerned that I would somehow expose deep dark secrets or skeletons best left in the closet. In a few cases, I did change the names to avoid harm or a potential lawsuit. It's the nature of memoir to tell what happened as the writer remembers it. There is really no such thing as objectivity in this, which is why one person's version of how something happened can seem quite different than another person's version.

When I chose to become a Muslim at twenty-two years old, it was not because of some fatal error or omission in my upbringing. I had a wonderful, privileged childhood with all the love and attention a child could want. I did not choose a lifestyle alien to my people because I hated my culture or because I wanted to spite my parents and relatives. I chose Islam because it reacquainted me with my God, my Creator, in a way no other religion or lifestyle was able to do.

Mom and Dad, you raised me well and prepared me for the steps I had to take. You nurtured a sensitive, intelligent child and helped her become confident, independent, and compassionate. There are no words to express the debt of thanks and gratitude I owe you both.

To my children, I'm so proud of the faith-filled adults you've become. You've been patient with your "gypsy mother" as she's traipsed around the world, graciously keeping a space for me in your homes whenever I end up in town. You've brought me the joy of grandchildren. I smile in my heart to see you happy in your lives, and I love you very much. Your father deserves equal credit for helping to raise you so well and also for teaching me that Islam is a way of life, not just a religion.

To Asad, my husband and soul mate, you were one of the few who said "Write the book" and then gave me the space and time to get it done. You are a living example of kindness, courtesy, and compassion to me. Without you there would be no Sitara. Without you I would never have spread my wings to fly so far from home.

Many people pushed me to finish this book: Carol Lynn with her visionary spirit, Zarinah El Amin Naeem of Niyah Press with her practical know-how and get-it-done attitude, my editor, Kenny B. Darling, for his supportive comments and exacting questions, and my dear friend Lisa Amowitz for her beautiful, eye-catching cover design. To my teachers, past and present, and all my family, friends and colleagues who helped and supported me with kind words, enthusiasm, and encouragement, thank you from the bottom of my heart.

Selected Resources

This memoir describes how I came to be a Muslim and how my life evolved and changed after embracing Islam. It is not meant to be a treatise on the religion or a detailed explanation of what Islam is and what Muslims practice. If you would like to know more about the transformative faith of Islam, here's a short selection of websites and books that might be of use.

Quranic Translations

A serious seeker of the truth about Islam should do their best to learn to read and gradually understand Quranic Arabic as a lifelong study. That said, many translations and explanations of the Quran are available in English, as well as in other languages. Some are classics, such as the Yusuf Ali and Mohammad Pickthall translations, available as books and e-books. I refer often to those, but also like the following translations and interpretations of the Holy Quran:

Decoding the Quran: A Unique Sufi Interpretation by Ahmad Hulusi, translated from the Turkish by Aliya Atalay, available as a book and an ebook (2013).

The Message of the Quran, translated and explained by Muhammad Asad, available as a book and an ebook, and originally published in 1982.

The Study Quran: A New Translation and Commentary by Seyyed Hosse-in Nasr, Caner K. Dagli, Maria Massi Dakake, Joseph E.B. Lumbard, and Mohammed Rustom, Harper Collins, 2015.

The Tajweedi Quran: With Meanings Rendered in Early 21st Century American English by A. Nooruddeen Durkee, An–Noor Publications, 2004. *Contains transliteration of the Arabic text.

Biographies of Prophet Muhammad

In the Footsteps of the Prophet: Lessons from the Life of Muhammad by Tariq Ramadan, Oxford University Press, 2007, digital and print.

Muhammad: His Life Based on the Earliest Sources by Martin Lings, ebook, 2007.

Muhammad by Yahya Emerick, Critical Lives Series, 2002, digital and print.

Revelation by Meraj Mohiuddin, 2015.

General Information

Being Muslim: A Practical Guide by Asad Tarsin, Sandala Press, www.beingmuslim.org.

No God but God: The Origins, Evolution and Future of Islam by Reza Aslan, Random House, LLC, updated edition, 2011 digital and print form.

What Everyone Needs to Know About Islam by John L. Esposito, Oxford
University Press, 2011, digital and print form.

Websites and Scholars

Hamza Yusuf, sandala.org
Nouman Ali Khan, nakcollection.com
Anse Tamara Gray, rabata.org

Organizations

Ta'leef Collective:	taleefcollective.org
Bayinnah:	bayinnah.com
ISNA:	isna.net
ICNA:	icna.net, whyislam.org
Islamic City:	islamicity.com

Glossary

Common Islamic Terms in Arabic

Abaya – loose-fitting over-garment similar in style to a cloak or a robe.

Alhamdulillah – All praise is to God (Allah).

Allah – Arabic name of God, the Creator. The only One worthy of worship.

Allahu Akbar – Allah is the Greatest of all.

Asalamu alaykum, walaykum as salam – Peace be upon you, and upon you peace. The prescribed greeting and response for Muslims.

Athan – Muslim call to prayer, recited loudly from the masjid to let the people know it is time for one of the five daily prayers. Translated as follows: *God is Great, God is Great, There is no God but Allah, Mohammad is the messenger of Allah, Come to the Prayer, Come to Success, God is Great, God is Great, There is no God but Allah.*

Bismillah – In the name of God, often said at the beginning of an activity to ask for Allah's blessing.

Bayaa – a pledge of loyalty to a teacher or a cause.

Buraq – a horse-like creature on which Prophet Muhammad ﷺ journeyed to the seven heavens during the miraculous Night Journey of *Israa and Miraj* (see below).

Burkini – a particular style of modest Islamic swimwear, designed like a diving suit to cover the whole body except the face, hands, and feet.

Dawah – inviting people to Islam.

Dhikr – remembrance of Allah usually through the repetition of short phrases or words.

Du'a – a supplication or prayer of asking God for something.

Eid – one of the two annual Islamic feast days, **Eid ul-Fitr,** ending the month of Ramadan, and **Eid ul-Adha** during the Hajj.

Fatiha, Al – first chapter of the Holy Quran, recited multiple times in the five daily prayers. The phrase itself means "the Opening."

Fitrah – the original nature of human beings, uncorrupted by any subsequent beliefs and practices imposed by family and society.

Habibti – honey or sweetheart (f.), habibi (m.).

Hadith – The collected sayings of Prophet Muhammad ﷺ.

Hajj – the pilgrimage to Mecca, one of the five pillars of Islam.

Halal – legal and lawful in Islam.

Haram – illegal, or not allowed according to Islamic law, forbidden.

Hijab – the Islamic dress code for women. Basic requirements are to cover the entire body excluding face and hands. Regardless of the style, clothing should be loose fitting so as not to reveal the shape of the body.

Kaaba – "the cube," in Mecca, the holiest site in Islam.

Kalima – literal meaning: word. Used to identify the declaration of faith, or shahadah.

Khutbah – sermon given by the imam at congregational prayers.

Iftar – food which is eaten at the end of the fast, right after sunset.

Imam – leader of a Muslim congregation or, simply, leader of a congregational prayer.

Iman – faith in Allah (SWT) reflected by correct beliefs and correct actions.

Inshallah – if Allah (SWT) wills.

Israa and Miraj – a miraculous night journey from Madinah to Jerusalem and from there to the heavens, undertaken by Prophet Muhammad ﷺ guided by the angel Jibril (Arabic name of angel Gabriel, the Angel of Revelation).

Istiqama – a word conveying uprightness and balance. related to the phrase *Ihdina siratal mustaqeem* in S. Fatiha, asking God to show us the straight, or balanced, path in life.

Istikhara – prescribed prayer for asking Allah's help in making a choice or decision.

Jazak Allahu khair – May Allah reward you. Used as a high form of thanks.

Jennah – paradise, heaven.

Jilbab – an over-garment styled like a long coat.

Jihad – to struggle or to strive against oneself or against an external enemy.

Mahram – male family member whom a woman cannot marry because of their blood relationship, and therefore in front of whom she does not have to wear hijab.

Masha'Allah – It was God's will, or whatever God wills An expression of joy and appreciation.

Masjid – Arabic word for mosque, a word which actually derives from Spanish and Greek.

Moathen – person who calls the athan (see above).

Mullah – an educated Muslim trained in religious law and doctrine and usually holding an official post.

Muslim – a follower of the religion of Islam. One who submits their will to Allah (God).

Nakba – the Arabic term for the events of 1948, when thousands of Palestinians were displaced from their homeland by the creation of the new state of Israel.

Naseya – forebrain, or foremost part of the frontal lobe, behind the forehead.

Niqab – face veil worn by Muslim women in some Muslim countries by custom and in others by choice.

Qibla – the direction of the Kaaba as determined from any point on the globe; the direction of prayer.

Quran – the Revelation from Allah to His prophet and messenger, Muhammad ﷺ over the course of twenty-three years, from 610 CE to 633 CE.

Radi Allahu anhu, anha – May Allah be pleased with him or her. Can be used after the name of any pious person who has passed away and is used in an abbreviated form (r.) after the name of the companions of the Prophet.

Ramadan (fast of) — obligatory annual fast in the lunar month of Ramadan. Abstinence from food, drink, and marital intimacy from dawn till dusk.

Riyal — currency of Saudi Arabia. In September 2016, the exchange rate is 3.75 riyals to $1.

Ruku — the bowing performed during *salat*.

✹ — Arabic phrase, transliteration: *sal Allahu alayhi wa sallam. May Allah's peace and blessings be upon him.* A term of respect used after the name of Prophet Muhammad ✹.

Sakinah — peace, serenity, tranquility.

Salat — The cycle of formal prayer, which includes certain postures and required recitations, obligatory formal prayer is performed five times daily by Muslims.

Salaam — peace.

Shahādah — The testimony of faith: *La ilaha illa Allah. Muhammadun rasulullah.* "There is no god but Allah. Muhammad is the messenger of Allah." Regarded as the first pillar of Islam.

Shaitan or Shaytan — Satan, the devil. Also known as Iblis.

Sheikh — a scholar, or a leader in a Muslim community or organization.

Shia — denomination of Islam that views Ali (r.), the fourth caliph of Islam, as Muhammad's rightful successor and therefore rejects the first three caliphs.

Shirk — the sin of deification or worship of anyone or anything other than the singular God, i.e. Allah. Literally, it means ascribing or the establishment of "partners" placed beside God.

Siraat — according to the hadith of Prophet Muhammad ✹, a very narrow bridge that must be crossed to enter Paradise on the Day of Judgment.

Sufism — mystical Islamic belief and practice in which Muslims seek to find the truth of divine love and knowledge through direct personal experience of God.

Sunni — denomination of Islam that regards Abu Bakr (r.), the first caliph, as the rightful successor to Muhammad ✹.

Subhanallah — Glory be to God.

Suhoor – the meal eaten by fasting Muslims just before dawn.

Sujud – position in prayer where the worshipper is kneeling with her forehead on the floor.

Sūrah – chapter; the Quran is composed of 114 surahs. When quoting from the Quran, I have listed the name of the chapter in Arabic transliteration and then its number and verse.

Suq – the old-fashioned type of bazaar selling a wide variety of merchandise in small shops or stalls.

SWT – when writing the name of God (Allah), Muslims often follow it with the abbreviation "SWT," which stands for the Arabic words *Subhanahu Wa Ta'ala* or "Glory to Him, the Exalted."

Tablighi Jamaat – global Sunni Islamic proselytizing and revivalist movement that focuses on urging Muslims to return to orthodox Sunni Islam.

Tarbiyah – the act of nurturing something to its full potential.

Tauhid – Oneness or Unity of Allah (SWT).

Tawwaf – circling around the Kaaba as part of the rituals of Hajj; circumambulation of the Kaaba, seven times in a counter-clockwise direction.

Thobe- a long gown or robe worn by men.

Umrah – the non-obligatory pilgrimage to Mecca undertaken outside the month of Dhul Hijjah.

Wahhabism – a puritanical form of Islam founded by Abdul Wahhab (1703-1792); today, known for its strict interpretation of the Quran.

Ya Allah – "Oh God," often uttered as part of a supplication.

Words or Phrases in Urdu

Angraz – word denoting the English language or English people.

Bhaaji – older sister, used as a term of respect when addressing a female who is older than you.

Chappals – sandals.

Chowkidar – security guard, often armed.

Dupatta – a long rectangular head cover that is wound around the head, chest, and shoulders. It often envelops a good portion of the upper body, front and back sides. It is the type of head-covering most prevalent among Pakistani, Indian, and Bengali Muslim women, though Hindu women also cover their heads in a similar fashion.

Farangi – used to denote a British person, but not widely used these days. I have heard people refer to me by this term, but since English is now so widespread, the word *foreign* is also common, as in the sentence, "Foreign *key hey,*" *She is from foreign.*

Itwar – Sunday.

Mai – a maid; someone who cleans the home, school, or office.

Mehndi – a natural dye that is used to decorate the body or color the hair, known as henna in Arabic.

Rehri – street cart pushed by a peddler.

Rupee – Pakistani currency (Rs.). In September 2016, there were Rs. 104 to $1.00 USD.

Shalwar kameez – South Asian style of Islamic dress consisting of a loose-fitting tunic top and baggy trousers, worn by both men and women in Pakistan and parts of India. Alternative spelling: *shalwar.*

Saree – a garment consisting of a length of cotton or silk elaborately draped around the body, traditionally worn by women from South Asia.

Sayb – apple.

Taweez — a piece of paper with prayers or Quranic verses written on it that is thought to act as an amulet or talisman for the person who keeps it.

Urdu — the language of Pakistan and certain parts of India.

Waala — a street vendor.

Words or Phrases in Other Languages

Ay Dios — Spanish, meaning "Oh God."

Bar Mitzvah, Bat Mitzvah — Hebrew name for a traditional coming of age ceremony for a boy (bar) or a girl (bat) in the Jewish faith; usually takes place at age thirteen. The adolescent is now considered old enough to be responsible for their prayers and to take part in public worship ceremonies at the synagogue.

Kaddish — Hebrew prayer to remember the dead; a part of Friday night Sabbath services.

Kibbutz — Hebrew term for a farming collective or Socialist commune.

Ulpan — intensive course for the study of the Hebrew language.

About the Author

If you'd asked her about career choices when she was a girl, Sommieh Stephanie Flower would never have chosen education. But now she looks back contentedly on a successful career as a teacher and school administrator who established several private religious schools for Muslim children in the United States and Pakistan. She has always wanted to tell her life story, from a happy childhood on Long Island to a little school in Islamabad. *Eye of the Heart* is that story. Sommieh currently divides her time between her extended family in North America, where she rediscovers the joys of life through her grandchildren, and Sitara School and Teachers' Institute, a free school for impoverished children and aspiring teachers in Pakistan, where she resides with her husband.

Sitara

Sitara School started, quite literally, with a dream. After meeting and befriending the children who collected recyclable trash in the streets of Chatha Bakhtawar, I saw them in a dream, laughing and playing and reading in the courtyard of my home. I woke up with the idea of starting a school, a safe haven where these impoverished girls and boys could come to play and learn.

I took this thought home with me to Canton, MI and began to tell my friends about my experiences in Pakistan and my intention to start a school there. A handful of supporters invited others to donate and dream of Sitara became a reality.

That first year there were 20 children. They came wide-eyed into the school room and saw the whiteboard, the desks, the crayons, pencils and books. They began with an undisciplined eagerness that left me and their teachers exhausted at the end of the day, but it the good kind of exhaustion that comes from doing something worthwhile.

With Allah's help and blessings, the school has grown from its humble beginnings. Generous donations have allowed us to rent a brand-new campus and to expand our classroom space and curriculum to include a future girl's high school, Inshallah.

Sitara School is the first venture of Sitara Institute, a non-profit group formed in the State of Michigan, USA, in January 2011. Sitara Institute currently has a small but growing donor base of about 200 people in North America and abroad.

We invite you to join us by visiting:
http://sitara-institute.org/
or sommiehflower.com

Also by Niyah Press

The Spiritual Adam by Imam Abdullah El-Amin

The Black Mzungu by Dr. Alexandria Osborne

Jihad of the Soul by Zarinah El-Amin Naeem

Like Glue: The Little Book of Marriage Advice by
Dr. Halim Naeem and Zarinah El-Amin Naeem

A Part of Me Refused to Die by Nisha Sulthana

Muslim in Transit by Mohammed Qamruzzaman

Speeches for the Soul by Hon. D. Neletha Butterfield

The Quran & Science by Ghiasuddin Ahmad

www.niyahpress.com
info@niyahpress.com

Group Discussion Questions

1. Memoirs are deeply personal. Why do you think Sommieh chose to share her story? Would you share yours?

2. The author discusses living in a secular Jewish home. How might her life have been different with a more religious upbringing?

3. Each chapter ends with a verse of the Quran or a spiritual quote. What do they tell you about Sommieh's thought process?

4. How do the poems shared by Flower as an opening to each of the three book parts provide insight into her way of thinking?

5. Sommieh's first encounter with the Quran was through a man she respected and loved. How did this affect her entrance into Islam?

6. What are some of the life lessons Sommieh seems to have learned between her first and second marriages?

7. Sommieh discusses "God-centered" education. What does that phrase mean to you? How do you think it might benefit (or harm) children growing up in our 21st century world?

8. Sommieh embraced Islam in 1979. Based on her description of the 1980's, do you think American society has changed in its views on Islam? Why/why not and in what ways?

9. After leaving the U.S. in 2010, Sommieh started a school that offers free education to impoverished children in Pakistan. Can you see yourself serving humanity on a more global scale in the future? What type of experiences would you be interested in?